DIMENSIONS
OF PSYCHOANALYSIS

DIMENSIONS
OF PSYCHOANALYSIS

edited by
Joseph Sandler

with contributions by
John Bowlby
Janine Chasseguet-Smirgel
William Gillespie
André Green
John Klauber
Christopher Lasch
Karl H. Pribram
Joseph Sandler
Roy Schafer
Hanna Segal
Albert J. Solnit

Foreword by
Sir James Lighthill
Provost
University College London

International Universities Press, Inc.
Madison   Connecticut

First published in 1989 by
H. Karnac (Books) Ltd.
58 Gloucester Road
London SW7 4QY

Library of Congress Cataloging-in-Publication Data

Dimensions of psychoanalysis / edited by Joseph Sandler; with
    contributions by John Bowlby . . . [et al.]; foreword by James
    Lighthill.
        p.   cm.
    Includes bibliographical references.
    ISBN 0-8236-1293-7
    1. Psychoanalysis.   2. Freud, Sigmund, 1857–1939.   I. Sandler,
    Joseph.   II. Bowlby, John.

BF173.D547   1990   89–77824
150.19′52—dc20   CIP

Manufactured in the United States of America

CONTENTS

ACKNOWLEDGEMENTS

I should first like to acknowledge the enormous support and encouragement I have received from Sir James Lighthill, FRS, Provost of University College. He, as well as the Hon. David Astor, who endowed the Freud Memorial Chair of Psychoanalysis in the University of London and the Psychoanalysis Unit at University College, have done a great deal for the development of psychoanalysis in Britain. I want also to thank Bryony Tanner for her help with the secretarial work involved in the preparation of this book and Jane Pettit for the great amount of work she put into checking my editing and into collating the references.

J.S.

The Freud Memorial Professorship at University College London

Sir James Lighthill

Background

University College, the oldest and largest of the Schools and Colleges of the University of London, has a long and distinguished record of academic excellence and innovation which began with its foundation in 1826. The basic principle behind the foundation of UCL was that higher education in a far broader sense than existed elsewhere at the time should be available to all who could profit by it without any restrictions based on religion or class background. The College sought, furthermore, to provide study facilities not existing in the more traditional universities and to this end established the first professorial chairs in England in English, French, Italian, German, English law, Jurisprudence, Political Economy and Geography as well as providing the beginning of English university teaching in chemistry, physics and scientific physiology.

In more modern times innovation continued with the founding of the first Faculty of Engineering in the United Kingdom and the pioneering of genetics, statistics, biochemistry, chemical engineering and phonetics as university disciplines.

It was with particular pleasure therefore that, adding to this list of 'firsts', the College in 1974 announced the establishment of a new visiting Chair, whose occupant would be known as the Freud Memorial Professor, and which was to be generously endowed by the Honourable Mr David Astor.

Mr Astor, then editor of *The Observer* newspaper, had developed an interest in psychoanalysis whilst at the University of Oxford and felt that students in general should have a chance to hear the discipline of psychoanalysis expounded by its most authentic exponents, psychoanalysts, since in most universities the subject was touched upon only by Professors of disciplines other than psychoanalysis. He wanted the actual views of Freud presented together with their ever-changing contemporary application.

The College at that time was fortunate in already having a gifted Freudian scholar, Cecily de Monchaux, on its staff as a Senior Lecturer in the Department of Psychology. It also possessed a lively Department of Philosophy within a Faculty of Arts that covered most subjects in the Humanities. On the other hand, the Clinical teaching of the College's medical students was carried out in an organization administratively separate from the College.

It was against this background that the formal aims of the development were expressed as

'to promote the study and critical examination of psychoanalysis including its theoretical aspects and its cultural implications' and 'generally to facilitate any studies or research into psychoanalysis'.

The broad approach that Mr Astor was keen to encourage was encapsulated in the constitution of the Board of Management for the Chair which included a member appointed by the British Psychoanalytical Society as well as the Head of the Department of Psychology in the College, the Grote Professor of Philosophy of Mind and Logic and the Lord Northcliffe Professor of Modern English Literature.

Holders of the Freud Memorial Visiting Professorship have traditionally given an inaugural lecture, which has normally been published, and a series of three or four other general lectures. Also they have conducted interdepartmental seminars in the College during their tenure which so far has never extended beyond one academic year.

The Freud Memorial Visiting Professors

The first Freud Professor was to have been the distinguished Erik Erikson, then Professor of Human Development and lecturer in psychiatry at Harvard, but ill health unfortunately prevented his taking up the appointment, and the College instead launched a Public Lectureship Programme in 1974/75 aimed at introducing a number of different aspects of the study of psychoanalysis, which would, it was hoped, be developed in future years.

The 1974/75 programme began with a series of lectures by Dr John Sutherland, who had been Medical Director of the Tavistock Clinic in London, entitled 'Developments in psychoanalysis, from mechanisms of the mind to dynamics of the person'. During the second term of the session topics covered were as follows:

'Freud and the interpretation of art', given by Richard Wollheim, Grote Professor of Mind and Logic at UCL;

'The inner world and its reflection in art', by Hanna Segal, a leading exponent of Kleinian theories, herself a practising analyst who was eventually to become President of the British Psychoanalytical Society and Freud Professor at UCL in 1977/78;

'Psychoanalysis and the literary imagination', by Charles Rycroft, a psychoanalyst and member of the British Psychoanalytical Society;

'Orestes and Oedipus: A structural analysis', by André Green, then an active clinical psychoanalyst in Paris and subsequently Freud Professor at UCL in 1979/80;

'The good society and the aims of psychoanalysis', by Professor Elliott Jaques, who was then Professor of Sociology and Director of the Institute of Organisation and Social Studies at Brunel University;

'Violent social change and the psychoanalyst', by H. P. Hildebrand, then a clinical psychologist at the Tavistock Clinic;

'The significance of Piaget's work for psychoanalysis', by Anne-Marie Sandler, a practising analyst and member of the British Psychoanalytical Society;

'The psychoanalyst and medicine', by Enid Balint, again an analyst and member of the British Psychoanalytical Society.

In term three Professor Erikson was able to honour the College with a visit and chose as his title for two lectures 'The child's toys and the old man's reasons', covering play and vision and shared visions.

This ambitious series of lectures, given to large audiences and well received both in the UK and internationally, established the reputation of the developments at UCL, which were further enhanced by the First Freud Memorial Professor in 1975/76.

He was Roy Schafer, a practising analyst, whose work had contributed greatly to psychoanalytical theory and who was then Chief Clinical Psychologist at Yale University Health Services and Professor of Psychiatric Psychology at Yale. His inaugural lecture was entitled 'The psychoanalytic life history', and he gave other public lectures on free association; self-control; impotence, fridigity and sexism; self-love and self-hatred. In addition, a series of interdepartmental lectures took place entitled 'Psychoanalytic interpretation: an introduction to Freud'.

During 1976/77 the Chair was held by William Gillespie, formerly President of the British Psychoanalytical Society and the International Psychoanalytical Association and Emeritus Physician at the Maudsley Hospital. His inaugural lecture was 'The legacy of Sigmund Freud', and there were other public lectures on Freud and science; Freud and culture; symbolism and language; Freud and sexuality; psychic structure and structuralism; and some controversial issues, including the death instinct.

Hanna Segal held the Chair in 1977/78, giving as her inaugural lecture 'Psychoanalysis and the freedom of thought', a series of public lectures on fantasy, dreams and symbolism plus a series of interdepartmental lectures providing an 'Introduction to psychoanalysis'.

In 1978/79 the College was fortunate in having Joseph Sandler, a leading exponent of Anna Freud's group, himself a practising analyst and then President of the European Psychoanalytical

Federation, to give as Freud Memorial Professor his inaugural lecture, 'Unconscious wishes and human relationships'. Public lectures followed, entitled:

'The inner world: a psychoanalytic view', 'The psychoanalytic psychology of adaptation' and 'Pain and depression: a psychoanalytic perspective', together with a series of interdepartmental lectures on psychoanalytic psychology.

André Green brought a continental European approach in 1979/80 with an inaugural lecture entitled 'Psychoanalysis and ordinary modes of thought'. He gave a wide-ranging series of public lectures in addition, as follows:

'Psychoanalytic theory—the language of experience'; 'Transference and metaphor'; 'Contradictory aspects of time in psychoanalysis'; 'The child and the dream'; 'Representation—a multiple function'; 'A hypothetical model of language in psychoanalysis'; 'Tertiary processes and symbolization'; 'Identity and difference'; 'Madness and psychosis'.

A rather different approach was adopted during 1980/81, when three distinguished contributors each spent roughly a term at the College. John Bowlby, then at the Tavistock, who had made valuable contributions to child psychiatry, lectured in the first term on 'Psychoanalysis as a natural science'. In term two Christopher Lasch, Professor of History at the University of Rochester, New York, and interested in the application of psychoanalysis to historical and sociological problems, lectured on 'The Freudian left and the theory of cultural revolution' and 'The transition from patriarchal authority to bureaucratic authority in Western Europe and America'. Karl Pribram of the Stanford University Medical Center, interested in the neurological basis of psychoanalytical theory, lectured in the third term on 'The concept of energy in psychology—late nineteenth- and twentieth-century views'.

Tragedy entered the programme before the beginning of the 1980/81 session when John Klauber, then President of the British Psychoanalytical Society and Freud Professor-elect, sadly died. Fortunately Dr Klauber's inaugural lecture was complete, and the lecture was read by a close colleague of his in October 1981, under the title 'The role of illusion in the psychoanalytic cure'. The response subsequent to the reading was such that the College realized what a successful occupant of the Chair John Klauber would have been.

For the 1982/83 session, Mme Janine Chasseguet-Smirgel, a practising analyst and past President of the Paris Psychoanalytical Society, who has interests in 'art and psychoanalysis' and also in 'politics, ideologies and psychoanalysis', accepted the Chair and gave a most illuminating series of lectures on the theme 'Perversion and the universal law'.

The last holder of the Freud Memorial Chair as a Visiting Professorship was the distinguished Professor Albert Solnit, then Sterling Professor of Paediatrics and Psychiatry and Director of the Child Study Center at Yale University, who had collaborated with Anna Freud on seminal works such as 'Beyond the best interests of the child'. While at UCL, he lectured in a penetrating fashion on 'Memory as preparation: developmental and psychoanalytic perspectives'.

The Freud Memorial Chair since 1984

The College and the Board of Management, recognizing the value of the Chair to the College community in particular, was by 1983 beginning to consider ways in which its occupants might be able to achieve still more for psychoanalysis as an academic discipline, have a more widely ranging influence within UCL and be able to play a more substantial role in undergraduate and postgraduate student education. Since 1980, moreover, the College had possessed a Faculty of Clinical Sciences (formerly the University College Hospital Medical School) and, accordingly, wished to offer students in the clinical phase of medical education the opportunity to benefit from contact with holders of the Chair.

After extensive discussion it was the unanimous decision of the Board of Management, which includes the College's benefactor, Mr Astor, that the best way forward was to extend the tenure of each holder of the Chair from one year to a substantially longer period (five years in the first instance was envisaged) from the start of the session 1984/85. The College would continue to recognize the essential need of the holder of the Chair to maintain a personal psychoanalytic practice and would wish the Professor to be concerned in developing a programme of activities by visiting lecturers so as to ensure that a proper variety of psychoanalytic viewpoints continues to be represented in UCL. At the same time the long-term character of the professorial appointment would provide opportunities for further exciting developments in the role of psychoanalysis as an academic discipline, along the general lines of those many other impressive innovative movements with which UCL has for so long been associated.

And so it has proved since the outstanding choice of Joseph Sandler as the first long-term holder of the Freud Memorial Chair. He has created an important research unit in Psychoanalysis and been active in the supervision of PhD students and also in many other new developments in postgraduate and undergraduate teaching, and he has made UCL a great centre for psychoanalytic study and exchange of ideas. The recent unification of UCL with the Middlesex Hospital Medical School, with its powerful tradition in psychiatric teaching, research and clinical practice, has brought many additional benefits and given exciting new opportunities to Joe Sandler as Freud Memorial Professor in the united institution.

This work celebrates 14 years of the Freud Memorial Professorship programme: ten years of the excellent Visiting Professorship arrangements, and four years since the inauguration of the vigorous and now well established UCL Psychoanalysis Unit under Professor Sandler's inspired direction. In this collection of Lectures associated with the programme (mainly Inaugural Lectures by the Professors—some of which I had the privilege of chairing) it is a pleasure to observe with admiration the special skills of exposition deployed by the authors as they 'professed' their subjects to general audiences gathered to listen and learn from them here at University College London.

James Lighthill
University College London
October 1988

DIMENSIONS OF PSYCHOANALYSIS

CHAPTER ONE

Introduction

Joseph Sandler

I t is a regrettable fact that many experts in fields outside psychoanalysis—in literature, philosophy, sociology, history, art, for example—equate psychoanalysis with the writings of Sigmund Freud and tend to neglect the enormous and significant developments that have taken place in psychoanalytic thinking since Freud's death. Christopher Lasch points out, in Chapter 8, that most socio-political writers of the left have shown little interest in Freud's later writings; but what Lasch describes is a widespread tendency among many intellectuals.

Fortunately it has been possible to bring together in this volume the thoughts and viewpoints of a number of scholars who, while not all psychoanalysts, have a deep acquaintance with current aspects of the field. The preparation of an inaugural lecture is something that is never taken lightly, and in each of the lectures the author has managed to convey his or her vision of psychoanalysis as a whole as well as making a significant new contribution.

One of the functions served by this collection is to demonstrate how much and how fruitfully psychoanalysis has developed. This advancement has not been an even one, and as a consequence a significant number of psychoanalytic concepts have not been fully integrated with other equally significant ones. Even within Freud's writings developments occurred in a number of different directions and have continued to do so since (this phenomenon is discussed at some length in Chapter 13.) The contents of this book bear testimony to this, for although it is evident that current psychoanalytic ideas share a set of basic assumptions (such as that of unconscious mental functioning), the relationship between these ideas is not always clear-cut. Yet even though the relative lack of integration of many analytic concepts with one another is from one point of view undesirable, it is their very diversity that provides an exciting and dynamic force in the dialectical development of the ideas that constitute psychoanalysis. *Dimensions of Psychoanalysis* is an appropriate title for this book, because the reader will be able to extract from it the common ground in different areas of psychoanalytic thinking, as well as the differences of approach, both explicit and implicit, in the 'position statements' that follow. Thus Roy Schafer, in 'The psychoanalytic life history' (Chapter 2) considers problems facing both psychoanalytic theory and clinical practice today and puts forward the view that psychoanalysis needs a new language. He proceeds from a consideration of the nature of clinical psychoanalysis and sees it as 'an interpretive discipline whose concern it is to construct life histories of human beings'. He traces the influence of existential and phenomenological thinkers and proposes an *action language* 'for Freudian psychoanalysis viewed as a life-historical discipline'.

Schafer points out that psychoanalysis constructs a very special sort of personal past for the patient as well as a present subjective world, and he relates these constructions to the way in which the person in analysis sees his or her life history. Schafer's presentation of the way in which the personal past of an analysand is constructed represents a development that has substantial implications for the psychoanalytic theory relating to the reconstruction of the childhood past of the patient. He shows how the infantile material brought by the patient is organized by analyst and patient working together and stresses the importance of a knowledge of child development and its relevance for the construction of the life history during the course of analysis.

Schafer differentiates the way in which a subjective world of the present is *constructed* in analysis from psychic reality. He shows how one establishes a perspective on the subjective world as 'primarily a child's atemporal, wishful, and frightened construction of reality'. In all of this the 'disturbing and disturbed present' is given new meaning, and the role and nature of insight in this context is assessed. Schafer then presents his thesis that the analyst develops a view of the analysand's life history as *action*. The idea of action includes the mental acts of wishing, imagining and remembering. Schafer argues that the 'action language' approach provides a gain in theoretical consistency, and he links this with his formulations about the construction of the patient's life history. The patient must take responsibility for his actions—'the analysand must be brought to recognize unconscious defence as personal activity'. Those in analysis have to 'reclaim their disclaimed actions'; the relevance of this to the problem of the mechanisms of change through psychoanalytic therapy is obvious.

In 'The legacy of Sigmund Freud' (Chapter 3) William Gillespie brings his long experience and personal knowledge of the development of psychoanalysis, particularly in Britain, to the understanding of Freud's achievements and the lines of progression that have followed from them. He gives a clear presentation of the essentials of Freudian theory and its later advancement, but Gillespie does not simply restate standard notions about psychoanalysis, for he raises and discusses a number of issues that are of significance for psychoanalysis today. Should analysis be judged primarily on the basis of its therapeutic results? Should the problem of man's nature be regarded as a biological or a psychological one? Are language and verbalization fundamental and essential features of the psychoanalytic process?

A major theme in this chapter is the way in which Freud's own history, his education, his self-analysis, the influence of various thinkers and colleagues, as well as the general intellectual and scientific climate of the time, have influenced psychoanalysis. Gillespie's presentation represents a bringing together of the fundamental findings and theoretical convictions characteristic of the early years of psychoanalysis with the ways in which psychoanalysis has subsequently branched out, both in its applications and in its theory.

Hanna Segal, in 'Psychoanalysis and freedom of thought' (Chapter 4), points out that the great step taken by Freud was his realization that thoughts that had previously been regarded as unthinkable were not. In this and in his achievements he can be compared with such thinkers as Copernicus and Darwin. Segal emphasizes that the battle for the freedom of thought has to be fought individually with every analysand, as well as within oneself. Whereas an external authority can make us afraid to speak, the fear of internal authority in the shape of the superego is a source of inhibition of thought. Segal reminds us how complex the superego is because it is so much more than the sum total of parental prohibitions, and 'its savagery goes far beyond that of most parents'. In agreement with Melanie Klein, she sees the superego not only as an internalization of parental prohibitions, but also as a result of the projection into those parental figures of some of one's own impulses and phantasies. So both the ideal and persecutory aspects of the superego have roots in the infant's own impulses. She makes the interesting point that the superego's prohibition against thoughts is also in part a projection of the infantile self's own antagonism to thought. Thinking limits the omnipotence of the infant's phantasy and is therefore attacked because of the longing to retain that omnipotence. Segal's use of clinical illustrations convincingly reinforces her argument.

Basing her work on that of Melanie Klein and Wilfred Bion, Segal then addresses herself to the nature and origin of thought and shows how hunger in the infant can be experienced as the presence of a bad attacking object. Such a bad object can only be dealt with by expulsion. The need for the absent object is linked with infantile hallucination and later childhood phantasies. For Segal omnipotent phantasy is not a thought because it is not recognized as such. A thought occurs when a phantasy is recognized as a product of one's own mind.

The hatred of thought processes can be active throughout life, and Segal demonstrates this graphically through a clinical example. She shows how conflict can occur between thoughts and the omnipotent unconscious phantasy of being at one with an ideal breast. Disillusion is necessary for thought to develop.

Following a discussion of the relation of belief to thought, Segal emphasizes the need for patients to face their omnipotent phantasies and to deal with the feelings of helplessness and dependence that result. The omnipotent phantasies have to be turned into thoughts, with the result that there can be a testing of the reality of the omnipotence of one's wishes. She then explores the notion of internal reality in regard to such feelings as love, gratitude and guilt and asks how these affect behaviour in the external world. She then reflects on the relation of integration to thinking. Thought allows conflict and seeks resolution, and integration is a step from phantasy to thinking. All this results in a change in the individual's sense of values. Finally, Segal reminds us that freedom of thought is also the freedom to know one's own thoughts, the bad as well as the good; but there are important forces, external and internal, that militate against this freedom.

In 'Unconscious wishes and human relationships' (Chapter 5), I point out that there has been an increasing tendency in recent years to consider normal and pathological processes in terms of the vicissitudes of the person's object relationships. This is often seen to be in conflict with the idea of sexual and aggressive instinctual drives and wishes as the prime motivating forces in human behaviour and development. The view put forward is that there is no necessary incompatibility between unconscious wishes (instinctual or otherwise) on the one hand, and object relationships on the other. Nevertheless, in order to bring the two together, psychoanalytic theory has to take a step forward.

To begin with, theoretical emphasis can be placed on *wishes* as opposed to drives, even though instinctual drives can be regarded as entering into many of the infant's wishes. Moreover, drives are not the only motivating forces in unconscious wishes. After a certain point in early development has been reached, wishes acquire a content that includes representations of self and object in interaction. Starting from the point of view that an object relationship can be a valued relation between oneself and another person, it is evident that such relationships begin early in life. Relationships as they exist in *phantasy* develop from very primitive feelings and perceptual experiences.

The idea that all wishes are instinctual is strongly contested, and attention is drawn to the role of, for example, narcissistic blows and threats to self-esteem, and the pain of object loss, as powerful motivators of unconscious wishes. I suggest that anxiety in its various forms is a very potent stimulus to wishful activity aimed at restoring feelings of safety and well-being. From this it follows that we can have a wish to establish (or to reestablish) particular types of relationship, and I elaborate the view that a psychoanalytic theory of motivation related to the control of feeling states should replace a psychoanalytic psychology that regards behaviour as predominantly motivated by the pressure towards sexual or aggressive instinctual drive discharge. The idea of wish fulfilment bringing about a change in one's perception of reality is discussed, leading to the conclusion that a signal or information theory of wish fulfilment is appropriate rather than one based on the discharge of drive energy. (In Chapter 9 Karl Pribram puts forward a different view.) If we accept the argument put forward here, we can bring together the idea of an object relations psychology and a psychology based on unconscious wishes. The chapter ends with a reference to the relevance of work on the 'meshing' of infant and mother, 'synchrony', mutual 'cuing', and the like. Object relationships become intimately connected with wish fulfilling 'meshing' between self and object.

André Green, in 'Psychoanalysis and ordinary modes of thought' (Chapter 6), argues that Freud had to recognize the existence of modes of thought that were much more extraordinary than he had anticipated. Green discusses a particular form of logic at work behind the scenes in the patient's free associations. We cannot say that primary and secondary processes are opposed to one another, nor that one is irrational and the other rational. Green refers to Freud's distinction between the primitive on the one hand, and the conscious and reasonable on the other, and suggests that the two can be united in a third form that is different from the sum of the other two. In the analytic situation, the discourse of the analysand is, and equally *is not*, the analysand, and we can see a particular form of reunion of these two aspects. What the analysand shows is the expression of a compromise between the unconscious and the conscious as well as a compromise between the desire to be in contact with the analyst and the desire to avoid this contact with him. The analyst has to decipher this compromise. Green elaborates the idea of a third category of processes, which, he suggests, can be called the instruments of liaison or connections—the *tertiary* processes. Green goes on to apply an alternative logic to what

Freud had said about the conflict between different psychic structures and proceeds to the notion that the only reality is the reality of what is *not* there, that which makes one suffer by its absence. Green asserts that the strange logic of the patient can inflict a narcissistic hurt on the analyst by imposing on him its extraordinary mode of thought.

Finally Green refers to Freud's distinction between historical truth and material truth. This can be connected with the notion of narrative truth, because for Green historical truth also involves a secret language, a secret system of thought. He then points out that Freud's work is historically true but not *materially* true. His solutions were compromises between a core of truth and a psychological construction that reflected his own training and experience.

John Bowlby, in 'Psychoanalysis as a natural science' (Chapter 7), recalls Freud's assertion that psychoanalysis can claim to be a science and goes on to consider this in the light of his own thinking. He is opposed to those who regard psychoanalysis as only being involved with the private internal world of thought, phantasy and feeling; it is equally concerned with real experiences in the external world. Both the internal and external have to be studied, as well as the interaction between the two.

Bowlby describes his research as it developed from the consideration of separation. He emphasizes the pathogenic effect of the loss of the mother figure and concludes that the first task for psychoanalytic theory is to understand the nature of the child's tie to his mother. He demonstrates the influence on his psychoanalytic thinking of ethological conceptions and then develops an essentially biological approach to dealing with the question of separation anxiety and attachment behaviour. He is able to show how different his view is from Freud's traditional one which involves ideas of libidinal phases, fixation and regression. Bowlby regards recent work on separation as highly relevant for the practice of psychoanalytic therapy.

The sort of natural science Bowlby has in mind for psychoanalysis is at variance with Karl Popper's model, and the experimental methods of the physical sciences. Psychoanalysis should rather conform as closely as possible to the methods of the biological scientists.

Christopher Lasch, in 'The Freudian left and the theory of cultural revolution' (Chapter 8), addresses himself to the 'improbable alliance of psychoanalysis and cultural radicalism, of Freud and Marx'. After the First World War and the rise of fascism, doubts arose in the intellectual left about the inevitability of historical progress, and there was a turning to psychoanalysis because it was set against the view that men are masters of themselves; the Freudian left took the view that as a consequence men *need* masters. Lasch is concerned with the psychology of power, with the sources of resistance to social change and with why attempts to get rid of authoritarianism result in its re-establishment. Lasch then embarks on a discussion of the view that psychoanalysis relates internal conflict to the internalization of social authority and to the institution of the patriarchal family, 'which crushes the revolt of the son against the father, saddles the son with a guilty conscience, and makes him grow up to become a tyrant in his own right'. All the diverse schools of the Freudian left make the assumption that the patriarchal family is the source of organized oppression. Revolution is linked with the overthrow of the father, and support is found for this in Freud's ideas about the primal horde. But, says Lasch, we are misled if we make use of the earlier psychoanalytic model of the mind, and a revision is necessary. In his ensuing discussion Lasch is clearly influenced by those post-Freudian psychoanalysts who have placed emphasis on the pre-oedipal phases of development. He is also influenced by Freudian feminism, which has drawn attention to the importance of the pre-oedipal mother. He finds himself in agreement with Janine Chasseguet-Smirgel, who suggests that many groups may share a phantasy of collective reunion with the mother and tend to choose as a leader someone who gives them the chance *not* to identify with the father. Lasch's presentation goes far to support his contention that psychoanalysis has much to contribute to social and political theory.

Karl Pribram, in 'Psychoanalysis and the natural sciences: the brain–behaviour connection from Freud to the present' (Chapter 9), indicates his agreement with both Freud and Bowlby that psychoanalysis *can* be characterized as a science, but in order to remain one it has to take account of recent work and to make use of observations made with techniques other than the psychoanalytic method.

After considering Freud's work in the context of end-of-century science, Pribram devotes particular attention to the concept of energy. Unlike those (like myself—see Chapter 13) who would now replace the energy theory with information-processing formulations, the abandoning of the energy concept, says Pribram, would be unfortunate. He relates motivation and emotion to quantitative aspects of energy and points out that the 'stop' and 'go' mechanisms in the brain are linked with energy-related functions. Pribram pays special attention to Freud's formulations in his 'Project for a scientific psychology' (Freud, 1950a) and clearly attaches great importance to that early work of Freud. He finds a resemblance between Freud's formulations there and his own ideas and contends that a comprehensive neuropsychological theory as extensive as that developed by Freud in the Project can be constructed on present evidence.

John Klauber, in 'The role of illusion in psychoanalytic cure' (Chapter 10), sees transference as an area in which truth and illusion are commingled. An increasingly important task of psychoanalytic therapy is to separate the two. Following a discussion of the transference concept, Klauber points out the difficulty both patient and analyst have in recognizing and accepting the transference, which is considered by Klauber as a therapeutic madness induced by psychoanalysis, producing confusional and delusional features. All of this is a form of illusion, which Klauber sees as a new piece of understanding expressing itself in the language of artistic creativity—it is the illusion that puts the patient in touch with the reality of his feelings.

Klauber stresses that clinical success is linked with the degree to which the analyst's humanity is coordinated with his analytic function. The analyst has to tolerate the patient's and his own emotions. Finally, 'as one discriminates one's feelings better, they can be experienced more sharply and therefore allow one to love another person, or an ideal, wholeheartedly.'

Janine Chasseguet-Smirgel, in 'Perversion and the universal law' (Chapter 11), sees the perversions 'not just as disorders of a sexual nature affecting a relatively small number of people but . . .

a temptation in the mind common to us all.' Perversion is a dimension of the mind that is connected with man's wish to escape from his condition, and Chasseguet-Smirgel notes that perversions appear to be particularly evident before major historical upheavals, as if the hope for the advent of a new world is reflected in a desire to escape from the genital universe of the father. Taking the Marquis de Sade's works as an example, she concludes that we consider the world of perversion as that of the sadistic bringing about of chaos. Chasseguet-Smirgel shows us how psychoanalytic thinking can be extended to the study of social conditions; indeed, the two areas interpenetrate, and the one cannot really be separated from the other.

In a chapter of a very different sort, 'Memory as preparation: developmental and psychoanalytic perspectives' (Chapter 12), Albert Solnit addresses himself to the problem of preparing a child for potentially traumatic experiences. Solnit's thinking is thoroughly embedded in a developmental point of view, and in this work he traces the role of remembering in a number of different areas. He presents us with several detailed case accounts and formulates a view of the function of memory that is a move forward from Freud's idea of abreacting a trauma through remembering. Solnit shows us how preparing a child or adult for a threatening event can be helpful because it organizes a set of memories that can function to protect the person's capacity to feel coherent and therefore safe. Solnit emphasizes the need for defences in normal life and points out that the therapeutic undoing of repression after a trauma is only appropriate when more tolerable alternatives are available.

Solnit also considers the question of historical truth and indicates how difficult it is to get at this; but a portion of historical truth, in addition to narrative truth, is necessary in order that reconstruction in therapy should lead to a greater coherence of the individual's self. Remembering, says Solnit, has two important functions: the first is the function of coping in order to master, while the second is to prepare the individual for future events and for future development. Each person has to know himself as worthwhile and to feel that he is in charge of himself.

The first part of 'The id—or the child within' (Chapter 13) is concerned with the need to take a historical approach if psychoanalytic concepts are to be fully understood, for it is only in the historical context that their full relation to one another becomes evident. Following a discussion of the aims of psychoanalysis and a consideration of the concept of unconscious conflict, I suggest that, from a clinical point of view, the notion of conflict between id and the other mental agencies can be simplistic and misleading, for what we see in our patients is unconscious conflict 'between some tendency or urge which was once acceptable ... to the patient's consciousness, and a counterforce which came into existence during the course of development'. This need not be a sexual or aggressive instinctual urge (though it may be), but can well be a peremptory urge to impose a childhood *solution* to an anxiety-arousing conflict. Clinical material is given to illustrate this thesis, and the value of considering 'the child within' rather than the id as the source of peremptory conflictual impulses is recommended.

I hope the reader will find this volume both informative and exciting. While it cannot cover the spectrum of what we understand by psychoanalysis today, it provides a sampling of a number of important trends in areas of current psychoanalytic interest.

CHAPTER TWO

The psychoanalytic life history

Roy Schafer

I n his wartime poem of 1940, 'In memory of Sigmund Freud (d. Sept. 1939)', the late W. H. Auden told how Freud was 'taken away'

> To go back to the earth in London,
> An important Jew who died in exile.

The poet hastened to add this cry of outrage:

> Only Hate was happy, hoping to augment
> His practice now, and his dingy clientele
>   Who think they can be cured by killing
>   And covering the gardens with ashes.

Against the figure of Hate, Auden was holding up the image of Freud's psychoanalysis. It was an image of love and enlightenment in a world overrun with ugliness: of forgiveness, restoration and reunion; of enthusiasm, delight and dedication; and of the preciousness of the honestly remembered and individualized life. Perhaps lacking the stern, uncompromising element, but still very true to its subject.

What, then, could be more appropriate than establishing the Freud Memorial Professorship here in London? London is appropriate, too, for its having long been the home and centre of creative work of Freud's distinguished daughter, Miss Anna Freud, and of so many other notable and dedicated psychoanalysts. And that this Inaugural is taking place at University College London adds all the more to the appropriateness of the occasion, for this College already proudly claims among its many humane and enlightened firsts its taking into its student body Jews, women and other victims of prejudice—the socially repressed who are the counterparts and often the symbols of the individually repressed. I can imagine no honour greater for a psychoanalyst, and none more moving, than to be chosen to inaugurate this Memorial Professorship.

For some years now the chief problem confronting psychoanalytic theoreticians has been the need to develop a new language in which to speak of their methods and findings and conduct their debates with one another and with members of other disciplines. This need has developed as a result of searching and successful critiques by psychoanalysts and philosophers of Freud's natural science language—what he called his metapsychology. Inevitably, successful critiques leave a void that must be filled. In the instance of psychoanalysis, the void can be filled neither by any ordinary or common-sense locutions nor by impressionistic, idiosyncratic, quasi-poetic rhetoric. Although both sorts of expression constitute the clinical dialogue, just as they make up communication and thought in daily life, they will not serve for systematic discourse. The reason why they will not serve is that these languages follow tacit, elusive and incompatible rules of every kind. They render psychological events both as entities and as processes, the one calling for nominative and adjectival designations and the other for verbal and adverbial designations. Additionally, their employment is characterized by frequent switching from the active voice to the passive, from plain description to metaphoric allusion, and from abstract to concrete terms.

What is especially important in this connection is that, when speaking either of these languages, the theoretician and lay person alike typically switch at those points where problems of logical consistency or else difficulties in thinking through and articulating some ambiguous notion are encountered—or, if not there, then at those points where switching helps modulate or avoid emotional tension. All of which we can appreciate as conducive to good work, good rapport and good spirits, but never as well suited for framing the systematic propositions that constitute a discipline.

With all its imperfections, metapsychology is systematic, and its durability has depended heavily on this fact. Its constituent terms, such as energy, force, structure and mechanism, imply definite and binding rules, which make possible a high degree of coherence within and among metapsychological propositions. A new language for psychoanalysis must do the same.

In deciding on a new language for psychoanalysis, one must first decide just what kind of discipline clinical psychoanalysis is. It has been becoming increasingly clear in recent years that clinical psychoanalysis is an interpretive discipline whose concern it is to construct life histories of human beings. The principal business of psychoanalysis is to interpret and to reinterpret in life-historical perspective the verbal and other utterances of the analysand during the psychoanalytic session. Psychoanalysis is used to establish meaning or significance where none has been apparent, as in the instance of seemingly senseless compulsions, and to increase the intelligibility of its data by establishing the life-historical contexts of that which is to be further understood, as in the instances of dreams and inhibitions. That its objects of study—the analysand primarily and the analyst secondarily—are human beings cannot be overemphasized. They are persons who have been shaped by language and who now use it to create new meanings and so new worlds. In this they are unlike atoms, stars, acids, bridges, machines, computers or lower organisms. Consequently, the discipline of psychoanalysis faces problems that are much more like those of the humanities than those of the natural sciences. These are the problems of perspective, subjective evidence and inference, and reliability and validity of interpretation. Specifically, the discipline must develop an ordered account of the doings of human beings in a special kind of relationship into which only language-using, historically oriented human beings can enter—the psychoanalytic relationship.

It was the modern existential and phenomenological thinkers who laid the groundwork for this revised conception of the nature of the psychoanalytic enterprise and who attempted to work out their own humanistic language for psychoanalysis. Their language, or rather their set of overlapping languages, reflects philosophical commitments and projects of many kinds, and, to my way of thinking, it is not well suited to the methods and data of clinical psychoanalysis. This is so perhaps chiefly because these thinkers seem to have used psychoanalysis for philosophical prescription; they have not investigated it as a discipline in its own right.

The project of which I shall speak is that of developing an action language specifically for Freudian psychoanalysis viewed as a life-historical discipline (Schafer, 1976). It is one by means of which psychoanalysts may hope to speak simply, systematically and nonmechanistically of human activities in general, and of the psychoanalytic relationship and its therapeutic effects in particular. The general nature and some of the justification for this language will become evident in the course of this lecture. In executing this project, I have drawn on contemporary philosophical studies of action concepts, mind and existence.

I shall be developing three interrelated theses concerning the nature of the clinical psychoanalytic enterprise: (1) that it constructs a personal past of a certain kind; (2) that it constructs a present subjective world of a certain kind; and (3) that both of these constructions require a relatively systematic transformation of the terms in which the analysand defines and understands his or her life history up to and including the present moment. I shall be considering only general distinguishing features of psychoanalytic interpretation as a method of history-making and world-defining. It is not implied that these three theses are the only general ones that should count in an understanding of psychoanalysis.

The first thesis is that a psychoanalysis consists of the construction of a personal past. It is not *the* personal past but *a* personal past. However convincing it may be, it remains a construction, merely a history of a certain kind. To construct any history that is coherent and more than a sprawling and stultifying chronicle, one must lay it out only along certain lines. In psycho-analytic work, for instance, one is not constructing physiological or narrowly linguistic life histories, nor is one simply arranging chronologically any kind of data stated in any kind of terms.

What is distinctive about this Freudian life history? My answer has two parts: one part concerns that which it is a history of, and the other, which I shall take up in presenting the third thesis, expresses a characteristic point of view we take of this life-historical material. The material itself is organized around personal versions of the major and typical sexual and aggressive conflicts of early childhood. The idea of conflict implies the infantile danger situations, such as loss of loved persons and loss of their love, and the anxieties and defences that are features of these situations. And the idea of danger situations is conceived subjectively; that is, it refers to the child's view of itself and its world, to what it experiences emotionally and often unconsciously. Further, one understands the child to be defining this experience largely in the terms of primitive bodily awareness and conceptualization—one might say in terms of infantile categories of understanding. The child's categories are based on organs (e.g., mouth, anus, genitalia), substances (e.g., faeces, urine, milk, blood), movements (e.g., sucking, fingering, straining, falling), and contacts (e.g., kissing, clinging, hitting). A good case in point is Freud's obsessional Rat Man, of whom one can say this, that unconsciously he was steadily constructing and maintaining a sadistic reality through the application of predominantly anal bodily categories.

In this light Freud's proposition that the ego is 'first and foremost a bodily ego' refers to the formative role played by the categories of psychosexual and aggressive understanding. It is in the terms of these categories that the child constitutes the primitive human reality of itself in its surroundings. The infantile issues of defining oneself and others, of loving and hating oneself and others, of activity and passivity, pleasure and pain, danger, idealization, identification, reparation, reality testing—all of these are constituted in the terms of these categories of understanding. Important as it is to trace the history of these issues throughout the child's development, one must not lose sight of the principle that they are, so to say, authored by the bodily ego.

Freud's suggestion that the infant's first act of judgement is deciding whether to swallow or spit out implies the oral category of
understanding, which, one might add, we keep on using to the last,
and not only unconsciously.

This infantile material is not transparent and simply waiting to
be organized. For even though the adult analysand may remember
some of it in these bodily terms, it is the analyst who starts
constituting much of it as analytic data by asking certain questions, following certain methods, and defining only certain contexts of meaning. Undoubtedly, the recovery of unconscious
memories and the reconstruction of infantile experience are essential to the method, but one should not confuse this clinical truth
with the methodological proposition that the analytic data have to
be constituted as such. That proposition says that one cannot
establish either the historical sense or the current significance of a
fact outside of some context of questions and methods for defining
and organizing the material in question. Only by steadily thinking
in terms of the infantile, body-based psychosexual and aggressive
conflicts can the Freudian analyst define, as psychoanalytically
relevant information, that which he or she will then use in
interpretations.

A complex relation exists between the child's bodily categorial
principles and the analyst's organizing concepts. I may have
seemed to be contradicting myself, saying on the one hand that the
categories are found in the analytic material and on the other hand
that they are applied to it by the analyst. To resolve this apparent
paradox one must consider another question about the psychoanalytic life history. This is the question whether it is a history that is
told forward from its beginning or backward from its ending in the
present. It has been said that it is the story of one's life told in
reverse and that the method is necessarily retrospective. Although
there is much truth in this view, it does not catch the whole
truth. Perhaps the chief point to make against it is that the analyst
does not approach each analysis as if having to rediscover psychoanalysis all over again. It is not just that, in all likelihood, the
analyst has already taken an anamnesis as part of his or her initial
assessment of the analysand's problems and suitability for the
psychoanalytic method. More important is the psychoanalytically

defined knowledge the analyst already possesses about the typical stages and conflicts of development, the typical modes of moving through these stages and resolving or repressing these conflicts, and the typical ways in which the child's resulting viewpoints on pleasure, danger, failure and success remain features of adult life.

Here, 'typical' includes more than is suggested by the words normal or favourable; it includes as well many abnormal, traumatic, disruptive features of development, such as severe illnesses and extreme deprivations. It also includes the disturbing family contexts in which, too often, the formative years are spent, such as cruel or seductive upbringing, loss of parents or siblings through death or separation, and radical changes in physical, social, and emotional milieu. Although psychoanalysts disagree among themselves on the exact nature and timing of the cognitive and emotional features of development and on the relative importance of psychic reality or unconscious fantasy on the one hand and the actual environment or external reality on the other, they nevertheless agree on a considerable body of accrued psychoanalytic knowledge about healthy and disturbed development. Here, psychoanalysts may lay some claim to being engaged in a scientific enterprise: they can say a lot about the conditions or causes of different types of development. In this respect, psychoanalysis is forward-looking rather than retrospective, developmental rather than historically reconstructive. It remains true, however, that this knowledge of development was in the first instance arrived at retrospectively or historically; its basic shape has been not so much altered by the findings of child analysis and psychoanalytic observation of infants as filled in, refined and confirmed by them.

The analyst uses this knowledge, in one or another of its versions, when listening to the analysand, thinking what that person is likely to have gone through in order to have arrived at his or her present distinctive plight. But at the same time the analyst is already conceiving of that present plight in terms that reflect the psychoanalytic account of human development. One may say that the analyst uses the general past to constitute the individualized present that is to be explained while using that present as a basis for inquiry into the individualized past. Thus, while moving with the analysand back and forth through time, the analyst bases interpretations on both present communication and a general knowledge of possible and probable pasts that have yet to be established and detailed in the specific case.

All of which is to say that for the psychoanalytic life-historical investigation there is no reverse direction. The life history, far from being linear or directional, is circular, for psychoanalytic interpretation is circular. Events may be recounted forward or backward, but what counts as an event in this kind of history is established by a circular kind of understanding. Alternatively, interpretation is a particularized creative action performed within a tradition of procedure and understanding. It has no beginning and no end.

To return now to the question of whether the fateful bodily categorial principles are found or applied, one must answer that they are both: the facts are what it is psychoanalytically meaningful and useful to designate, and what it is meaningful to designate is established by the facts; one looks for idiosyncratic versions of what has usually been found and one finds the sort of thing that one is looking for. Plenty of room is left for unexpected findings and new puzzles. Like the historian, the analyst works within this interpretive or hermeneutical circle. Although Freud approached this point when, in discussing early sexuality, he said very simply (1933a) 'Enough can be seen in the children if one knows how to look', he did not reach it owing to his taking a natural science view of psychoanalytic investigation.

What is therapeutic about the construction of this life history, I shall come to later. At this point I want to move on to the second thesis, which is that a psychoanalysis consists of the construction of a present subjective world of a certain kind. Again, not *the* present world but *a* present world. Like the past, the psychoanalytic present is not more than one of a number of possible constructions. To be systematic, it must be realized through the consistent application of one set of categories. By this is meant the Freudian present achieved through the Freudian categories.

This present subjective world is not identical with what, in psychoanalytic writing, has been called psychic reality. For the concept of psychic reality implies the following three points: first, all the relevant mental processes have already taken place and have organized themselves, unconsciously at least; second, this mental activity has been carried on in the very terms of Freudian analysis; and third, the business of interpretation is, therefore, simply to uncover hidden ideas or experiences so that the analysand may then deal with them consciously and rationally. I shall bypass the epistemological difficulties of this idea of psychic reality and say only that it does not convey the clinical analyst's interpretive activities accurately or fully. It is not being questioned that psychoanalysis uncovers already established and unconsciously maintained ideas and experiences; nor is it being questioned that this is the case especially for archaic and potentially highly emotional features of existence. It may be accepted that this is the psychic reality the psychoanalyst takes up under the aspects of transference, resistance and acting out. But with the concept of the present subjective world one is considering the nature of psychoanalytic knowledge itself. And here the point is that the psychoanalyst constructs this world through those aspects of interpretation that implement the Freudian strategy of defining significance, interrelatedness and context. By means of this strategy one also makes of psychic reality something more than, and something different from, what it has been. Among other things, one establishes for the analysand a perspective on it as primarily a child's atemporal, wishful and frightened construction of reality and as such a construction that is in principle modifiable. To accept this modifiability is itself a new action and one of the most important a person can ever perform.

The psychoanalyst also establishes that the analysand continues to construct this kind of reality out of present circumstance, necessity and happening. It is only in this connection that one can truly appreciate the importance of constructing the psychoanalytic life history. For, working within the Freudian circle, one cannot investigate and interpret the present subjective world without the understanding to be gained through historical investigation and interpretation. The disturbances of the present life, whether they be symptoms, inhibitions, other functional disruptions or character malformations, are doomed to remain unintelligible without coordinate historical analysis. The point of the historical inquiry is the elucidation of the present world, especially in its disturbed aspects. As a therapist, one is not interested in establishing historical explanations for their own sake;

nor is one usually preoccupied with undisturbed functioning, which anyway tends to remain mostly opaque to psychoanalytic scrutiny. The therapist aims to be practical, not theoretical. Basically, he or she is trying to establish the ways in which the disturbed psychosexual and aggressive past has not yet become the past. Here one thinks of Freud's emphasizing the timelessness of unconscious mental processes. One wants to establish how the disturbed past has continued to be, unconsciously, the disturbing present.

In this way, one gives new meaning and organization to the disturbing and disturbed present. One wants especially to show, through what has customarily been called the analysis of the ego, and of transference, resistance and acting out, that the analysand's mode of establishing meaning in the present is based unconsciously on his or her persisting and disturbing application of certain infantile categorial principles. For example, and here I am speaking schematically, one wants to show how analysand X repetitively makes of his marriage and his analysis the same old painful oedipal defeat, how analysand Y makes of his masturbation and his psychoanalysis the sadistic activity of his defensive obsessional regression, and how analysand Z disparages her achievements and gratifications, both within and outside the psychoanalysis, as her masochistic way of confirming her castrated status. The analyst is studying the making of psychic reality as well as the product.

Thus one analyses the disturbed and disturbing past-as-the-present and seeks to construct a present that encompasses the past recognized as such. Here is an answer to a possible objection that the analysand, after all, comes with a past and a present, though obviously with defective accounts of these. What, it must now be asked, are these defects? How are they to be defined? Are they simply gaps, misrepresentations and distortions of emphasis? Must one not confront and understand the analysand as defective self-observer as well as defective life-historian, and also as someone who has a desperate interest in blocking or restricting the Freudian type of understanding and who, unconsciously, exercises great skill and perserverance in obscuring, fragmenting, diverting, and othewise interfering with the psychoanalytic investigation?

The psychoanalyst sees in these defects and strategies the analysand's attempts to achieve and maintain personal discontinuity, both historical and in present psychic reality, and also to impose this discontinuity on others, denying them their own life histories and present worlds. The analysand does not tolerate the idea that the present can only be some comprehensive, even if modified, version of the past—in the end, one hopes, a less fragmented, confining, anguished and self-destructive modification of that version. Through interpretation, one helps the analysand to abandon the goal of radical discontinuity, of rejection and obliteration of personal pasts and of major features of present existences. It is part of psychoanalytic insight to realize that that goal, which requires a narrow and superficial synthesis at great personal expense, was born of frightening love, hatred, excitement and depression. At the same time, the psychoanalyst helps the analysand to abandon the goal of thoroughgoing personal continuity, or, in other words, the goal of 'cure' without change. The contradictory goals of radical historical discontinuity and total contemporary continuity regularly co-exist; this must be so, for they imply each other.

Thus, when psychoanalysts speak of insight, they necessarily imply emotionally experienced transformation of the analysand, not only as life history and present world, but as life-historian and world-maker. It is the analysand's transformation and not his or her intellectual recitation of explanations that demonstrates the attainment of useful insight. The analysand has gained a past history and present world that are more intelligible and tolerable than before, even if still not very enjoyable or tranquil. This past and present are considerably more extensive, cohesive, consistent, humane, and convincingly felt than they were before. But these gains are based as much on knowing *how* as on knowing *that*. Insight is as much a way of looking as it is of seeing anything in particular.

Having now presented a general idea of the distinctively Freudian past and present, I shall go on to discuss the third thesis, which concerns the characteristic point of view taken of this past and present. The thesis is this: the psychoanalyst develops a view of the analysand's life history as action. The term action will be used in the philosophically well-established sense that includes wishing, imagining, remembering, and other such mental acts along with physical acts in and on the environment. Under 'environment' is to be included one's own physical body, for while it is true that one acts with this body in many instances, it is also the case that one acts in relation to it as an object as well.

In this comprehensive sense of action, both the setting of aims and one's pursuing them are actions; both sitting still and moving are actions; both remembering and repressing are actions. Neurotic symptoms are especially complex actions that simultaneously feature pleasure-seeking, aggression, self-punishment, defense, synthesis and some adjustment to environmental circumstances in whatever way the analysand views them. To say this is to restate the psychoanalytic principle of multiple function in the terms of action; that is, it is to give an account in terms of the systems id, ego and superego, and their mutual relations. On this basis, when patients present symptoms as afflictions or happenings, as by definition they must, psychoanalysts on their part understand them to be disclaiming certain intricate actions that they are performing unconsciously. Other such disclaimings of action include so-called slips, overwhelming impulses and thoughts that have popped into mind.

In order to speak in terms of action, one must also use the idea of modes of action; for example, there are the modes sadly, impetuously and curiously. Foremost among the modes of action are the topographic classifications that Freud finally treated adjectivally, that is, as *qualities* of mental acts, and that, in the design of action language, one must treat adverbially, that is, as *modes* of psychological action. There is no loss of clinical significance in saying consciously, preconsciously, and unconsciously instead of conscious, preconscious, and unconscious; there is a gain in theoretical consistency.

One may define any action in multiple ways. The psychoanalyst regularly establishes that the analysand has defined certain characteristically disturbing actions in a number of contradictory ways. In this regard Freud referred to the tolerance of contradiction in the system Ucs. or the id. For example, in the choice of a husband, a woman may, unconsciously, both repudiate *and* realize her wish to possess the oedipal father and additionally may be making a homosexual 'object choice' of a mothering figure. Customarily, the psychoanalyst refers to the multiple definitions of single actions as their overdetermination, even though according to the views now being developed he or she is referring to meanings rather than causes and even though it cannot and need not be demonstrated that the analysand has been acting in terms of every one of these meanings, unconsciously or otherwise.

By developing through interpretation a conception of past and continuing life-historical features as actions, one introduces new and significant actions into the analysand's history. But one is not necessarily adding thereby to the explanation of the initial performance of the actions in question. The point is that psychoanalytic interpretation expands the conception of actions and that this expansion is an essential constituent of insight. Insight combines both the old and the new. The new comprises all those conceptions of life-historical actions, relations and situations that the analysand may never before have defined as such.

For example, in repressing and reacting against her wishing to possess her mother's breast exclusively and totally, a girl may be performing an action that furthers the development of an altruistic mode of existence: there is no absurdity in the psychoanalyst's saying to her as an adult analysand that this was the course of action on which she embarked from early on, though at the time she could not have realized that this was the case. Absurdity enters at the point where one ascribes this retrospective designation of the action to the early infantile mind, as when one maintains that the very young infant can be so sophisticated as to conceive of altruism, altruistic intentions or motives, or a self that is altruistic. Put in historical perspective, there is far more to an action than could have entered into its creation at the moment of its execution. It is the same as the effect of a new and significant literary work or critical approach on all previous literature: inevitably, fresh possibilities of understanding and creation alter the literary past.

Logically, the idea of multiple and new definitions of individual actions implies multiple and changeable life histories and multiple and changeable present subjective worlds for one and the same person. To entertain this consequence is no more complex an intellectual job than to entertain, as psychoanalysts customarily do, multiple and changeable determinants and multiple and changeable self- and object-representations. Ultimately, of course, the analysand should not be employing these different perspectives in a way that keeps them emotionally isolated from one another or forever in great flux.

The reconceptualization of psychoanalytic theory and interpretation in the terms of action follows Otto Fenichel's (1941) technical argument that the analysand must be brought to recognize unconscious defence as personal activity. In action terms, the scope of disclaimed action then shrinks progressively. One sees that this is so upon observing that those analysands who are benefiting from analysis regard and present themselves more and more as the authors or agents of significant factors in their past and present lives and less and less as victims and patients in the sense of passive sufferers. They then enter more freely into emotionally interactive personal relationships recognized as such.

To emphasize action is not to deny the place of necessity and accident in the lives of human beings. Through interpretation, analysands get to know, for example, that they have not created their parents' physical and psychological limitations and excesses or the traumatic events of their own infancies. Among other results, interpretation typically helps them feel less painfully inferior or unworthy because, among other necessities, their parents could not love them well or at all.

Nevertheless, these same analysands also get to recognize the extent to which, and the manner in which, they once put certain constructions on infantile events, such as the primal scene, the birth of siblings, weaning, toilet training, anguished losses—and not being well-loved. Further, they get to see that, unconsciously, they have been continuing to put the same basic constructions on significant events and relationships in their current lives. And so they come to regard themselves, not as helpless objects who have found themselves cut off by hostile forces, unyielding barriers or remorseless enemies from large segments of actual or possible pleasure and security, but as people who have, for certain reasons, been seeing to it that they remain cut off from these experiences, and who, subtly or crudely, have enlisted others to aid them in this irrational enterprise. Moreover, the others whom they have enlisted exist not only in the present actual world but in the imagined world of inner or surrounding infantile personal relations; indeed, these imagined internal and surrounding presences and interactions are often the most important figures and events of all. I am referring here to such phenomena as the unconsciously imagined presence of the devouring mother, the castrating father, their idealized or damaged breasts, penises, and other organs and their blows, caresses and withdrawals.

Thus, in the course of personal transformation, analysands discover, acknowledge and transcend their infantile categories and their defects as life-historians and world-makers. They see that they have been, not the vehicles of a blind repetition compulsion, but the perpetrators of repetition at all costs. They reclaim their disclaimed actions, including their so-called mechanisms of defence, and in so doing they revise them and are in a position to limit their use of them or in some instances to discontinue using them altogether.

Increasingly, though not of course unfailingly, the analysand and analyst proceed on the strength of a shared recognition that subjective experience itself is a construction. Together, they examine and try to understand the historically founded archaic principles and categories that characterize the analysand's current construction of experience. They no longer think of past or present experience solely or mainly as that which is given and is to be consulted introspectively for clues or answers. Thinking in the new way, they realize that interpretation can only be reinterpretation. On this basis, the past and the present can be altered radically, and so can the anticipated future.

I am saying that the psychoanalyst interprets, not raw experience, but interpretations. Psychoanalysts imply just this point when they speak of phase-specificity, for they use this term to refer to two things; first, the child's construction, out of whatever was given at the time, of infantile versions of reality, and, second, their own psychoanalytic reinterpretation of that infantile construction. In this view, and contrary to the common criticism, it is the analysands, not their analysts, who are the reductionists; it is the analysands who repeatedly make of the world a toilet, a spanking, a brothel, a cold breast or any of the other scenes, objects, or interactions with which psychoanalysts regularly concern themselves. Through life-historical interpretation, the psychoanalyst both defines this reductionism and establishes a perspective on it that curtails its scope and urgency.

There is a special advantage to be gained from viewing the changes facilitated by psychoanalytic therapy as the extension and stabilization of the analysand's commitment to personal agency. In taking this view, one is better able to frame an answer to the question of what difference it makes to become conscious of so many disturbing and hitherto unconscious conflicts or, as it would now be preferable to say, to consider consciously those paradoxical actions that previously one had performed unconsciously, repetitively and in utter futility. In another form, this question asks how anything is changed, or changed for the better, by the construction of a Freudian life history and present subjective world.

To develop an answer, one must bear in mind that these constructions both presuppose and further the process of changing the analysand's point of view of himself or herself in relation to others; that is to say, in the interpretive circle, the significant observations, memories, insights and modes of feeling that are made possible by the Freudian constructions also document and extend these very constructions. Under the influence of the psychoanalytic perspective, the analysand not only begins to live in another world but learns how to go on constructing it. It is a transformed world, a world with systematically interrelated vantage points or rules of understanding. It is a world of greater personal authority and acknowledged responsibility. It is more coherent and includes a greater range of constructed experience. It is more socialized and intelligible. At its best it has nothing to do with Freudian jargon, social complacency or conformity.

And *that* is the difference it makes! For whoever sceptically questions what difference it makes to confront conflicts consciously is presupposing a static reality, an unalterable personal history and world, a life that allows only one interpretation and requires simple either–or choices. That sceptic is also pre-supposing a subject who cannot be the agent of his or her own experience and life situation and who at best can be no more than a recaller or witness of happenings and impersonal inner conflicting forces in a fixed reality, a creature inhabiting a world in which one is fated to be without personal authority or responsibility and so, in an ultimate sense, must be passive and existentially incoherent. On that basis, 'making the unconscious conscious', if it were possible at all, could only lead to extreme situations—chaos, orgy, panic, mayhem and self-destruction. But to the extent that the Freudian analysand is learning, devising and following new rules of understanding, he or she is no longer exactly the same person with respect to whom insight was to be developed; also, that analysand is no longer creating exactly the same set of desperate situations that were to be rendered intelligible. The person, the reality, the analytic situation all are correlatives, and all are constantly in flux. Increased intelligibility of persons and situations implies the transformation of agents and their situations.

The Freudian idea of the primacy of person-as-agent does not indict or preclude passive modes of experience with their frequently pleasurable, restorative, and otherwise adaptive aspects. One thinks here of the point made by the distinguished psychoanalytic theoretician, Heinz Hartmann (1939): with reference to certain forms of personal rigidity, he emphasized the adaptive significance of one's being able to yield to biological automatisms, as in the instance of the sexual climax. But this yielding is now to be seen as an action; far from being inactivity, it is something one does. Not everyone does it, at least not always and not in every respect. While it is of some interest to note that this sort of yielding entails refraining from doing other actions, specifically those actions that would block the automatism, it is also to be remarked that we must designate refraining itself an action. In the same way, we must designate as actions delaying, regulating, choosing and other members of that family of words. Choice or choosing is not a prerequisite of action; it is a form of action. And refraining from interfering is one kind of refraining action, as psychoanalysts know all too well from the method they usually follow in their work.

As much as by its basic categories of past and present life-history and experience, Freudian interpretation is distinguished by its conception of personal existence as actions with multiple and transformable meanings.

The terms of a theory should be wedded to the methods that generate its data. On this basis one may claim that it is the language of action rather than mechanism that is the natural, sufficient and parsimonious expression of the psychoanalytic method. The terms or rules of action suit a life-historical discipline as the terms of metapsychology do not, for clinical psychoanalysis never has been and never could be a laboratory science dealing in mindless objects and experimentally controlled processes. Psychoanalysis suffers no loss of dignity on this account, and the vast and consequential discoveries that testify to Freud's genius are preserved intact, if not seen in a clearer light. Indeed, in a further unification of one's thinking, one will, as psychoanalyst, now be regarding the analysand's activities just as one regards one's own: not as the resultants of the operation of the functions, energies, forces and structures of a mental apparatus, but as meaningful and complex actions taken by a person who simultaneously finds and makes a world in which to act. So construed, this is a person who can to a considerable degree remake and refresh that world, both as it is and as it was in the infantile past. And this is the theme of Auden's homage to Freud.

CHAPTER THREE

The legacy of Sigmund Freud

William Gillespie

W e have it on high authority that a prophet is not without honour save in his own country, and this saying applies, I think, not merely to prophets. To be honoured in one's own country is therefore indeed remarkable; and so, as the first British-born holder of this Chair, I am profoundly aware of the personal distinction that has been accorded me. My appreciation of the honour is matched by a feeling of great responsibility; my main justification for undertaking the task is the 45 years that I have spent in attempting to absorb the subject and practise the art of psychoanalysis since I went to Vienna at the end of 1930. Inasmuch as psychoanalysis is based ultimately on the clinical data that emerge from the encounter of patient and analyst in the psychoanalytic setting, this qualification is more important than might appear at first sight. Indeed it is not too much to say that a personal experience of psychoanalysis is a necessary condition for a truly informed discussion of it—and under the term 'personal experience' I include experience from both ends: that is, experience on the couch as the analysand, and experience in the analyst's chair with patients. I say 'patients' advisedly, because an analytic subject who is participating in the process for reasons other than

31

his personal suffering is unlikely to be able to reveal to the analyst and to himself the depths of his being which constitute the real subject-matter of psychoanalysis. This is, I know, a hard saying for those who are academically minded rather than clinically active, but it has long been well recognized by psychoanalysts. Wide-ranging as are its academic implications, the basis of psycho-analysis is to be sought not in the study but in the consulting room.

I have said that personal experience of psychoanalysis is a necessary condition for its informed discussion, but of course it is not a sufficient condition. Some capacity for conceptual and logical thinking and some capacity for criticism are no doubt also called for if one is to be able to understand Freud's ideas and to take up a reasonable attitude towards them. And here the very excellence of Freud's presentation and his consummate literary mastery do present a certain difficulty, I believe, for they make it hard some-times to suspend one's judgement quite as much as one should. Whatever some may say, psychoanalysis is not a system of belief, like a religion or a political faith; it is properly to be regarded as a branch of human knowledge, whether or not your criteria admit to to the category of empirical science. In any case, just as with other sciences, its findings have in the same way to be tested and modi-fied if and when experience shows them to be untenable.

My feeling of responsibility is reflected in the title I have chosen for my inaugural lecture, namely, *The Legacy of Sigmund Freud*. The spirit of what I want to say is well epitomized in a couplet from Goethe's *Faust*, which Freud quoted more than once in his works:

> *Was du ererbt von deinen Vätern hast*
> *Erwirb es um zu besitzen.*

In Louis MacNeice's translation:

> Whatever legacy your fathers left you,
> To own it you must earn it dear.

First, then, we must try to understand and master Freud's achievement in penetrating into the mysterious workings of human behaviour and experience; only then should we attempt to evaluate that achievement and follow its further development and refinement in the hands of others as well as in the hands of Freud himself.

Many of my audience certainly know how enormous is the litera-ture concerned with this subject. The psychological writings of Freud alone extend to 23 large volumes in the English Standard Edition. The general range of psychoanalytic writings is indicated by the fact that Grinstein's cumulative index of them already runs to 14 volumes. Perhaps it is as well for the purpose of these lectures that my own reading has been relatively sparse and selective, and what I have been able to absorb is very much more limited still.

In deciding what to present to you and how to do it I have had to consider what is likely to be useful, comprehensible and interest-ing to my audience; but the only thing I can feel sure about is that a self-selected audience will be very heterogeneous. Some of you will certainly be better versed than I in certain aspects of my subject matter, whereas others may have much interest in it but little previous knowledge. I can only hope that my account of the work and ideas of Freud and his collaborators and successors will be of some use to some of you. On the whole, my aim will be to err on the side of simplicity, and you will, I hope, forgive my enormous sins of omission.

Before I proceed further, I think it may be helpful if I hint very briefly at the nature of some of the themes relevant to our topic. That may be reassuring to those who are afraid, because of some of my opening remarks, that what I am offering will turn out to be one more rather tedious restatement of the development of Freud's thought. Certainly, it would be strange if a Freud Memorial Pro-fessor did not have a good deal to say about Freud; and it would also be remarkable if someone who had accepted the Chair were to take a predominantly negative attitude to his subject. This Chair, after all, constitutes a memorial to Freud, not a burial of him. My own view is that I am here neither to bury Sigmund Freud nor to praise him, except in so far as this latter may be unavoidable; but rather to look at Freud, his work and his views as objectively as possible, putting the truth above all else, as Freud himself charac-teristically did.

I will therefore sketch in a preliminary way a few of the themes that I have in mind. First, then, are there good reasons to consider that Freud and his work are so important as to justify the setting up of this Chair at University College? If so, is this principally because he discovered a very valuable new method of medical treatment for the psychoneuroses and possibly for other mental ills as well—something that might be compared, for example, with the discovery of penicillin? But the therapeutic value of the method has been seriously questioned in some quarters, and it was by no means unduly stressed by Freud himself, particularly in his latter years. He once said, adapting a witticism, that it is like women—in spite of all its shortcomings, yet the best thing we have—of its kind. Should psychoanalysis in fact be judged primarily by its therapeutic results, and if so, has there been up to now any proper assessment of those results that has even a remote claim to validity? Was Freud's increasingly modest estimate of the therapeutic efficacy of his method due mainly to subjective factors, the changing outlook of an ageing man, or was it realistically justified by his widened experience, which might be considered to have corrected the optimism and enthusiasm of the relatively young Freud? I say 'relatively young', because he was about forty years of age when he embarked properly on his psychoanalytic voyage. And after all, was he in fact filled with such overweening therapeutic arrogance at the beginning? Let me remind you of what he wrote in his first important analytic publication, the *Studies on Hysteria* (Breuer & Freud, 1893–95): Replying to an imaginary patient, he makes this response: 'No doubt fate would find it easier than I do to relieve you of your illness. But you will be able to convince yourself that much will be gained if we succeed in transforming your hysterical misery into common unhappiness. With a mental life that has been restored to health you will be better armed against that unhappiness.' However, I would not deny the possibility that during the following years, say between 1895 and 1910, as he refined the psychoanalytic instrument and became increasingly expert in its use, Freud may well have developed much more sanguine and ambitious views about its therapeutic efficacy; certainly, some of his more enthusiastic followers began to hope that the result of a successful analysis would be not merely to relieve the patient of his illness but to transform him into something perhaps little short of a Nietzschian superman.

Should we then perhaps see Freud's principal achievement less as the discovery of a potent therapeutic tool but rather as the invention of a new method of exploring the human being, and thus finding unsuspected powers for good and evil hitherto undiscovered by science? Is it the creation as a result of these discoveries of a new kind of psychology, a 'depth' psychology, and the development of an abstract theoretical framework which he called 'metapsychology'?

Another question that I should like to raise is this: was Freud right to abide so faithfully by the view that *in principle* the problem of man's nature is a biological one and that underlying psychology there will eventually be found a biological basis? We know that in spite of this opinion he developed into a supremely psychological psychologist. Are those analysts in the right who maintain that psychoanalysis should abandon all temptation to look over its shoulder at other disciplines, such as animal psychology (and here I am thinking of such lines of research as ethology rather than the learning of rats), physiology, embryology, hereditary genetics and the theory of evolution? Undoubtedly for Freud evolution and the necessity to take a historical and developmental point of view were central to his thinking; indeed, he considered that what he called instincts or drives were essentially derived from remote ancestral experience. This idea seems to imply a readiness to accept the possibility that acquired characteristics can be inherited, in other words a Lamarckian point of view, and Freud has often been castigated for this old-fashioned and supposedly exploded belief, even if it was shared by Darwin himself. Freud's excursions into anthropology and the origins of religion will also come under review; he was certainly much influenced here by the kind of approach that I have just mentioned, but also by the analogies that he demonstrated between primitive practices and religions on the one hand and various clinical manifestations of neurosis on the other hand.

You will remember, I am sure, the famous patient of Breuer known as Anna O. It was her treatment, as related by Breuer to Freud, that started Freud on the momentous journey that led him to psychoanalysis. One of the names that Anna O invented for Breuer's new method of treatment was 'the talking cure'. I mention this as an introduction to another topic, namely the part played by language and verbalization in psychoanalysis. To what extent is this a fundamental and essential feature? How much is it a result of Freud's own undoubted mastery of the verbal and literary medium and the cultural background in which he grew up? And is it in fact accorded the same pre-eminent position today as in the earlier period of psychoanalysis? In Freud's original formulations he devoted much thought to the part played in human psychology by the function of verbalization, particularly as a characteristic of conscious as contrasted with unconscious mental activity. Since then, of course, a vast amount of work has been done in other related fields, for example in the study of linguistics, semantics, meaning, logical positivism, to mention but a few. One should consider what bearing these researches have on psychoanalysis, and how much psychoanalysis ought to contribute to them.

Then there are the concepts going under the general name of structuralism, which has assumed such importance recently in numerous fields of study. Such concepts raise fundamental issues and controversies of a philosophical nature which Freud perhaps tries to avoid; but it is hard to refute the assertion that he perhaps unwittingly made certain assumptions that could be described as philosophical attitudes; did he, like M. Jourdain, talk philosophy without knowing it? Certainly concepts like those of unconscious mental functioning, a mental apparatus, a structural model of the mind and innate drives derived from ancestral experience imply that there is a great deal that cannot be directly observed underlying the phenomena of human behaviour and in a sense more fundamental than behaviour as such.

A different line of thought which is also an essential feature of psychoanalytic thinking is to be found in the idea of *process*, which looks in a way to be opposed to the idea of structure. In other words, everything mental is in the nature of a process, a change occurring in the dimension of time. The essence of this idea can be traced back at least as far as Heraclitus and his famous dictum '*Panta rhei*' [everything is in flux]—and if everything, then obviously mental events too. And the concept of process or change in time is of the essence of evolution as well as of individual development, both of which figure very significantly in Freud's thought.

No doubt the development of verbal communication is the most fundamental event in the evolution of man, the one that distinguishes him from all other animals, for without it tradition and the development of human societies would have been impossible.

The invention of writing certainly came much later in the evolutionary development of human societies, and what we call less primitive societies would be inconceivable without it. But I think we should beware of attaching exclusive importance to speech and writing when considering human psychology and social development. We should surely not forget the plastic arts and music, even if it may be argued that this last form of expression is one that we share with the birds. In this connection it is remarkable that Freud's interest in and appreciation of the arts did not extend to music—remarkable because he spent nearly his whole life in that supremely musical city, Vienna. He has told us that his relative indifference to music was due to his inability to understand it in verbal terms; this might, I suppose, be used to substantiate the charge sometimes made against him, for example, by George Steiner, that he was too much biased by the literary tradition in which he and most of his patients had been educated.

So much for the topics one could discuss at much greater length. For the moment, however, I wish to make some remarks about the development of Freud himself and some of his leading ideas and theories.

The origins of psychoanalysis

Despite the vast development and many-sidedness of present-day psychoanalysis, its creation and conception is unequivocally the work of one man, Sigmund Freud, who worked alone at it for about ten years, beginning in 1895; this was the year in which his joint publication with Josef Breuer, *Studies on Hysteria* (Breuer & Freud, 1893–95), appeared. The fact of Freud's early isolation certainly simplifies the attempt to understand how psychoanalysis originated; but the simplicity is merely relative, as will become apparent when we consider what Freud accomplished in those ten years. Of course, it would be an error to suppose that psychoanalysis sprang from the brain of Freud by some kind of spontaneous generation. We need to examine some of the background, intellectual, medical and social, which helped to mould even a genius like Freud. A great deal could be said about this background, and it has been dealt with by various writers on

Freud. Among these writings the first volume of Jones's (1953) biography is, of course, outstanding; others have added to his account and have questioned the accuracy of some of his statements. My own aim will be to pick out selectively what strike me as the most interesting and the most significant facts.

Freud was the eldest child of a young mother and a much older father who already had two sons by his first marriage. At the time of Sigmund's birth his father was a wool merchant in the small town of Freiberg in Moravia (now Pribor). Jakob Freud's business did not prosper, and the family moved to Vienna when Sigmund was four years old. However, the move failed to bring any great improvement in their financial situation, and this was a source of mortification to Sigmund, even if the outcome was an intensification of his own ambitious fantasies and their ultimate realization in a field far removed from business, though it was for this that his father had at first destined him.

But we should ask ourselves about other aspects of Freud's background, aspects that were more important than the purely economic ones. For example, the fact that his family was a Jewish one was certainly of central importance in his life, and it had far-reaching influences on his career and achievement; his last great work was devoted to Moses and monotheism (Freud, 1939a). It may well be that his father, Jakob, was brought up in an orthodox religious manner; there is some reason to believe that Hasidic mystical views played a part in Jakob's background and that Sigmund himself took an interest in Cabbalistic writings, for these occupied a place in his library. This background may perhaps explain Freud's seemingly superstitious belief in the magic of numbers; and no doubt this propensity played a part in his ready acceptance of some of the theories of Wilhelm Fliess, whose friendship and support meant so much to him during some of the most crucial years of his scientific career.

However, by the time of Sigmund's birth in 1856, when his father was 40, Jakob, if not a freethinker, was certainly liberal-minded and very far from orthodox, even though when Sigmund was 35 Jakob presented him with a Bible which he had inscribed in Hebrew, saying that in Sigmund's seventh year the spirit of God began to move him to learning; that he had seen in this book the vision of the Almighty and had tried to fly high upon the wings of the Holy Spirit. Certainly it appeared that Jakob Freud was far from being militantly anti-religious, as some might say his son became. In this connection it is of interest that Freud's adverse criticisms of established religion were directed chiefly against the Roman Catholic form of Christianity rather than Judaism; for an early influence in his life came from a Catholic nanny who used to take him to church and tell him about such things as hellfire. She was removed from him on being convicted of stealing when Sigmund was 2½ years old. Later, of course, he became painfully aware of the anti-semitism of Vienna's predominantly Catholic population.

But there is a theme more central in Freud's thinking than religion—the theme to which he gave the name of the Oedipus complex. Intimations of it in mythology and legend no doubt go back to the beginnings of recorded history; but it is the Oedipus Rex of Sophocles that Freud had in mind when he applied the term 'Oedipus complex' to a constellation of attitudes and wishes, loves and hates related to father and mother, a constellation that he first clearly recognized in the course of his own self-analysis—a momentous undertaking which I shall discuss later. I mention it now in connection with the actual circumstances of Freud's early childhood. These were unusual and by no means corresponded to the straightforward triangular relationship that Freud postulated for the classical positive Oedipus complex, where the little boy loves his mother and regards his father as the hated rival and wishes to get rid of that rival, indeed to kill him, just as Oedipus killed Laius, however unwittingly. Sigmund Freud's situation was much more complicated; his father produced two families, and when Sigmund appeared as the first-born of his father's second marriage, he was so much younger than his two half-brothers that it was possible for him to believe, as a little boy, that it was one of these half-brothers who was his real Oedipal rival and the father of his mother's younger children, of whom there were eventually six survivors—five girls and last of all a brother, ten years younger than Sigmund. He himself, as the first-born and a boy, was well aware that he was his mother's favourite; his brother was too much younger to be a serious rival. This unusual family background perhaps illustrates one of the principles to which Freud's work led him, namely, that pathology often illuminates normality.

At school in Vienna Sigmund was an outstanding pupil; one of the Greek works which he studied was Oedipus Rex—a school experience, as it happens, that I shared with him. It may well have made a deep impression on him, treating as it does not only of an oedipal situation, but also of a systematic and relentless investigation of the unknown past, which bears an unmistakable resemblance to a psychoanalytic treatment. It was no doubt also at school that Freud first developed his admiration for Goethe, an author whom he quoted so frequently and so appositely in his own works. One of Goethe's supposed writings in particular fired his imagination; he tells us in *The Interpretation of Dreams* (1900a) that when he was hesitating over the choice of a career, it was hearing a reading of Goethe's essay on Nature that decided him to take up the study of natural science. He was moved, he says, not by any particular predilection for the career of a physician, but rather by a sort of curiosity directed more towards human concerns than towards natural objects. His early familiarity with the Bible story also had an effect on the direction of his interest. A further very important influence was Darwin, whose theories were then, in the 1870s, of popular interest. *The Origin of Species* had appeared in 1859, *The Descent of Man and Selection in Relation to Sex* in 1871. Freud also tells us: 'In my youth I felt an overpowering need to understand some of the riddles of the world in which we live and perhaps even to contribute something to their solution. The most hopeful means of achieving this end seemed to be to enrol myself in the medical faculty; but even after that I experimented unsuccessfully—with zoology and chemistry, till at last, under the influence of Brücke, who carried more weight with me than anyone else in my whole life, I settled down to physiology. . . . I took no interest in anything to do with medicine till the teacher whom I so deeply respected warned me that in view of my impoverished material circumstances I could not possibly take up a theoretical career' (Freud, 1926e, pp. 253–254). And so Freud's histological studies of the nervous system led him, by way of neuropathology, to the neuroses and the living human patients who suffered from them.

It is easy to understand that a man with Freud's solid scientific background, together with his 'overpowering need to understand some of the riddles of the world', soon found himself profoundly dissatisfied with the prevailing professional approach to the understanding and treatment of these problems. A sojourn of some months in Paris brought about a great enthusiasm for the work and personality of Charcot, who appeared to have advanced some way towards the understanding of hysteria on a quasi-neurological basis; and Freud followed this up by studying the methods of other French hypnotists. But the decisive influence came from nearer home. Josef Breuer, a prominent physician in Vienna, a friend of Freud although considerably older, had much earlier recounted to Freud the remarkable story of one of his patients who has become famous under the name of Anna O. What was revolutionary about this case was that together Breuer and this very intelligent hysterical girl worked out a method of treatment which she called 'the talking cure', whereby, with the help of hypnosis, each of her symptoms was traced back to some forgotten but emotionally significant and indeed traumatic event in her life; and when this was successfully accomplished, that particular symptom disappeared. The essential fact was that it was thereby demonstrated that hysterical symptoms have a meaning—that they constitute, in effect, a kind of cryptic language. This fundamental discovery of Breuer would probably never have been communicated to the world had it not been for the insistence of Freud. We can today surmise with near certainty that it was the manifestations of an erotic transference to her physician, culminating in the fantasy of being pregnant, which frightened Breuer so much that he fought shy of the whole affair, and it was only with great reluctance that he finally agreed to a joint publication with Freud; this included the description of a number of other patients treated by Freud, as well as theoretical chapters by both authors. The book was *Studies on Hysteria*, which appeared in 1895 (Breuer & Freud, 1893–95) and this event may be said to mark the beginning of psychoanalysis. It was only much later that the phenomenon of transference was explicitly recognized, and much later still before it was accorded the dominating place in the theory and practice of analytic therapy that it now holds. It is interesting, therefore, to note that it was transference—or more precisely Breuer's reaction of horror to erotic transference—that played so prominent a part in this first tentative approach to psychoanalysis and brought it temporarily to an untimely end. Had it not been for Freud's intervention, it is possible that the whole story might have ended there, so that psychoanalysis as we know it might never have been discovered.

As is well known, Freud gradually abandoned the use of hypnosis and the abreactive technique developed first by Breuer, then by Freud himself. He came to rely instead on the method of free association, so-called. It is unfortunate that Freud's word '*Einfall*', which really implies a sudden flash of thought, has no proper English equivalent and has had to be rendered by the academic-sounding word 'association'. It has often been objected that really free association is an impossibility. Indeed, as a means of gaining access to mental contents—thoughts, wishes, fears and so on—of which the patient is unaware, the efficacy of the method depends precisely on the fact that the associations of the patient are *not* free but are influenced by these unconscious factors. Nevertheless, it is the *attempt* to associate freely which makes possible that widening and loosening of the thinking process which enables patient and analyst together to reach some of that unconscious mental content, and in this sense we can reasonably say that the aim at free association was and still is an essential element in psychoanalytic technique. It can also be seen as an honest effort to be as nearly truthful as is humanly possible. You will remember how, in *The Mikado*, Ko-Ko, as Lord High Executioner, faced with the duty of self-decapitation, protests, 'I don't see how a man *can* cut off his own head'; to which Pooh-Bah replies dryly, 'A man might try'. Similarly, a man can *try* to associate freely, and this honest effort is what is needed in psychoanalysis. But just as Ko-Ko raised objections against even attempting to cut off his own head, sooner or later every patient comes up against a strong *resistance* against saying something that comes into his head; or although he may not be aware of his resistance, he may have the experience that his mind goes blank at a certain point. Or again, when the analyst points out an obvious link between two items in the patient's associations, the patient may refuse to accept that there is a connection. Such experiences with patients led Freud to the general concept of resistance, and from it he postulated the existence of a defensive process to which he gave the name 'repression'.

This simple and primitive example illustrates how clinical observation of the exchanges between patient and analyst led Freud towards a theory of how the mind functions, and to the conviction that a vitally important part of that mental functioning goes on without any conscious awareness—to a theory, that is, of unconscious but dynamic mental processes. The theory was not an armchair product but stemmed directly from observations of the behaviour of patients, thus illustrating a fact that I stressed at the beginning.

Another quite unexpected clinical fact that emerged when Freud applied the new method of investigation was the prevalence of sexual themes in the patients' associations. These frequently led back to childhood; and at first, led astray by the assumption widely held at that time and shared by Freud that childhood was the age of sexual innocence, Freud believed that his patients had been sexually seduced and traumatized by their elders, and in particular by their fathers. He erected a considerable theoretical edifice on this mistaken basis, and when he discovered his error he suffered a shattering blow. It was only his dogged persistence and strength of character that prevented him from throwing in his hand at that point. Eventually, however, he recognized that what he had been taking as objective fact in his patients' stories was really to be understood as fantasy but, furthermore, that fantasy was no less important than external events; indeed, he began to see that it was more important, since it was an expression of internally arising impulses, ultimately of instinctual origin. The fantasies in fact led him to the discovery of what he called infantile sexuality, which had to be regarded as a general phenomenon of human development.

This radical change of viewpoint which attributed much less weight to traumatic factors was in large part the result of Freud's decision to undertake an analysis of himself—a task that he began in 1897, only two years after the publication of *Studies on Hysteria*. He had already discovered that in the course of their associations patients frequently recounted their dreams, and that when these dreams were studied in detail by asking the patient to bring associations to the individual elements of the dream as it was related to him by the patient, then many unsuspected thoughts came to light. In this way something new began to emerge, and a vitally important distinction was recognized by Freud between, on the one hand, the manifest dream as it was related and, behind that, the latent dream thoughts. These did not merely embrace a much wider material than the manifest dream—it also became evident that a new *meaning* began to appear from a manifest dream which itself might seem to be senseless or of little significance in connection with the patient's life and interests. Of course it had been thought from olden times that dreams might have a meaning, which skilled interpretation could reveal—the classical example of a brilliant interpreter of dreams is Joseph of the Old Testament. However, nineteenth-century scientists were much more inclined to scoff at such ideas and to regard dreams as no more than the valueless product of a sleeping, poorly functioning brain, and to endorse the popular German saying: *'Träume sind Schäume'*—dreams are mere froth. This is not a suitable occasion to discuss the elaborate theory of dreams at which Freud finally arrived. I mention the subject now because of its relevance to Freud's self-analysis, which was made possible by the circumstances that he was a good and prolific dreamer, and that with all his customary dogged persistence he pursued the study of his own dreams in the manner I have briefly described. These researches into his own dreams and those of his patients led Freud to the view expressed in his statement that 'dreams are the royal road to the unconscious'. It was his dreams that led Freud to the discovery of 'infantile sexuality' or the forgotten sexual life of early childhood and to his abandoning the theory of early seduction by fathers, for it was impossible for him to conceive of his own father playing such a role; and in turn he recognized the inherent improbability that paternal misbehaviour of this sort was anywhere near so widespread as his analysis of patients had led him to believe.

For Freud dreams were of special interest for another reason—namely, that dreaming is generally acknowledged to be a perfectly normal product of mental activity, unlike so-called pathological conditions, such as the neuroses, with which his studies had begun; and yet it became clear that they had much in common with neurotic symptoms. His results, therefore, promised to illuminate not merely psychopathology but also normal psychology. Further support for Freud's theories of unconscious mental functioning, the role of repudiated wishes and defences against them, and so on came from the study of everyday mistakes such as slips of the tongue as well as from the analysis of jokes and witticisms. Thus

Freud's self-analysis, begun in 1897, opened up rich areas for the development of his thought, and this was reflected in the books he produced—*The Interpretation of Dreams* (1900a) in the first place, but also *The Psychopathology of Everyday Life* (1901b), *Jokes and their Relation to the Unconscious* (1905c) and the *Three Essays on the Theory of Sexuality* (1905d); in this last he discussed not only the development of sexuality in childhood but also its deviations in adult life and the paths it must follow during adolescence if it is to eventuate in what is generally accepted as normal adult sexuality. In this way, by 1905 Freud had established firmly the basis of psychoanalytic psychology.

Let me therefore outline some of the fundamental findings and convictions that were characteristic of psychoanalysis at that time—findings that are still at the centre of its approach to the study of human behaviour and experience.

(1)   First among these is the hypothesis that what is mental or psychical is by no means limited to those things of which we are consciously aware—that many, indeed most, of the processes that go on in us proceed without our being aware of them, and yet these unconscious processes are so akin to conscious ones that it is difficult or impossible to deny them the designation 'mental'.

(2)   It frequently happens that a conflict of interests arises between different mental processes, intentions or wishes. This conflict is itself often not conscious, since one or more of the conflicting tendencies is likely to be an unconscious one.

(3)   What is going on mentally here and now is strongly influenced by the past life and experiences of the individual, and this influence is something of which he is in most cases not immediately aware; frequently he is in fact incapable of knowing it except after arduous analytic work. Underlying this fact is the broad principle of developmental influence—the principle, that is, that present behaviour and experience cannot be understood or accounted for meaningfully except in relation to the past history of the person in question.

(4)   This past history is in large part the history of the person's relationships and experiences with other persons, and most funda-

mentally the history of his childhood and his relationships with his parents or those who carried out the parental function. Without parents or their surrogates no infant can, after all, survive.

(5)   These early relationships are by no means limited to the provision by the parents of the means of survival in the purely material sense. Man does not live by bread alone, and an essential building material for the child's development—certainly for his successful development—is the presence of love and devotion on the part of the parents, which is a condition for the possibility of the child's developing fully his own capacity for loving, affectionate relationships. The development of such relationships cannot be properly understood without some familiarity with the unfolding of sexual impulses and wishes in the growing child and without the recognition of the fact that these do not begin at puberty but express themselves from early infancy onwards in different forms that vary greatly with the growth of the child and the stage of development he has reached.

(6)   Although the development of sexuality is undoubtedly influenced by the child's environment and experiences, an innate or instinctual factor is postulated, and in this there is a constitutional element that varies from one child to another. This instinctual element brings us to the boundary between the psychological and the biological and sets a limit to what we should expect to be able to achieve by purely psychological therapeutic influence.

In an encyclopaedia article written in 1922, Freud (1923a) summarized more succinctly what he described as 'The corner-stones of psychoanalytic theory' as follows: 'The assumption that there are unconscious mental processes, the recognition of the theory of resistance and repression, the appreciation of the importance of sexuality and of the Oedipus complex—these constitute the principal subject-matter of psychoanalysis and the formulations of its theory. No one who cannot accept them all should count himself a psychoanalyst.'

All these formulations, I think, were either explicit or implicit in the views that Freud had already reached by 1905, the end of the ten years of 'splendid isolation' during which Freud worked virtually on his own. If the development of psychoanalysis can be likened to the growth of a great tree, then Freud's constructive achievement during those first ten years can be regarded as the establishment of the main trunk, on which all further developments depended. One may go on to say that numerous great boughs began to grow out from the trunk in various directions, and that this growth no longer stemmed solely from Freud himself but that it owed some of the strength and the direction it took to a number of important figures who became associated with him. In some cases the direction of growth came to diverge more and more from the main line of development; the best-known examples are to be found in the work of Jung and Adler, both of whom could have made very valuable contributions to psychoanalysis itself had they not overemphasized their disagreements—Jung, for example, by denying the importance of sexuality and equating the libido with psychic energy in general, Adler by denying sexuality in a different way and laying all the stress on the struggle for power and on social factors generally. His development of ego psychology anticipated in some areas later psychoanalytic views, and some of this could well have been incorporated. In both cases, as Freud put it, the trouble was not with those things that they asserted so much as with what they chose to deny.

For a number of reasons I have spoken here mainly about Freud himself and about the earlier stages in the development of psychoanalysis. Even this much may have strained your patience, and any attempt to give an overall picture of the eighty years since the Studies on Hysteria would have been not only foolish but impossible, for I should have needed to draw your attention to so many and such varied topics. It would have been necessary, for instance, to trace the marked changes that have taken place in the therapeutic method, with the increasingly prominent position accorded to the analysis of the transference phenomena occurring between patient and analyst—and not solely in one direction, as is evidenced by the lively attention now paid to the analyst's countertransference. Furthermore, one would have to discuss the change in the type of patient who now comes to analysis and the technical changes that some analysts have adopted to meet this challenge. I refer here not merely to the so-called borderline patient and to those with narcissistic personality disorders, which at present appear to be much commoner in analytic practice than the classi-

cal case of hysteria and obsessional neurosis that Freud described.
I have in mind also disorders of a frankly psychotic nature, which
some analysts find it possible to treat with or without modifications of the classical technique.

On the more theoretical side—but remember that in psychoanalysis theory and practice go hand in hand and exert much
mutual influence—the already wide concept of the libido was
widened still further with the introduction of the theory of narcissism and the distinction of narcissistic disorders from those
classified as transference neuroses. The enormously important
role of aggression became increasingly recognized, and Freud was
led by discoveries in this area to a new classification of instincts
into two great divisions—life instincts and death instincts, Eros
and Thanatos. But whereas the importance of aggression has been
universally accepted, Freud's concept of a death instinct directed
in the first instance against oneself, and taking the form of out-
wardly directed aggression only secondarily, has met with a much
more lukewarm reception in general, though the theory and its
clinical application have been warmly embraced by some analysts,
notably by Melanie Klein and her followers. Then there was the
radical change in Freud's theory of neurotic anxiety, such a central
issue for psychopathology. Whereas for many years Freud had
believed that neurotic anxiety came about as a result of the repression of libidinal impulses, he recognized this as an error, and in his
new formulation he postulated that anxiety, whose seat was in the
ego, is the agent that leads to repression. Furthermore, he no
longer accorded such an exclusive role to the mechanism of repression but recognized that repression is only one of a number of
defence mechanisms, and he thus revived the old term 'defence', to
include besides repression other mechanisms such as projection,
introjection and denial and, later still, splitting of the ego. Some of
these more primitive mechanisms were found to play a vital part
especially in psychotic disorders. All this was closely linked with
the devotion of greatly increased attention to the ego and to a
theoretical elaboration of its development, nature and functions,
an elaboration carried out particularly vigorously in the United
States thanks to the stimulation of Heinz Hartmann's work. The
large and controversial topic of the analysis of children would also
need to be discussed, associated as it is with much work related to

the particularly difficult elucidation of the earliest years and months.

This imaginary inaugural lecture would have had to go on to a discussion of the very wide-ranging applications of psycho-analysis—for example, to problems of anthropology, religion, art, education, and so on. One could hardly omit the subject of those inexplicable occurrences that are sometimes called occult; for a number of analysts, and notably Freud himself, have attempted to throw light in this very dark corner of scientific study. I could go on with this mere catalogue almost indefinitely, and I must ask you to be grateful to me that I have not attempted to cover too many subjects all at once.

CHAPTER FOUR

Psychoanalysis and freedom of thought

Hanna Segal

Psychoanalysis belongs to the great scientific tradition of freeing thought from dogma, whether religious or arising out of an established scientific tradition itself. Claude Bernard said: 'An idea must always remain independent. It must not be chained by scientific beliefs any more than by those that are philosophical or religious.' Such freedom, however, is hard to attain. In any culture certain thoughts or ideas are inadmissible.

Copernicus and Galileo's work met with emotional resistance. It was unthinkable that earth should be anything but the centre of the universe, with stars revolving round it. Darwin's work was equally inadmissible. Of course, I know that I am over-simplifying here. Copernicus, Galileo and Darwin, like Freud, had predecessors. And in the case of astronomy there was the added problem that scientific conclusions ran against the evidence of the senses. The earth is flat. But be that as it may, however well documented was the evidence, their discoveries were resisted because they conflicted basically with the accepted view of the place of God and man in the Universe. Before Freud, it was unthinkable that incestuous wishes were part of human nature and not the privilege of a few perverts. It was unthinkable that children, and even infants, had sexual wishes, phantasies and even activities, even though, unlike in the case of astronomy or biology, much of the evidence was around, both from observation and self-observation. The notion of infantile sexuality was so unthinkable that Freud himself, when first coming upon the evidence, assumed that all his patients had been seduced in childhood by an adult. Judging from a letter to Fliess, he was helped in allowing himself to contemplate the new idea because it released him from the burden of another inadmissible idea. In this letter he says that when his views about childhood seduction were disproved by his own evidence, instead of feeling depressed about it, he felt surprisingly excited and relieved. The excitement was due to the feeling of being on the brink of a great discovery. But the relief came from being able to discard another horrifying thought—namely, that so many respectable fathers, among them *his own father*, had been perverts. So his acceptance of one painful idea was somewhat facilitated by his relief at its freeing him from another. But it is important to note that while both thoughts were painful, to Freud they were not unthinkable. He could think about them and test them against the evidence. The acceptance of the hitherto unthinkable thoughts about the child's sexual nature was a major breakthrough in his thinking. Before Freud, it was unthinkable that human beings regularly held, not only incestuous, but cruel wishes and death wishes against their nearest and dearest and that they invariably harboured death wishes against their parents. To make such unthinkable thoughts thinkable, it takes a genius and a hero of the stamp of Copernicus, of Darwin, of Freud, someone of his time and yet stepping sufficiently outside what is thinkable in his time, to formulate hypotheses hitherto unthinkable.

Once such hypotheses are formulated, there is a long battle with emotional resistances and a long process of working through, of overcoming, first one's own inner resistances, then those of the scientific establishment, then the world at large, until, finally, they may become part of accepted scientific thought and eventually of the general culture.

With psychoanalysis, however, the problem is not only a social one. Even though psychoanalytic ideas gained some general acceptance, the battle for the freedom of thought has to be fought individually with every analysand on the couch, as well within one's self. And that is where it started. Freud did not set out to revolutionize culture, he set out to treat patients. Recognizing that the hysterical pathology hinged on the conversion into symptoms of thoughts that were not allowed into consciousness, he set about to free his individual patients' thoughts from inner resistances and prohibitions. His work, even the early work before his elaboration of the psychoanalytical method, abounds in examples.

What is the origin of such inhibitions of thought? Most immediately evident is the fear of the superego. In the same way in which the fear of an external authority can make us afraid to speak, the fear of an internal authority can make us afraid to think. The superego, according to Freud, is the internalized parental figure carrying the parental prohibitions, which becomes a structure in our unconscious mind, but while the external authority can forbid only actions, including speech, this internal authority can forbid thought. The prohibition may be directed not only to certain thoughts—say, hostile thoughts directed against the parents and siblings—it may also be against searching for knowledge, and thought itself. Some myths lead themselves to this interpretation—for instance, the myth of the Garden of Eden. Eating from the tree of knowledge is the first sin and leads to a fall from grace. The myth of the Tower of Babel—the pursuit of knowledge of god is punished by an attack on language—that is, verbal thought—an attack that leads to confusion of thought. The myth of Prometheus, punished for seeking fire—light. One root of the inhibition of thought and searching for knowledge is the demand felt to emanate from the superego that it be deified. The superego becomes a god who cannot tolerate enlightenment. When Oedipus finds the answer to the riddle of the Sphinx, the Sphinx has to kill herself. A god cannot survive being known too well. Such a god is also a terrible god. The Sphinx ate her victims. That aspect of the superego felt to be directed against knowledge and thought was particularly investigated and described by Wilfred Bion.

The superego is, however, a complex structure. It is more than the sum total of parental prohibitions, and its savagery goes far beyond that of most parents. In his later works Freud expresses the view, partly in agreement with Melanie Klein and others, who emphasized the point that the superego is not only an internalization of parental prohibitions, but that it is also and mainly a result of the projection into those parental figures of some of one's own impulses and phantasies. Both the ideal and the persecutory aspects of that superego have their roots in the infant's own impulses. For example, in the case of the Wolf Man, if his superego was a wolf with staring eyes, we would now say that this was largely because he attributed to his internal parents his own biting and voyeuristic impulses. Similarly, the demand of the superego to be treated as a god, never exposed to critical thought, is rooted in the infant's own needs for such a perfect parent.

The prohibition against thoughts that seem to emanate from the superego is also in part a projection of the infantile self's own antagonism to thought. If we eat from the tree of knowledge of good and evil, we exile ourselves from paradise. Copernicus and Darwin dealt great blows to human vanity. It was not only the superego vested in religion and authority that protested against their discoveries, but also human vanity and egocentricity. Man does not like losing his special and august place in the universe as god's elect. Freud refers in several papers to the blow Darwin and Copernicus dealt to man's self-love, and he adds: 'But human megalomania will have suffered its third and most wounding blow from the psychological research of the present time, which seeks to prove to the ego that it is not even master in its own house' (1916–17, p. 285). And the third blow is of a more personal nature. It is easier to accept Freud's theories in general than to accept the knowledge of one's self individually and specifically.

Thinking puts a limit on the omnipotence of phantasy and is attacked because of our longing for that omnipotence.

A patient dreamt that he was breaking the links in a chain with great fury. He associated to it that in the previous session the analyst had referred to a train of thought and had also used the expression, 'links', in pointing something out to him; when she had said 'a train of thought', he had had the angry thought that he had not verbalized: 'it's not a train, it's a chain'. He had been in a temper after the session. He did not want, he said, to be chained by his thoughts. He wanted to tear the chain apart and to be free of it.

He felt his own train of linked thoughts as a prison and a persecution because it interfered with the belief in his omnipotence. It led him to realize things he did not want to know. Paradoxically, the freedom of thought that gradually emerged in his analysis was felt by him as a chain on his freedom to think what he liked. Free thought becomes, for instance, subject to perceptual evidence, laws of consistency, logic, and so forth.

I think that at this point I have to say something about what I mean by those terms 'omnipotence', 'omnipotence phantasy' and 'thought', and how they are related. In Freud's view, expressed most tellingly and succinctly in his paper 'Formulations on the two principles of mental functioning' (1911b, pp. 213–226) it is related to the emergence of thought, to the loss of omnipotence and the experience of frustration, and the move from what he calls the pleasure principle to the reality principle. The infant's peace of mind is disturbed by peremptory inner needs, such as hunger. His first response is by hallucinatory wish fulfilment, an omnipotent phantasy of a need-satisfying object—a hallucination. His other response is by motor discharge, trying to rid himself of the experience by discharging it through muscular action. Eventually, however, he discovers that neither the hallucination nor the discharge satisfied the need. 'It was only the non-occurrence of the expected satisfaction, the disappointment experienced that led to the abandonment of this attempt at satisfaction by means of hallucination. Instead of it, the psychic apparatus had to decide to form a conception of the real circumstances in the external world and to endeavour to make a real alteration in them. The new principle of mental functioning was thus introduced. What was presented in the mind was no longer what was agreeable, but what was real, even if it happened to be disagreeable. This setting up of the reality principle proved to be a momentous step' (ibid., p. 219). To form a conception of the real circumstances and to endeavour to make a real alteration in them could be called a first step in thinking. It takes the place of the mindless motor discharge. Freud says: 'Restraint upon motor discharge (or an action) which would then become necessary, was provided by means of the process of thinking' (ibid., p. 221). According to Freud, it is thinking that makes it possible for the mental apparatus to tolerate an increased tension and to delay action. He calls it 'essentially an experimental kind of acting'. Thus, thinking evolves in the gap between the experience of the need and its satisfaction.

On this hypothesis there is a distinction between hallucination and thought. I shall come back to that. A further extension of this hypothesis on the origin and nature of thought emerges from the work of Melanie Klein, particularly with very young children, and that of Wilfred Bion, particularly with psychotics. In Klein's view, the response to hunger is a hallucination of an all-satisfying breast, as suggested by Freud, but she adds that when this cannot ward off the hunger, hunger itself is experienced also as the presence of an object, but a bad one, gnawing, tearing, attacking—a hallucinated bad object. According to Bion, such an experience, felt to be a bad object, can only be dealt with by expulsion. I think that the motor discharge, as described by Freud, may be a way of dealing with bad hallucinations, an attempt to expel them. It is, I think, the realization that this discharge does not relieve the need, that brings in the realization that a need is not an object that can be got rid of, but is something intrinsic to one's self, something originating within one's self, not a bad object, but the need for an object that is absent. The hallucinations are recognized as the product of one's mind. A phantasy of an ideal object or a persecutory one is recognized as a phantasy. So long as a phantasy is omnipotent, it is not a thought because it is not recognized as such. When a phantasy is recognized as a product of one's own mind, it moves into the realm of thought. One then can say: I phantasied this or that, or I thought such and such. In that, thought differs from hallucination, or delusion. Freud says that the reality principle is nothing but the pleasure principle subjected to reality testing. I would add that thinking evolves from omnipotent phantasy, and it is a phantasy recognized as such and one that can be subjected to reality testing.

Thinking first starts with, and then promotes, reality testing. It starts with the realization—this is not what is, it is what I made it to be in my mind. But it also promotes reality testing, in that omnipotent phantasy cannot be used for reality testing. Its very aim is to deny the reality of the experience. Thinking is not only an experimental action, as described by Freud, it is also an experimental hypothesis about the nature of things—a constant checking of what one phantasied against the evidence. Primitive thought starts at the pre-verbal level and is eventually encompassed in a word or a phrase: 'Mummy—Daddy—Mummy gone'. A word or sentence encompasses a complex experience.

Both the omnipotent phantasy—hallucination—and thinking enable one to bear the gap between need and satisfaction—the absence and the need for a satisfying object. But whilst omnipotent phantasy denies the experience of need, thought, which admits the need, can be used to explore external and internal realities and deal with them. But thought, because it springs from and admits frustration, can be attacked at its very inception.

This hatred of thought processes, deeply rooted in the unconscious, can be active throughout life. For example, I had a patient who was highly intelligent and articulate in some ways, but certain areas of his personality were functioning at a very primitive level. He had psychosomatic symptoms—a gastric ulcer—and at times of tension thinking was replaced by impulsive acting out. He had become aware in the course of his analysis of how he was obsessed with women's breasts. Towards the end of one session he reported a dream in which a woman was giving the breast to a baby. They were so close to the patient that he could fondle the woman's breasts. Then the woman went away, but she left the breast with the baby and the patient, who continued the sucking and fondling. He added that the baby must also be himself, as it was so close to him. He started the next session with a great deal of irritation with himself. He said that he had plenty of important problems in his adult life which he wanted to talk about, but the moment he set eyes on the analyst he noticed she was wearing a white blouse and started thinking about her breasts and he said with exasperation: 'I am not only obsessed with breasts, I am mad. I am obviously mad about breasts.' He then spoke of how he was always sucking something, like his toes and his thumb in his childhood, and now sweets, chewing gum, cigarettes, anything that he could put into his mouth. As he was talking, he was getting more and more dreamy and remote. I drew his attention to this and reminded him of the dream in which the baby–he sucked and fondled the breast while the woman went away. He interrupted me angrily, saying: 'Don't make me think. I don't want to think. I want to suck. I hate thoughts. When I have thoughts, it means I have nothing to suck.' My making the comment about his state of mind made him aware that what he was experiencing was a living-through of the dream that he had possession of the breast, and it made him aware of my presence. I was the woman with the white blouse, and there was a gap between us, necessitating speech for communication. The moment he became aware of that, he became aware that he was having thoughts, not a breast in his mouth, and he hated it. He hated the fact that he needed thinking to deal with this gap and with the problems he referred to at the beginning of the session, not the least of them being an impending psychoanalytic holiday break.

The nascent thought conflicts with the illusion that the infant is merged with, or in possession of, an ideal breast. And disillusion must be tolerated for thought to develop. An element of this disillusion persists in sophisticated thought.

Towards the end of his analysis, another patient brought the two following dreams. In the first dream he saw himself. He was slim, but otherwise unchanged—a balding middle-aged man. On waking from the dream he thought that his dream meant that being slimmer did not actually make him be any younger. This patient, with a tendency to corpulence, used periodically to diet and to slim, and as he lost weight he used to become very manic. He had had a near-conscious phantasy that being slim made him again into an adolescent, young and beautiful. In his association to the dream, he recognized with a certain sadness that it was no longer so. He was still pleased at having lost weight in the last week, but he could not feel as he used to, that it had changed him. His belief in the magic rejuvenating power of slimming and the elation associated with it have gone.

The following day he brought a more complex dream. He was saying goodbye at the door to an adolescent. He felt very tender towards him and sad at parting. In the background stood X, the adolescent's father, a cripple, and still further in the background, the patient's parental family. He had many associations to the dream. The first one was that the adolescent was himself, and he was saying goodbye to his phantasies of being still an adolescent and goodbye to the picture of himself as still dependent on his original family. The associations to X were more complex. X was a rich, extremely mean, successful businessman, now crippled through a disease of the central nervous system. The patient himself had been a businessman, successful and ruthlessly greedy. When he came to analysis, being successful in business was equated in his mind with being not only powerful, omnipotently so, but also very righteous. It was part of the culture he grew up in to believe that people were poor only because of their own fecklessness. Wealth was equated with godliness. Unconsciously, however, this greed and ruthlessness gave rise to a great deal of guilt, persecution and feelings of emptiness, which eventually brought him to analysis. In the course of his analysis he recognized how crippling to his mental development were those attitudes. The cripple in the dream represents his past self and an aspect of his father, who had the same set of values in a less extreme form. In the dream he says goodbye, not only to the adolescent self, but to the set of values and ideas that he can no longer entertain. Now he is no longer free to think that being rich is equivalent to being righteous. Nor can he think any more that that aspect of his father is admirable and to be emulated. So whilst analysis freed his perceptions and thoughts from the rigid set of values he was brought up in and which also suited his own greed and envy, he felt regret and sadness at the loss of a set of thoughts and beliefs belonging to the past. He mourned the lost idealization of his father and mostly of himself. Aspects of his personality, which he had used to think of as marvellous, he now thought of as crippling to his whole central nervous system. Certain ideas he could still think but could no longer believe.

I am aware that I seem to be confusing here belief with thought, but among its other functions, thinking has that of examining belief. He could still think about the ideas he used to have and sometimes regret that he could no longer hold them any more as true, but he could no longer use them in thinking about the world and base his action on them. Similarly, once we learned that the earth is a planet revolving around the sun, we are not quite free to think that it is flat. Or, rather, we can entertain such a thought as an intriguing phantasy—we can even, if we have the talent and inclination, write a science fiction novel about a flat world—but we have to recognize it as a phantasy thought.

If thinking, as I suggested, is related to matching phantasies with realities, phantasies lose their omnipotent character.

The patient I referred to came to recognize that many of his views of himself and the world, and sometimes irrational actions that sprang from them, were based on omnipotent unconscious phantasies. For instance, he had a phantasy that his faeces had magic powers and were superior as food to mother's milk, and in potency to his father's penis. When this omnipotent phantasy had become a clear thought, he had to face his real feeling of helplessness and dependence as a child in relation to his parents and, now, as a patient in relation to me. Freud links thinking with 'forming a conception of the reality circumstances in the external world'. This involves also forming a conception about one's self, one's needs, and one's impulses—that is to say, forming some conception of one's own internal world. The patient's belief in the magic of his faeces had been linked with another omnipotent phantasy. He had a phantasy, amply illustrated in many dreams, that he had swallowed me up (as in the past, he had phantasied about his mother) and inside himself had emptied me of all my supposed riches and attributes, physical and mental, so that in his manic state he felt the owner of all power and riches and contained me as an impoverished object full of greed and envy. This omnipotent phantasy underlay both his states of manic elation and those of persecution. This state of affairs was experienced, not as thoughts, but as a reality. Very schematically, one could say that there were three steps in his gaining of insight in that area:

1. My faeces are everything (omnipotent).
2. This is so because my internal parents are empty and I have it all—that is also why they persecute me.
3. This is so because I wished it so; in my mind I made it so by imagining that I had swallowed them up and emptied them.

This third step brings him in touch with the fact that the state of affairs he experiences is something he phantasied because he wished it. He begins to recognize that these are the thoughts he has, and he can no longer believe them as separating reality perceptions. The omnipotent phantasies turn into thoughts that can be expressed as: This is what I wished, or, this is what I wish. This is what I thought I had done, or could do. At that point reality testing, 'can I do it', begins to play a part, and it plays a part in two ways. One is a reality testing of the omnipotence of one's wishes—

for instance, the realization by that patient that it was a phantasy that he could possess himself of my attributes in that way. But another equally important element of reality comes into play—an internal reality testing in relation to other feelings and wishes that one may have—in the case of that patient, for instance, such feelings as love, gratitude, a wish to preserve inside himself a good perception of me, guilt about his greedy and envious thoughts and concern about what it was doing to his internal world, and how it was affecting his behaviour in the external world. All those feelings were in conflict with his omnipotent megalomania.

I have been led by this example to bring in several additional problems—awareness of impulses, sense of guilt, the problem of values. Are they relevant to my theme? I think I have to introduce here the concept of integration and its relation to thinking. An omnipotent phantasy can, and indeed must, be split off from certain perceptions, external and internal, that conflict with it. When a phantasy loses its omnipotent character and becomes thought, a hypothesis to be tested or a wish recognized as such, it becomes integrated with other thoughts and wishes. Thought allows conflict and seeks resolution. I cannot here go into the difference between having thoughts and thinking—suffice it to say that such an integration—comparing and matching and judging—is also a step from the state of having thoughts to the state of thinking. In the case of the patient, in a simplified way, a megalomanic phantasy, lived as a reality, began to give way to thoughts, to the appraising of himself, me and the world and an appraisal of his contradictory wishes.

This was linked with a change in his sense of values, because a sense of values and thinking are inextricably bound up. The sense of values naturally influences all thinking, but conversely, too, the sense of values is determined by what we think. Money-Kyrle explored this theme in such works as 'Psycho-analysis and ethics' (1952) and *Man's Picture of His World* (1961). My patient's view of the world was based on the phantasy that he had robbed his object and therefore feared that his object would rob and annihilate him; it led to a sense of values based on the idea: You have to kill if you are not to be killed. With the emergence of integration and thinking and a changed view of himself and the world, his sense of values unavoidably had to alter. A paradoxical and complex situation arises in relation to the superego. When integration begins and thinking takes the place of split-off omnipotent phantasies, guilt is in some way lessened and in others augmented. In my patient, the omnipotent phantasy of his superiority was linked with a terrifying superego, a parental figure, stripped of all positive assets and seething with greed and envy. His thinking was not only constricted by the infantile need to annihilate any thought that would conflict with his own omnipotence, it was also under continuous attack by an equally omnipotent envious and hostile superego, which did not allow him any real enrichment in feeling, thought or knowledge.

When the phantasies are recognized as phantasies, they are allowed to exist in thought. The less the omnipotence, the more permissible a thought becomes, as it does not have the omnipotent power to change the object into a monster superego figure. On the other hand, however, this inner persecution by a monstrous superego is replaced by a feeling of responsibility for one's own thought and more conscious guilt, which I think is unavoidable, even if the thoughts are recognized as not omnipotent.

In the case of the last patient I spoke about, the megalomanic phantasy and the accompanying fears, both mutilating his capacity to think, were replaced by realizations that, for instance, there were people he depended on, that this often stimulated in him greedy, envious and hostile thoughts and phantasies, and that the existence of those thoughts gave him some pain, both of guilt and of disillusionment in his view of himself.

What then is the freedom of thought? Nietzsche says: 'The thought does not come when we want it, it comes when it wants.' We could add: It is not what we want, it is what it wants. This, of course, is rather personifying thought, as though it were a being with a will of its own. There is such a category of thought—those attributed to and felt as emanating from an internal object, as an inspiration or a persecution. But more generally thought and thinking are the outcome of a complex interaction of our impulses, wishes, phantasies and perceptions—and as such, they are not necessarily what we would wish them to be.

Freedom of thought—and at best, I think we still have a very limited freedom in that respect—means the freedom to know our own thoughts, and that means knowing the unwelcome as well as the welcome, anxious thoughts, those felt as 'bad' or 'mad', as well as constructive thoughts and those felt as 'good' or 'sane', and being able to examine their validity in terms of external or internal realities. The freer we are to think, the better we can judge these realities, and the richer our experience. But like all freedoms, it is also felt as a bind in that it makes us feel responsible for our own thoughts.

And formidable forces, external and internal, militate against this freedom. The psychoanalyst sets himself the task of helping the patient first of all to recognize the immeasurable value of such freedom and the worthwhileness of struggling for it and then to achieve such freedom in a greater measure.

CHAPTER FIVE

Unconscious wishes and human relationships

Joseph Sandler

T raditional accounts of psychoanalytic psychology usually emphasize the way in which crude sexual and aggressive impulses attempt to force their way towards the surface of the mind, to find expression in the individual's subjective experience and overt behaviour. On the path from the depths to the surface such impulses may be felt to be dangerous, may arouse conflict in the mind and have to be defended against or censored—distorted, so that their true meaning is hidden from the person's own consciousness. Although such defensive distortion and censorship is a normal process, a consequence of the child's progressive socialization, the *outcome* of conflict and defence may under certain circumstances be regarded as pathological.

Within the traditional theoretical framework of psychoanalysis, the persons towards whom the impulses are directed, either in fantasy or reality, are the *objects* of the drives—hence, of course, the term object relationships. Such object relationships have been accounted for in classical psychoanalytic theory in terms of the investment of the object (or its mental representation) with instinctual drive energy, either in its original crude state or in a neutralized, purified or sublimated form.

In contrast to the linking of psychopathology with conflict over primitive instinctual impulses, there has been an increasing tendency over the past few decades to describe and explain both normal and pathological processes in terms of the vicissitudes of the individual's object relationships. The viewing of psychological processes from the vantage point of object relations (and, in particular, *early* object relations) has often been contrasted with the view stressing unconscious wish-fulfillment, and indeed violent and often strident ideological battles have been waged in psychoanalytic circles over this very issue. These battles erupted in the so-called 'controversial discussions' in the British Psycho-Analytical Society in 1943, but the divergence of standpoints was evident before that. I shall cite one relatively simple example. In 1941 the late Dr John Rickman published an account (Rickman, 1941) of hysterical paralysis and anaesthesia in a soldier of 28 who had previously sustained superficial gunshot wounds of the right arm and leg. He noted that, in this particular case, the patient was preoccupied with his arm, nursed and stroked it and tried to make it warm. After the patient had begun to talk about himself, it became evident that the 'poor arm' represented in his mind a person who was dead. This could be linked with the recent loss of his best friend, who had been killed in the action that had also wounded *him*. Through his symptom he seemed to mourn his friend, and at the same time he nursed his own damaged self. When the patient was shown that a process of mourning was going on inside himself, expressed in his concern for the dead arm, he first became resentful, and then depressed, presenting signs of grief and a need for sympathy. Within a few weeks he had recovered, having partly unburdened himself of his unhappiness at the loss of his comrade. Rickman went on to comment that the pathology of such a patient could now be seen in terms of his relationships to people, in the present as well as in the past, and in his continuing unconscious fantasy life.

Rickman's paper was an indication of the differences of opinion in regard to both theory and technique that developed and crystallized within the psychoanalytic movement in England since the 1930s. One of the most significant of these differences centred around the very question of object relationships. Those who saw mental functioning in terms of such present and past relationships, relationships existing in reality or in fantasy life, felt (as Rickman had done) that they had moved forward to a richer and more fruitful view of psychopathology than the 'classical' one, which they tended to regard as simply a psychology of conflict over instinctual expression. Here Melanie Klein's theories about very early object relationships in the infant's fantasies in the first few months of life had a profound influence. On the other hand, the so-called 'classical' analysts, grouped for the most part around Anna Freud, believed that the emphasis on object relationships led to an underestimation of the importance of persisting childhood sexuality and oedipal conflict in adult psychic life, as well as to an under-valuation of the child's potential for development. There were also, of course, many other areas of disagreement, and for many years people of different psychoanalytic persuasions caricatured the views of their opponents while staunchly defending their own; and of course they still do.

In what follows I want to try to clarify the links between unconscious wishes on the one hand and object relationships on the other, and to attempt by this to diminish what I believe is a theoretical hiatus as well as an area of unnecessary conflict in our current psychoanalytic thinking.

Freud's realization in 1897 that the traumatic memories recalled by his hysterical patients were really memories of wish-fulfilling daydream fantasies, and his intensive self-analysis and interest in his own and in his patient's dreams, introduced the point of view that the individual was, to a large degree, at the mercy of his instincts or his drives. However, civilized man struggles to contain these drives, often at great cost to himself. Early in the development of psychoanalysis, these drives were seen to be predominantly sexual in nature, although for a while Freud postulated a class of self-preservative drives (the so-called 'ego instincts'), which included aggression. Later, aggression was placed alongside sexual libido as a major component of the individual's instinctual life. Hysterical and obsessional symptoms were regarded as the outcome of an inner struggle against sexual impulses that would be *perverse* if they were openly expressed or experienced in the adult. Normal in infancy or childhood, they developed in a definite sequence through the well-known phases of psycho-sexual development—oral, anal and so on. Neurosis was seen as 'the negative of perversion'. The 'perverse' childhood sexual impulses were usually repressed by about the age of five or six, although they could be stimulated or revived later in life, leading to conflict and possible neurosis.

Although I have referred to 'instincts' and 'drives' thus far, these are constructs relating to basic psycho-biological tendencies of the individual, and to the force and energy implicit in these tendencies. From a psychological point of view it is sufficient for us to take, as a basic unit, the *wish*. We can regard the instinct or drive as a complex series of stimuli which not only propel the individual towards relatively automatic, biologically based action, but which arouse *wishes* in the mind. As Freud put it, the drives represent a 'demand for work' on the mental apparatus. The wishes aroused by the early sexual tendencies of the child contain a specific psychological content based upon the memories of previous satisfaction. Thus, for example, from the very beginning although the oral drive has, as its biological object, the breast, the *wish* to suck at the breast and to gain oral satisfaction must, in early psychological life, be a particular gestalt of sensations and feelings based upon the child's subjective experiences of sucking. The psychological object that *we* call the breast will be, for the infant, based on a sequence of sensory experiences closely bound to feeling states.

As the child develops, and the psychological processes that can take place in his mind become more sophisticated, he becomes more able to distinguish between self and object, between himself and other persons. With this development, there is equally a development in the nature of his wishes. In the instinctual wishes described earlier, for example, we can say that every wish comes to include a representation of the person's own self and a representation of the object who also has a role to play in the fulfilment of the wish. The wish contains representations of self and object in interaction. One does not simply have a wish to exhibit oneself, for instance, but the hoped-for reaction of the audience is equally part of the wish. This has been put as follows:

> ... the child who has a wish to cling to the mother, has, as part of this wish, a mental representation of himself clinging to the mother. But he also has, in the content of his wish, a representation of the mother or her substitute responding to his clinging in

a particular way, possibly by bending down and embracing him. This formulation is rather different from the traditional idea of a wish consisting of a wishful aim being directed towards an object. The idea of an aim that seeks gratification has to be supplemented by the idea of a *wished-for interaction*, with the wished-for or imagined response of the object being as much a part of the wishful fantasy as the activity of the subject in that wish or fantasy. [Sandler & Sandler, 1978]

I have just quoted the term 'wishful fantasy' in addition to 'wish', and this deserves some explanation. For Freud, fantasy had an intimate relation to the wish. Conscious fantasy was simply the wish-fulfilling conscious day-dream, but the term unconscious fantasy had a variety of meanings. In more recent years the range of such meanings has been so broadened that the term appears to embrace practically every type of unconscious mental content or activity. However, as it has become increasingly obvious that the term 'unconscious fantasy' is here to stay, in spite of its variety of meanings, it seems to me that it might best be conceived of as something that is constructed by the unconscious organized part of the mental apparatus from material relating to the whole variety of wishes that, at any one time, are seeking expression or satisfaction. The term *unconscious* is used here in a purely descriptive sense, because unconscious fantasy thoughts involve organized thinking (secondary process functioning) at a variety of levels of complexity. I would suggest that the term *unconscious fantasy* is now perhaps best reserved for what Freud referred to as an unconscious wishful fantasy. Such a fantasy is not in itself a satisfaction of a wish (or of a set of wishes), but it can be regarded as a step *towards wish-fulfilment* in that it is a worked-out *plan* for gaining the satisfaction of these wishes, a step in the direction of satisfaction, which is usually a compromise solution aimed at gratifying several different wishes simultaneously. It is clear, however, that the great bulk of unconscious fantasies is not acceptable to consciousness without even further censorship and distortion through defensive activity.

At this point I want to add a word or two about the role of the defences in the formation of unconscious fantasies, in particular those defences that involve processes of externalization or identification. Anna Freud has shown us how a wish to be the passive experiencer of, for example, sexual penetration may be disguised by the mechanism of 'turning passive into active', so that the wishful fantasy takes the form of the other person being the active partner. By the use of 'identification with the aggressor' one can deal with a threatening situation by changing one's image of oneself into that of the person who threatens. One can dissociate oneself from some unwanted impulse by attributing it to another person by means of the mechanism of projection, or one can gain possession of an admired and coveted attribute of another person by changing one's self-image in one's fantasy life by means of identification. One can deal with conflicting impulses in oneself by splitting the self-image into 'good' and 'bad' parts, and so on. Melanie Klein has been able to show us how we often dissociate aspects of our own selves, place these aspects in the mental representation of another person, and then, in the wishful fantasy, attempt to *control* that person's activities, in that way unconsciously attempting to achieve control over the unwanted aspects of one's own self now located in the object—this is the mechanism of projective identification. In presenting the mechanisms of defence to you in this way, I am well aware that this is not the usual way in which it is done, for psychoanalysts tend to speak rather concretely of, for example, the various different types of projection and will talk of 'putting an aspect of oneself into another person' or of 'using another person as a "container"', a mechanism described by Wilfred Bion.

We can regard an object relationship as being a valued relationship between oneself and another person. Such relationships start early in life, and also exist in our wishful fantasy lives. We continually create new relationships that we value, but these new object relationships are often new editions of older relationships. There is an obvious parallel between the setting up of an object relationship in ordinary life and what goes on in the transference situation in psychoanalytic therapy, although in the latter the analyst uses his particular technique to bring to the surface whatever is occurring unconsciously in the patient. However, even in the analytic situation the analyst is not entirely passive, and we have a situation in which each party is trying to externalize, to impose upon the other, an *intrapsychic role relationship*. A person's object relationships contain, as an essential component, a role relationship between the individuals concerned. If we refer to our clinical experience, it is striking that a type of relationship might be repeated over and over again and may have a very definite pattern inherent in it. We all know of cases in which someone gets on well with an employer or a lover, and after a certain number of months the person is suddenly disappointed and disillusioned. In analysis we can often trace this either to a pattern that had occurred in childhood or to a defensive wishful fantasy that had been constructed at some time in the past. In and through such a fantasy the individual is protected, for example, against dangerous closeness to some person in the present who represents a loved but threatening figure of the past. It is important to note that there is a definite sequence, a temporal dimension, in the pattern of interaction.

A clinical illustration may be useful here (Sandler, 1976): This was a patient in her late twenties, a schoolteacher. She came to treatment because of social and sexual difficulties, and after some time it became clear that she was terrified of her penis-envy and of her hostility towards her mother, had multiple phobic anxieties and needed, mainly through intellectualization and organizational control of others, including her teaching, to 'structure' her world so that she always knew exactly 'where she was'. Her need to do this emerged in the transference, and after some three years of analytic work her psychopathology had become very much clearer, and she was much improved and happier. However, there was one strand of material that had remained rather obscure. From the beginning she had cried during each session, and I had routinely passed her the box of tissues whenever she began to cry. Now I did not know why I did this, but having begun the practice, I did not feel inclined to change it without some good reason. Without knowing why, I had not felt it appropriate to take up her failure to bring her own tissues or a handkerchief, although with other patients I would have done this. There were many determinants of her crying, including her mourning for the mother she wanted to kill off, for the father she felt she had to give up, and so on. It transpired that when she was about two years old, a second child, a brother, had been born, and she felt that she had lost her mother's attention; she remembered that at about two and a half years of age she was relegated to playing on her own in the back-yard while her brother was being washed and changed. At this time she had also been sent to a kindergarten, and she had the memory of being very withdrawn and climbing into the rabbit hutch at the nursery school and cuddling a white rabbit. She then told me that she had later learned that after a short while at this school she was diagnosed as 'autistic' by the school psychologist and was apparently very regressed and had uncontrollable rages and tantrums. By this point in her analysis we were able to get at the repetition in the present of her fear of soiling and disgracing herself and her need to control her objects as she had to control her sphincters. However, there was clearly something that was an important unconscious fantasy for her which had not been elicited. I had the feeling that we were somewhat 'stuck' in the analytic work. One day something rather unusual happened in the analysis. She had begun to cry silently, but this time I failed to respond, and she suddenly began to upbraid me and criticize me for not having passed her the tissues. She became quite panicky and began to accuse me of being callous and uncaring. I responded by saying that I did not know why I had not passed her the tissues at that particular point, but if she could go on talking perhaps we could both understand more about it. What emerged then was material that lent a great deal of specificity to something that we had not been able to crystallize previously. It became clear that her great need for control and for 'structures' in her life was based not on a fear of soiling herself, but rather on a fear that she would soil or wet herself *and that there would not be an adult around to clean her up.* This turned out to be the fear that dominated her life. It was connected with a specific fantasy that seemed to have been elaborated during the late anal phase, under the impact of the mother's withdrawal from her because of the birth of her second child. The discovery and working-through of this specific fantasy marked a crucial point in her analysis. I do not want to go into any more detail about her material, except to say that I think that I must have picked up unconscious cues from the patient, which prompted me to behave in a certain way in her analysis—both to keep passing her the tissues and then to omit doing so. (It would be pure speculation to link the two-and-a-half years of analysis with the age when her anxiety started.) I believe that this patient had, quite unconsciously on her part and on mine, forced me into a role—a role corresponding to that of a parental introject ... in which I enacted the part, first of the attentive mother, and then suddenly that of the parent who did not clean her up. In the session I was not around to make sure that she was clean, just as she felt that, with the birth of her brother, her mother had not been around to clean her, being busy paying attention to the new baby.

I need hardly add that what occurred in the clinical situation must occur even more readily outside it, in the whole sphere of human relationships.

Because psychoanalytic theory and practice have placed so much emphasis on sexual and aggressive wishes, and because psychoanalysis has had to defend its findings in regard to the prevalence of such wishes, there has been a tendency to see *all* wishes as being instinctual. With developments in ego psychology after the war, psychoanalytic theoreticians have gone through the most tremendous intellectual contortions to try to derive *all* wishes from sexual and aggressive impulses, and they have attempted to maintain a position in which any unconscious wish is seen as being powered either by instinctual energy or by a desexualized or neutralized form of that energy. This position is simply no longer tenable, and our clinical experience with those cases of personality disturbance called by psychoanalysts 'character disorder', in particular narcissistic character disorder, has made it abundantly clear to us that we need to modify this very rigid position. Just as the tension produced by drive stimuli may evoke wishes, so can other stimuli (e.g. external stimuli) call forth the wish. If, for some reason, there is a lessening of our background feeling of safety, appropriate wishes to do something that would restore that feeling of security are evoked. If self-esteem is threatened, compensatory narcissistic wishful fantasies may result. Such fantasies form a very large part of our mental life and are typified in the various derivatives of the 'superman' fantasies of the child. The pain of *loss* will evoke wishes to restore the relation to the lost object in some way. Anxiety in its various forms (I include feelings of shame and guilt) is a most potent stimulus to wishful activity, the aim of the wish being to restore feelings of well-being. If a particular way of comforting oneself was successful in childhood, the urge to impose this particular method of dealing with discomfort or anxiety (or sadness or pain) may be the content of an unconscious wish. This, in turn, may have come to be defended against, subsequently emerging on the surface, possibly in its opposite form, as in the refusal of food in certain forms of anorexia. I want to stress that wishes to establish and re-establish certain types of relationship with others need not be motivated by sexual or aggressive drives alone, but may primarily represent attempts to restore or maintain feelings of well-being and security. The need to maintain or sustain such feelings is an over-riding one in mental functioning, and the urge to obtain direct erotic grati-fication may have to be sacrificed in the interest of preserving safety or well-being. A psychoanalytic psychology of motivation related to the control of feeling states should, I believe, replace a psychology based on the idea of instinctual drive discharge.

What of wish-fulfilment? If we do not accept the idea that wishes are gratified or fulfilled by discharging energy, then we need to put some other formulation in its place. The clue to what this might be may be found, curiously enough, in Freud's *The Interpretation of Dreams*. There, in speaking of wish-fulfilment, he also mentions the attainment of satisfaction (classically in the dream) through what he calls an identity of perception. In its simplest form the wish represents a striving to re-experience a memory of something that was satisfactory in the past; if an identical perception is reached in the present, then wish-fulfilment has been brought about. It is true that the biological needs of the individual may not be gratified by this, but for a short period of time the *psychological* wishes aroused by such biological needs will be satisfied. The dream, which can be regarded as a hallucination at night, provides such an identity of perception. However, what is curious here is that it provides a concealed and distorted identity of perception, because the unconscious work of the dream—the so-called dream-work—has censored the wishful (but conflictual) fantasies behind the dream, and wish-fulfilment is thus obtained in a way that deceives consciousness. It is a major function of the unconscious part of the mind to protect consciousness from a whole variety of unpleasant and unacceptable experiences.

How then is wish-fulfilment brought about? My own suggestion in this context is that there is an *understanding work* that pro-ceeds in a parallel but opposite direction to the dream work, so that the content of the dream, its symbolic and disguised meaning, can be unconsciously understood; and this unconscious understanding is the signal that the wish need no longer press towards fulfilment. I do not want to elaborate this here, except to say that this would imply a signal theory of wish-fulfilment, a systems theory, a model that is, moreover, consistent with present-day neurological thinking. I have spoken of the hallucination in the dream, but what is true of the dream can also be regarded as true for other 'derivatives of the unconscious', for other surface expressions of unconscious wishes and wishful fantasies. We can speak here of *actualization*, which is no more than the process of creating an experience that is felt to be 'real' or 'actual'. The simplest way to do this is to *act* upon the real world in such a way that our perceptions come to correspond to the wished-for reality. We may also act upon ourselves in order to attain this correspondence. Normally we do both, but there are also other methods of actualization. We may include *illusional* actualization, in which the perceptual process distorts the sensory data arising from the external world in the direction of wish-fulfilment, although normally such an illusion can be corrected by later experience. If it cannot, we have *delusional* actualization, a process that is not only restricted to psychotics. Wish-fulfilment through *hallucinatory* actualization is, of course, common in psychosis and normal in the dream. Actualization through *daydreams* is normally less satisfying than actualization by way of direct perceptual experience, although much will depend on the sensory intensity of the daydream images and the capacity of the individual to suspend 'disbelief' temporarily during daydreaming. We have actualization in art and literature, and even in some of our social rituals. I believe that the concept can be fruitfully applied in the study of totemism, for example.

If we take the view that wish-fulfilment can come about through actualization and remind ourselves that the content of an unconscious wish or wishful fantasy normally includes a representation of self and object in interacting roles, we are then close to bridging the gap between wishes and relationships. We are obliged to assume, however, that the individual constantly scans his environment, in particular the reactions of others, in the often subtle 'transactions' that go on between people in ordinary social relations. The responses of others to 'trial' signals or to behavioural indications of our own is constantly assessed by us. Similarly we respond, often quite unconsciously, to the signals inviting us to assume particular roles for others. If, on the basis of such unconscious 'scanning', 'trials' and 'signals', we find that the situation does not permit the gratification of an unconscious wishful fantasy through identity of perception, then we may discard a particular course of action (or seek other partners) in the attempt to attain unconscious wish-fulfilment.

The case of Mrs B (Sandler, 1959) illustrates the way in which responses from the environment that actualize unconscious wishful fantasies can be elicited. Mrs B came to analysis some considerable time ago, at the age of 35. Her main complaint was that she was unable to have intercourse with her husband because her vagina 'went into spasm', and her husband could not achieve penetration. She had been married for 15 years and was still virgin. She was leading, as she put it, 'a cat and dog life' with her husband.

Her symptom was first brought to the attention of the medical profession when, in her late teens, a medical student attempted to have intercourse with her. In spite of her willingness to co-operate he could not penetrate and expressed the view that she was physically deformed. Later, a diagnosis of 'vaginismus' was made, and she underwent a surgical operation that was unsuccessful. She also complained of backache and occasional severe attacks of cramp-like pains in her hands. Further symptoms included social anxieties, which revealed a marked fear of exposing herself, and she had anxiety dreams that she would be found naked in the street. She reported work difficulties, mainly revolving around her fear of responsibility. She had been working in a restaurant, and on being promoted to manageress had been so overcome by fear and guilt that she managed to engineer herself out of a job.

Mrs B was an identical twin, whose mother had died when she was a few months old. After being cared for by a succession of women, the twins were left with the maternal grandparents in Scotland. Mrs B's grandmother was an irritable and aggressive woman who dominated her husband and her own grown-up children and who, the patient felt, resented having to look after the twins and hated their irresponsible father while idealizing their perfect mother, who was always described as a 'saint'. Living in the household was an uncle who was weak and ineffectual, a drunkard like Mrs B's father, yet someone towards whom Mrs B was able to feel love and who played, in her fantasy life, the role of her father.

Mrs B's later choice of a husband was, it soon appeared, based entirely on her relationship to her father-image and her uncle. Her husband, too, was dissolute and drunken and had spent some time in a mental hospital.

The analysis, which lasted in the first instance just over two years, progressed well. In particular, Mrs B was able to bring her main relations to her childhood figures directly into the treatment situation. The first sign of this transference came in the form of an obstinate but intermittent tendency to silence—a silence that was due partly to a difficulty in thinking, and partly to an inhibition of speech. It soon became clear that this paralleled, on a psychological level, the physical symptom of vaginismus. The similarity between the two was striking, and it seemed as if she suffered an involuntary spasm of a mental sphincter. In time we could understand something of her inability to tolerate penetration of a mental or a physical kind, and as the silence disappeared in the course of the analysis, so there was an easing of her physical symptom. It became clear that she wished me to attack her to make her speak and to force my interpretations upon her. She was able to recall how her sexual fantasies in childhood had been rape fantasies, and the thought of being raped by the drunken uncle had been a very exciting one. It was evident that with her symptom she nightly provoked her husband, who stood for her uncle and her father, to assault her. She had shared a single narrow bed with her husband from the beginning of their marriage, although she said she had always meant to change to twin beds. If, in her analysis, when she was silent I was silent too, she would, after a while, berate me for my lack of co-operation.

I do not propose to go into the many aspects of Mrs B's psychopathology that revealed themselves during her analysis, but rather to summarize one or two of these very briefly. A central feature was her intensely masochistic character, and an inordinate, highly sexualized 'need for punishment'. On one occasion when promoted at work, she had felt so guilty that she had set herself on fire and had spent several months in hospital. All her relationships were coloured by this tendency. Cramp-like pains in the hands would occur in the analytic session whenever she felt guilty about feelings of violence towards me.

We were able to trace her hostility towards her mother, grandmother and sister and could understand how, through feelings of guilt and a need for punishment, she made herself the object of her own aggressive wishes. With the discovery of her hostility she was able to permit herself to be promoted at work and to manage more-or-less successfully without having to damage herself too much.

What was particularly striking in this patient was her intense resentment of men, which existed side by side with her sexual attachment to them. It transpired that she had thought as a child that if she had not been a twin she would have been a boy, and that her younger twin sister was her broken-off penis. Her resentment of men for having their power is striking, and it became clear that with her symptom of vaginismus she regularly provoked and then emasculated her husband. Similarly, in the analytic session she would provoke me to ask questions and would then snub me. In relation to her silence, she would often say that there was something in her mind that blocked her thoughts, and this matched her fantasy that a broken-off stump of a penis remained in her vagina, preventing successful penetration.

Following the analysis of this and much other material she was able to leave her husband, who was in fact most disturbed, and to take a lover with whom she now had satisfactory intercourse. The analysis of her exhibitionistic fears (she was afraid of a strong wish to excite men by exhibiting her body) enabled her to take a new job demonstrating frozen food in a large department store.

Certainly her analysis was far from complete, but for various reasons it was expedient to stop at this point. A year later she wrote that her improvement was maintained and that she was enjoying a happy sexual relationship.

Four years later Mrs B wrote asking to see me as she was extremely worried. Although her improvement had been maintained (she was now working full-time as an artist's model and was more-or-less satisfied with her sexual life with the man with whom she was living), her husband, from whom she had remained separated, had been writing many letters to her in which he threatened suicide if she did not rejoin him. I agreed to see her and did so for a year. The details of this further period of work need not detain us here, except for one feature. In place of her vaginismus, she was now mildly but noticeably deaf.

Her deafness had been diagnosed as 'nerve deafness' at a London hospital, but it soon seemed likely that this new symptom derived from the same unconscious processes that had led to her vaginal spasm. In spite of working through all this material again, her deafness persisted. However, an understanding of her deafness occurred suddenly and rather unexpectedly. I suddenly became aware that my need to talk loudly so that she could hear me also caused me to shout pedantically, as if to a naughty child. This realization led me to the understanding that by being deaf my patient could force me to shout at her as her grandmother had done when she was very small. It became clear that she was unconsciously recreating, in her relationship with me, an earlier relationship to the grandmother, who had been, in spite of her unkindness to and constant irritation with the patient, the most permanent and stable figure in Mrs B's childhood. With the working-through of feelings of loss of her grandmother and her need to recreate her presence in many different ways, Mrs B's hearing improved.

We could now see that Mrs B was not only obtaining masochistic gratification through her symptoms but was also defending against an intense fear of abandonment by recreating, in the analytic session and out of it, a feeling of the physical presence of her grandmother, whose mode of contact with the child had been predominantly one of verbal criticism or of physical punishment. In the symptom of vaginismus she had, among many other things, provoked shouting and physical assault, in order to obtain the feeling that the grandmother was physically present. It seemed that the pain and suffering was the price she paid for a bodily feeling of safety, for the reassurance that she would not undergo the miserable loneliness and separation that had characterized her first year of life, and which she felt would be her lot if she showed any hostility at all.

Finally, I want to turn briefly to the question of the role relationships that I believe to be central to the concept of object relationship (in reality or as reflected in fantasy life). We can start with the idea that the individual constantly obtains a special form of *grati-fication* through his interaction with others, consciously or uncon-sciously, in real life or in fantasy, and in so doing provides himself with a variety of reassuring feelings. The level of this 'nourish-ment', of good feelings obtained through affirmation and reassur-ance, has to be constantly maintained, because if it drops below a certain value, wishes will be aroused connected with restoring the necessary level of basic comfort about oneself. Such wishes are very closely linked to objects, and it is enough to think of the toddler who glances at mother from time to time, eliciting a reas-suring smile, to see the mechanism whereby an unconscious wish to perceive the presence of the mother, to gain safety, may be satisfied. The interchange involved provides a feeling of security and well-being, and if for some reason it is interrupted, distress will result. What we have here is a *dialogue*, an interaction that is of the essence in any relationship between two people. Years ago Rene Spitz showed how such a dialogue occurred between infant and mother in relation to such things as the smiling response, but there is increasing evidence that the very young infant can man-ifest extremely complicated behavioural responses to external events and circumstances, and that co-ordination of various parts of the body exists early on to a greater degree than we would expect, even in the first days and weeks of life. What is highly significant in all the studies on the infant's interaction with things and persons in its environment is the very young infant's depen-dence on experiencing appropriate sensorial and affective feed-back. This applies *par excellence* to social interactions.

Recently, workers in the field of mother–child interaction have spoken of the 'meshing' of infant and mother, of their developing 'synchrony', of their mutual cueing, and so on. It has become increasingly clear that many of the earliest interactions between mother and infant tend to start with the infant's spontaneous behaviour and are then continued on the basis of the mother's readiness to respond. Further, the child, very soon after birth, begins to show differential reactions (e.g. in the number of attempts to make eye-to-eye contact), reactions that depend upon the behavioural style and role-requirements of the mother. As the infant grows, he will create increasingly complex representations in his mind of the interactions and relationships, the dialogues between himself and his object. These dialogues with the object later become an integral part of his fantasy life and of his wishes to obtain satisfaction, to avoid unpleasant feelings and, above all, to feel safe. The negotiations of early infancy continue into adulthood as an important part of mental life.

The child's early role-relationships with his caretakers create in him a need to have objects 'mesh' with him in order for him to feel secure. The interaction with objects, in reality but also in wishful fantasy, provides an affirmation, with a resulting feeling of security. We are dependent to an enormous degree upon others for the minute nods of agreement and approval, for signs that friendliness rather than hostility is present, for safety signals. (There are some people who systematically avoid providing such signals, and their effect on their social environment can be quite devastating.)

It is important to note that the individual does not necessarily seek a replica of what he experienced in childhood. The need to obtain forms of actualization acceptable to the conscience, and to the person's developing sense of reality, leads him to disguise and distort the role relationships he wants to impose upon others, and the needs of others force him to create and accept compromises. Nevertheless, his unconscious wishes, whether they be sexual or aggressive or related to the preservation of self-esteem and safety, will profoundly affect his relationships with others. These wishes and their fantasy elaborations are continually being revised and modified, even though they retain a central and enduring core that is highly specific to the person concerned.

I want to conclude by expressing the hope that all of this may allow an essentially intrapsychic psychoanalytic psychology to contribute to a more general psychology of human relationships.

CHAPTER SIX

Psychoanalysis
and ordinary modes of thought

André Green

I n an unfinished work written in London during the Autumn of
1938—'Some elementary lessons in psychoanalysis'—Freud
wrote: 'Psycho-analysis has little prospect of becoming liked
or popular. It is not merely that much of what it has to say offends
people's feelings. Almost as much difficulty is created by the fact
that our science involves a number of hypotheses— it is hard to say
whether they should be regarded as postulates or as products of our
researches—which are bound to seem very strange to ordinary
modes of thought and which fundamentally contradict current
views. But there is no help for it' (Freud, 1940b).

Freud is alluding here to the unconscious. He explains that the
resistances to the unconscious are not only due to a moral censorship but to an intellectual one as well, as if its existence threatened
reason and logic. In this chapter I will try to show that the progression of Freud's work compelled him to recognize the existence
of modes of thought even more extraordinary than he could have
expected when he proposed his first hypothesis on the unconscious.

When we advise the analysand to avoid censoring his thoughts
and to say all that comes into his mind, the censoring pertains to
both moral and intellectual categories. The analysand's use of free

associations implies that he has accepted the surrender of all claim to the rational connection of thoughts so that another type of connection can be established by means of the analyst's freely floating attention. The relationships established by the analyst's mind between different parts of the material communicated by the analysand's free association, including some missing links that are implicitly active in silence, suggest that a certain form of logic is at work behind the scenes, which does not obey the rules of common reason. Would it not be the case that there would be either no latent content at all, or, if such a content existed, it would not be intelligible at all.

I do not intend to summarize the various stages that lead to the demonstration of this other logic. I will simply remind you that this double logic was theorized by Freud in his classical opposition between primary and secondary processes. Although it is well known that secondary processes are the processes of traditional logical thought and obey the reality principle, it has not always been made clear that primary processes, which obey the pleasure–unpleasure principle, also have an implicit logic. Forgive me if I recall its main characteristics. It ignores time. It does not take negation into account. It operates by condensation and displacement. Finally, it does not tolerate any expectation or delay. It succeeds in expressing itself by turning around the obstacles that would attempt to prevent it from making itself known; in other words, it permits our unconscious desires to experience a certain form of realization.

This point is the capital one. In spite of the censorship, the repressed wishes succeed in finding satisfaction through a special mode of thought to ensure the victory of the pleasure principle. My feeling is that we have underestimated the healthy aspect of that achievement and overemphasized its pathological aspect.

The primary and secondary processes are not opposed to one another in such a way that we could say that the primary processes are irrational and the secondary processes rational. Instead, we find that they are competitive and complementary processes that obey different types of reason. We can draw two important conclusions from this.

First, the psychical unity of man is fallacious. The validity of the equation psychical–conscious was contested by the idea of the unconscious. The subject was no longer One but Two, or if you prefer the only unity we could think of was that of a couple living in tolerable conflict or relative harmony. The second idea proceeding from the former is that the existence of a couple of conflicting terms tends towards the creation of compromise formations that endeavour to build a bridge between the two terms. Such is the case for rationalization and for interpretation.

I feel that if Freud was so strongly attached to maintaining a dualist point of view concerning instinct theory, for example, it is because he had understood intuitively that the duality at the outset was the condition necessary for the production of something else born from the relationship between the two generic terms.

What I mean to say is not that the duality is primitive, but that the duality is the limit of the greatest possible reduction as far as intelligibility is concerned. The necessary and adequate condition for establishing a relationship is that there be two terms. This simple declaration has many implications. It sets up the couple as a theoretical reference that is more fruitful than all those that use unity as a base. If we reflect even further on the implications of this fundamental duality as the condition for the production of a third part, we find the basis of symbolic activity. In fact the creation of a symbol demands that two separate elements be reunited in order to form a third element, which borrows its characteristics from the two others but which will be different from the sum of these characters nonetheless.

All this brings us to the analytic situation. In this situation the two parts that are its very essence are both brought together and kept apart. There is no physical contact between them. Contact can be established through the emotional climate of the silent session, but we know that silence can be experienced differently by each of the partners. A form of contact is also established through speech, indicating which part of himself the analysand wishes to place into contact with the analyst. Still, can we say that the discourse of the analysand *is* the analysand? Clearly we cannot, since rationalization and negation are at work. Nevertheless, if we did not believe that the analysand's speech tries to tell us something about himself, we would not have decided to prefer this particular form of relationship. Thus, we must say that the analysand's discourse *is* and *is not* the analysand and that it is produced by his symbolic activity, which attempts to bring together that which is separated. Separation becomes a new opportunity for another form of reunion.

That which is separated calls for a double separation. First of all, there is a separation between the analysand and the analyst. But this separation is reiterated by each of the partners since each has an unconscious separated from his own conscious. The analysand's discourse will result then from a double compromise. It will be the expression of a compromise between the unconscious and the conscious, as well as the expression of a compromise between the desire to be in contact with the analyst and the desire to avoid this contact with him.

In much the same way the analyst's listening must work on all of these areas at the same time, since he must also acknowledge that what he hears is a compromise between what he deciphers with the help of his conscious and is able to understand by means of his unconscious. It would be wrong to say that the analyst does not share the desire of contact with the analysand or is not similarly tempted to respond symmetrically to the movements by which the analysand attempts to break this contact. The interpretation strives to be the best possible compromise during these movements of come and go. The interpretation is expressed with paradoxical goals since it must maintain the contact with the analysand while allowing the necessary distance so that this form of contact can lead to an insight. As for its content, the interpretation is also a compromise formation: it condenses the modes of reasoning that belong to both rational logical thought and to this form of logic which obeys another type of rationality. In fact our interpretations include statements that imply if, then, so, because, however, and so on. At the same time our interpretations also tell that this expressed hostility is a sign of love, this apparent love hides a lot of hate, that this indifference translates feelings of despair, that this wish to die actually wishes to have someone else die, or to merge with him eternally, and so forth.

The situation I have just described implies that the ego can prove itself capable of recognizing the existence of the primary processes of subjective reason without withdrawing all claims to the secondary processes of objective reason. Above all, it implies that the ego can go from one to the other without denying its psychic reality and without repudiating material reality. The ego must chiefly be able to establish flexible connections which alternately are going to be done, forming temporary hypotheses and conclusions, and be undone, in order to leave room for others who give a better representation of the situation. I believe that it is useful to think that a third category of processes exists. I propose to call these instruments of liaison or connections, *tertiary processes*. For, in opposition to what Freud thought, it is not so much a question of the secondary processes dominating the primary processes, but rather that the analysand can make the most creative use of their coexistence and do so in the most elaborate activities of the mind, just as he does in everyday life. Perhaps this is asking a great deal.

As long as Freud had the feeling that he could call upon the ego to lead him towards an awareness of the unconscious through the return of the repressed, he could consider that he was in a position to solve the difficulties inherent in psychoanalytic treatment. But he came to the conclusion that a great part of the ego was itself unconscious, and this was, without doubt, a disappointing discovery for him. Up until then the unconscious gave itself away through the manifestation that proved its existence: slips of the tongue, parapraxes, fantasies, dreams, symptoms, transferences ... which once analysed should have forced the ego to conclude that the unconscious was not a fiction. When Freud discovered that the ego is not only the seat of resistance but is unconscious of its resistances and that its defence mechanisms remained opaque to himself, he relied upon signs that he could hear, but these signs remained silent for the analysand. Freud did not find the means at his disposal to logically analyse this non-repressed unconscious. He had made the ego's integrity into a preliminary condition for the possibility of undertaking an analysis. In 'Analysis terminable and interminable' (1937c) he was forced to admit the hard truth:

> The ego, if we are to be able to make such a pact with it, must be a normal one. But a normal ego of this sort is, like normality in general, an ideal fiction. The abnormal ego, which is unserviceable for our purposes, is unfortunately no fiction. Every normal person, in fact, is only normal on the average. His ego approx-

imates to that of the psychotic in some part or other and to a greater or lesser extent. [Freud, 1937c, p. 235]

We can observe that Freud refers to psychosis here and not to neurosis. This means that he is obliged to admit that the normal ego includes a certain number of distortions in its relationship to reality, which question its capacity of integration or its power of synthesis. We could think that this alteration of the ego is also responsible for the defection of the second ally: transference. Positive or even ambivalent transference was based on the idea that with the help of the analyst a better compromise could be found between the demands made by the id and the ego which must also take into consideration both the superego and the reality principle. The negative therapeutic reaction contradicts this presupposition.

No stronger impression arises from the resistances during the work of analysis than of there being a force which is defending itself by every possible means against recovery and which is absolutely resolved to hold on to illness and suffering. One portion of this force has been recognized by us, undoubtedly with justice, as the sense of guilt and need for punishment, and has been localized by us in the ego's relation to the superego. But this is only the portion of it which is, as it were, psychically bound by the superego, and thus becomes recognizable; other quotas of the same force, whether bound or free, may be at work in other, unspecified places. If we take into consideration the total picture made up of the phenomena of masochism immanent in so many people, the negative therapeutic reaction and the sense of guilt found in so many neurotics, we shall no longer be able to adhere to the belief that mental events are exclusively governed by the desire for pleasure. These phenomena are unmistakable indications of the presence of a power in mental life which we call the instinct of aggression or of destruction according to its aims, and which we trace back to the original death instinct of living matter. [Freud, 1940b, pp. 242–243]

In this quotation Freud holds the destructive instincts responsible for this state of affairs. I shall not discuss here the concept of the death instinct, but I shall note that in fact it is because the ego appears to have surrendered to this reversal of life values that the happy ending does not come about.

Two serious grounds pertaining to the ego and the instinct of aggression cause the analyst's action to fail. But if we try to understand what Freud says about these two situations according to the perspective I have chosen—that is, the existence of a different logic—perhaps it would be possible to go beyond the stage of mere declarations.

Let us go back to Freud's quotation. What seems to take place with these analysands is that the pleasure–displeasure principle governing psychic activity has transposed the order of these terms. Namely, the search for pleasure has substituted itself for the search for displeasure, and the avoidance of displeasure has become avoidance of pleasure. It is as if the subject says 'Yes' to displeasure and 'No' to pleasure. In many cases the analyst thinks that the 'No' to pleasure is merely on the surface and that there are hidden satisfactions for this maintenance of suffering. But there are other cases where psychic pain is such that it appears difficult to believe that the subject receives any satisfaction from it at all. We can ask the following question: what are the unconscious thoughts of these patients made out of? In short, what does their psychic reality look like, if we do not give up considering their manifest discourse as a cover-up discourse?

The psychic reality of these patients is not less complicated than the psychic reality in those cases where the pleasure principle dominates. Disguises use condensation and displacement here as well. Doubtless, the difference lies in the fact that the logic presiding over these operations is a logic of despair. Freud said that psychic reality is the only true reality. It is also exact in the case we are dealing with. Melanie Klein showed us the importance of reparation processes in depression, and I believe that the cases Freud refers to are impregnated with depressive features. But there is even more. Winnicott showed that for certain patients the only reality is the reality of that which is not there, that which makes one suffer by its very absence. Absence leads not to hope but to despair. Here we can infer that the unconscious thought processes of the patients displaying the features described by Freud refer back to a psychic reality—the only true one for them—formed by objects that only exist through the disappointment or displeasure they create. The emptiness of the ego is more consistent than its achievements. All the self-hatred that dwells in these analysands reflects a compromise between the desire to carry out an unquenchable revenge and, co-existing with this, the desire to protect the object from these hostile wishes directed towards him. This revenge is born from a wound that hit these patients in their very being, which disabled their narcissism. Their failure to realize this stems in great part from the fact that their thoughts do not know how to distinguish between the harm they want to impose upon themselves—and of which they are often unconscious—and the harm they want to inflict upon their object. They do not forgive the object for its inability to value them, for its absence at the time when they most needed it and the fact that this object has other sources of pleasure than themselves. This logic of despair has one constant goal: to produce evidence that the object is really bad, uncomprehending and rejecting because of the extent to which these patients entreat rejection by others. When they attain their goal, they have proof not only that they are not able to instill love, but that the love of others is merely a superficial front behind which they hide their hatred. In short, love is always uncertain, hatred is always sure. Likewise, they make arrangements to perpetuate this form of sado-masochistic relationship which they have chosen for as long as possible, as long as they can find a partner who accepts the role they have assigned to him.

If analysis is based on the possibility of establishing new bonds in psychic activity with that which is separated by repression, we can declare that this ability to establish bonds is not destroyed here as in psychosis, but that these bonds always establish themselves in a way that confirms that the result of this bond is never positive. While the analytic work provides these patients with additional meaning, the result of an increase in meaning is always a reduction in being. Paradoxically, these analysands only have the feeling of a 'more-being' in the lessening of their well-being, which is always—in the end—an implicit accusation against those who brought them into the world, since they never asked to be born.

The answer to this situation tends to show the patient that his need to create despair in the analyst is necessary for him to be able to verify that the analyst can survive this hatred and continue to analyse what goes on in the patient's psychic world. This is the best proof of love that the analyst can give. That is to help him, the patient, in recognizing that this self-hatred is a sacrifice, and that this hatred directed towards the object is perhaps, as Winnicott believes, a ruthless love. For the extreme ambivalence of these patients goes hand in hand with their extraordinary intolerance of ambivalence, just as their unconscious guilt feelings reflect a refusal to feel guilty and an extreme idealization of the image they have of themselves, symmetrical to the image of the ideal object they look for in vain on this earth.

The logic explained earlier, that of primary processes, as Freud defined it, was, in a way, a logic based on the idea of a couple of opposites formed by desire, on the one hand, and prohibition on the other. If the prohibition were suspended, we could presume that nothing would prevent a happy union with the object. In short, it was not conceivable that the object could not love the subject, or hate it. In this perspective, the logic of primary processes is a logic of hope—a case opposite to what I have called the logic of despair. Here the object is in the forefront, not the wish, not the prohibition. If the happy union is experienced as being impossible, it is because the subject cannot feel loved by the object or cannot love the object. It is a different logic in regard to the conflict between the wish and the prohibition because the conflict between the ego and the object about love and hate prevails. Of course when I speak of the object, I refer to the internal object which is so profoundly internal that it is a narcissistic object shaped on the subject's wounded narcissism.

The negative therapeutic reaction teaches us that the fixations on hatred are much more tenacious than the fixations on love. The first is the conviction of having been deprived of a love to which one has as much right as to the air one breathes. Under these conditions it is difficult to give up an object without wanting to obtain this love up until the end. The second reason is that hatred is accompanied by guilt. To give up the object is to give up hating, but to discover a possibility of love with another object not only means letting the primitive object of the fixation follow its own destiny, it also means making it literally disappear from the self and, in a way, abandoning it. There is guilt in hating the object, but there is just as much guilt, if not more, when the subject no longer hates the object in order to love another object. The solution then consists in perpetuating the internal bond with it, for it is better to have a bad internal object than to risk losing it forever. The correspondence between the relationship of the ego with the object and the ego with the superego is striking.

Let us return now to Freud's assertion concerning the psychotic distortions of the ego. Up until this point we only had to deal with hope and despair in a mirror-like system, with two terms, opposite to and symmetrical to the other. We can understand that, contrary to what we have said before, no third term is created, no symbolization occurs effectively. Tertiary processes are missing.

When Freud spoke of the repression of reality in psychosis and of its transformation, he wrote the following in his paper, 'The loss of reality in neurosis and psychosis' (1924e):

> In a psychosis, the transforming of reality is carried out upon the physical precipitates of former relations to it—that is, upon the memory-traces, ideas and judgements which have been previously derived from reality and by which reality was represented in the mind. [p. 185]

In very severe forms of psychosis, such as the one he studies in the Schreber case, we can see the enormous development of this transformation, which creates a feeling of strangeness for us. But usually we have to cope with patients less severely disturbed than Schreber, the so-called borderline cases.

In 'Neurosis and psychosis', Freud (1924b) writes:

> It will be possible for the ego to avoid a rupture in any direction by deforming itself, by submitting to encroachments on its own unity and even perhaps by effecting a cleavage or division of itself. In this way the inconsistencies, eccentricities and follies of men would appear in a similar light to their sexual perversions, through the acceptance of which they spare themselves repressions. [pp. 152–153]

This quotation justifies the importance that splitting takes on in the last part of Freud's work. If during the course of an analysis it is necessary to depend on the cooperation of the ego, the analyst must know this ego is two-sided: split. In one of his last papers, 'The splitting of ego in the process of defence', Freud (1940e) describes the situation thus: between the demands made by an instinct and the prohibition by reality 'the child takes neither course, or rather he takes both simultaneously, which come to the same thing' (p. 275). In other words, according to Freud, the child's ego does not decide, that is to say, it does not judge: it admits to two contradictory judgements *at the same time*. We can see how this operation is different from repression. In the latter a choice is made which apparently decides that reality must get the upper hand on the instinctive demands. Freud (1940e) insists on this simultaneous co-existence, when splitting occurs:

> On the one hand, with the help of certain mechanisms he [the child] rejects reality and refuses to accept any prohibition; on the other hand, in the same breath he recognizes the danger of reality, takes over the fear of that danger as a pathological symptom and tries subsequently to divest himself of the fear. . . . The two contrary reactions to the conflict persist as the centre-point of a splitting of the ego. [pp. 275–276]

In repression the relationship between the ego as representative of reality and the instinctive demands as representative of plea-sure are vertical. Repression dominates the instinctive impulse by pushing it down towards the depth, while the instinctual impulse pushes in the opposite direction towards the top. The unconscious is underground in relationship to the conscious. In splitting the relations are horizontal; the reason of the ego and the reason of the instinctive demands coexist in the same psychic space. A coexistence such as this constitutes a stagnation factor when it takes place during the analytic cure. It is as though the analysand only hears the analyst's interpretations with one ear. The other ear continues to let itself be rocked and cradled by the instinctual impulse mermaid song, completely ignoring the message received by the other ear. The two logics are in contradiction with one another. There is a refusal to choose any of the items. Prior to the discovery of the ego's unconsciousness, unconscious repression had to disguise itself in order to express itself.

Behind the conscious 'No' we can reveal the unconscious 'Yes'. In the present case the ego's strategy changes. It says 'Yes' and 'No' at the same time. What is important is not so much the double game the ego plays by splitting, it is that the splitting is unconscious. We find a paradox here. In repression the unconscious is separate from the conscious, but the return of the repressed enables us to establish a bridge between the two. The repressed is hidden, but sometimes it shows itself through its disguises. While the two types of thoughts appear to the naked eye to coexist in splitting, the ego appears to totally misjudge its dual way of functioning. There is no communication between the split parts, no tertiary process. We find an extension of this situation in the analysand's associations. For the analyst these associations are significant enough so that the interpretation springing from them is conclusive. But the patient cannot establish the bonds that would allow him to arrive at the proper conclusion. It is as though the sequence of thoughts is made of independent pieces. In this case it would appear that the analyst's tertiary processes must be placed at the patient's disposal. After the logics of hope and despair we have now described the logic of indecision.

All of these new concepts were born from the disappointments of Freud's analytic practice, which lessened his therapeutic ambitions. Freud believed that he had inflicted a terrible narcissistic wound upon mankind by showing that the rational ego is not the master in man. But time has shown that the ego's strange logic of the patient can also inflict a narcissistic wound on the analyst by opposing him with its extraordinary modes of thought.

In view of so many accumulated difficulties, what is the solution? For a long time the analyst's work consisted of discovering the unconscious wish in order to integrate this thought with that of the ego and teach it to recognize the other part of its mind, which refuses to submit to common reason and reality. But now we are dealing with something else. It is a matter of reasoning, according to the processes of a deeply hidden madness of the ego. Consequently, the analyst must train himself to use kinds of thought further and further removed from rational logic. The logic of the pleasure principle as Freud found it in the primary processes appears much too simple in relation to the logic found in the difficult borderline cases. These cases reveal the existence of what I have called the analysand's *private madness*. This private madness is only revealed in the intimate transferential relationship. Outside this relationship the patient is more or less like many others, neither more nor less insane than anyone else. He is able to carry out the tasks he is set. He is far from lacking a sense of responsibility. But in the light of the transference he reveals an entirely different kind of psychic functioning in his inner world.

Transference has the power of revealing the extreme sensitivity of these patients to both loss and intrusion. They are always seeking to establish a psychic distance that will permit them to feel safe from the double threat of invasion by the other and its definitive loss. Thus a permanent contradiction evolves, causing them to desire what they are scared of losing and to reject what is already in their possession, but whose invasion they fear.

In fact, these attitudes hide something else. If there is a struggle against the invading intrusion, it is because there is a secret desire to be completely invaded by the object, not only to be united with it but also to be reduced to total passivity like a baby in his mother's womb. This wish can be counterbalanced by the desire to invade the mother and entirely occupy her body and thoughts. In the same way, if the relinquishment or the loss of the object is feared so much, it is also because there is a desire to kill the object in order to find shelter in a mythic self-sufficiency which will set the subject free from all the variations that the object imposes upon him and which deprive the subject of any constancy in his relationship with the object.

I believe we have not adequately taken into consideration the way in which the greatest contributions to modern psychoanalysis have added to our knowledge. They have taught us less in terms of the psychic contents, since we always deal with the same themes but with varying outward appearances. They have contributed to our knowledge in terms of kinds of forms of thought. That which we call defence mechanisms are also ways of thinking.

When, for example, Winnicott describes transitional phenomena and transitional objects, he creates a class of objects and a type of space where the judgement of existence has no place. Such objects are and are not the breast or the mother. Despite what Freud thought, the suspension of judgement is not always prejudicial to the ego. All depends on the constructive or destructive value of these new types of objects.

The analysis of the Wolf Man (1918b) showed Freud the destructive effects of splitting. Freud's interpretations on the unconscious homosexuality of the patient were not able to resolve the case's riddle. Ruth Mack Brunswick was unquestionably much closer to the truth when she wrote that the Wolf Man's problem was that he did not want to be either a man or a woman.

It is not only by chance that Freud discovered splitting in connection with fetishism, nor that we return to sexuality or, more exactly, bisexuality in referring to the Wolf Man. Freud constantly underlined the fact that the vulnerability of the ego is linked to its relationship with the sexual function. But we have to remember that the sexual function is tightly connected with object relationships. Because they are relationships, they can always be considered in terms of oneness, duality, trinity, conjunctions, disjunctions, fusion, separations etc. . . . which involve a reference to an archaic logic, the logic of passion.

At the very end of his work, that is to say in 'Constructions in analysis' (1937d) and *Moses and Monotheism* (1939a), Freud strives to make an important distinction between historical truth and material truth. He does not give a formal definition of these two notions, but he specifies that historical truth is that which was considered as being true by an individual at a given time of his history during childhood. This is precisely what the analyst must reconstruct through his work. On the other hand, material truth refers to objective truth. Historical truth is a subjective interpretation, which forms a system of beliefs and modes of thinking that in turn fastens itself on the individual and on which any further evolution will have no effect, coexisting with the evolution of rational processes of development. As for material truth, it is unknown as such. It is only accessible through the discovery of the distortion of historical truth.

That psychic truth can be reached only by the analysis of distortion could be the motto for all of Freudian theory. We are bound to distortion because we are born in a state of prematurity; we depend on the love and the protection of those who watch over us until we can free ourselves from them. The agency that should give us access to material truth, the ego, undergoes the influence of forces—passions of love and hate—which go beyond its weak power and compel it to make compromises that always imply an inevitable distortion. It is not mere chance if the ego's power is at its best when trying to understand and master inanimate objects of reality.

This distortion is so deeply rooted and so solidly and firmly established that today many analysts contend that we can never attain this material truth by reducing the distortion of the historical truth. We can only oppose another construction, which is a hypothetical approximation (Bion) to the construction of historical truth. In short, we cannot do any better than to propose an additional hypothetical construction to the patient's construction. It would not be the true but rather the probable, compatible with the unknown truth. In this way we present the analysand with another version of the personal myth to which he adheres. It now forms the truth shared by him and us. It is a truth he can recognize as his own and which we convey to him, just as we could recognize through transference this truth he carried in himself without knowing it.

Now, this truth was not only a mass a secret contents—it was also a secret language, a secret system of thought. In order to arrive at the desired result, it is indispensable for the patient to be able to succeed in accounting for not only what we had to hide, but also how it could have been hidden. If it was indispensable to get rid of it, it was no less indispensable to keep it. Content and form are inseparable. Likewise, is psychoanalysis today an analysis of the container at least as much as an analysis of the contents? This requires that psychoanalysts go much further in the handling of the stranger mode of thought to which Freud initiated us. This does not mean that we will become less rational. On the contrary, we will expand the field of reason by admitting that many types of rationality coexist in the human mind which mutually penetrate one another. We will not become more mystical, but rather more comprehensive, while waiting to become more wise, if possible.

The more our psychoanalytic work reaches deep layers of the mind, the more it is likely that our hypotheses will appear far distant from ordinary thought, and even from forms of thought that Freud has already brought to light, and which enlightened the relationships between the unconscious and the conscious. It will not make communications between analysts and non-analysts any easier. The patient is not the only one to rationalize and deny. Like Freud, we can say 'There is no help for it'. That which stirs up reservations and even resistances among psychoanalysts themselves today will become evident within a few decades.

What Freud took for material truth will perhaps be historical truth in the near future in the light of psychoanalytic knowledge. And we will be able to say that Freud's work is historically true, but not materially true. His answers were compromises between a core of truth—which permitted it to last—and an intense psychic construction which remained limited by both the confines of his experience and his faithfulness to a form of rationality too rigorous to allow him to understand the kinds or forms of reasoning that lead astray. I have no doubt that he was prepared to accept this idea, and, being his heirs, we must train ourselves to deal with these baffling modes of reason in order to extort a piece of territory from the still unknown continent of the human mind.

CHAPTER SEVEN

Psychoanalysis as a natural science

John Bowlby

F from 1895, when Freud made his first attempt to sketch a theoretical framework for psychoanalysis, until 1938, the year before he died, Freud was determined that his new discipline should conform to the requirements of a natural science. Thus, in the opening sentence of his *Project* (Freud, 1887–1902), he writes: 'The intention is to furnish a psychology that shall be a natural science ...'; whilst in the *Outline* (Freud, 1940a) we find a passage in which he asserts that, once the concept of psychical processes being unconscious is granted, 'psychology is enabled to take its place as a natural science like any other'.

Admittedly, during the intervening years Freud's ideas about the scope of his science had changed considerably from his early ambition 'to represent psychical processes as quantitatively determinate states of specifiable material particles' (1887–1902) to his later definition of psychoanalysis as 'the science of unconscious mental processes' (1925d, p. 70). But from first to last there can be no doubt what sort of discipline Freud intended psychoanalysis to be.

Nevertheless, despite Freud's unwavering intention, the scientific status of psychoanalysis remains equivocal. On the one hand, philosophers of science have dubbed it a pseudoscience on the grounds that, however large a measure of truth they may contain, psychoanalytic theories are cast in so elastic a form that they are unfalsifiable—e.g. Popper (1963). On the other, many psychoanalysts, for example, Home (1966), Ricoeur (1970), and others in Europe, disillusioned by the inadequacies of Freud's metapsychology and preoccupied with the personal perspective that is unquestionably required in clinical work, have abandoned Freud's aims and claims and have declared that psychoanalysis is miscast as a science and should be conceived instead, as one of the humanities. Both Schafer (1976) and George Klein (1976), espousing this view, have advanced proposals alternative to Freud's; but each of their reformulations, different though they be, seems a version of Hamlet without the Prince. Gone are all concepts of causality and theories of biologically rooted impulse, and, in Schafer's version, gone also are concepts of repression and unconscious mental activity.[1]

Melanie Klein (1948) has made very different proposals, ones that certainly do not suffer from these defects; but it would be difficult to claim that the form they take or the research they have engendered meet scientific requirements.

Yet by no means do all analysts despair of developing their discipline as a natural science. Alive to the deficiencies of Freud's metapsychology, especially his concepts of psychic energy and drive, a few are attempting to replace it with a new conceptual framework consistent with current scientific thinking. Central to these new proposals are ideas drawn from systems theory and the study of human information processing. Those active in this enterprise include Rubinstein (1967), Peterfreund (1971, 1980), Rosenblatt and Thickstun (1977), Gedo (1979) and myself (Bowlby, 1969, 1980). Meanwhile there are also a number of analysts who have been seeking to extend the discipline's database by studying children's social and emotional development using direct observation. Some of these studies have been atheoretical, e.g. Offer (1969). The authors of others have attempted to put new empirical wine into the old theoretical bottles, e.g. Spitz (1946, 1957), Mahler (Mahler, Pine & Bergman, 1975); whilst others again, e.g. Sander (1964) and myself (Bowlby, 1958, 1969, 1973),[2] have searched for new theoretical models. My own search has led not only to control theory and information processing, but also to the biologically rooted disciplines of ethology and comparative psychology. Thus there is no lack of new initiatives, and it will take time to see which of them, or perhaps which combinations of them, prove most productive of scientific advance.

Here my aim is to describe one such initiative—my own—and why I think it promising; and to indicate also some of the difficult problems that lie ahead. Let me start by giving a brief account of the course of my work and the problems I have been trying to solve.

A principal reason for my undertaking training as an analyst was an interest in personality development born whilst I was reading natural sciences and psychology at Cambridge during the 1920s. This led me to work for six months in what would now be called a school for maladjusted children before completing my medical training. The experience, though short, was invaluable, since it exposed me to children and adolescents whose difficulties I know now to be typical of much personality disorder and also to hypotheses regarding the role of family experience in their origin. Subsequently, my work in a child guidance clinic whilst specializing in psychiatry strengthened my confidence that these hypotheses were of great promise. By the time I had qualified as an analyst in 1937, however, it was already clear that my interest in the part played by family experience in determining how a child or adolescent develops was not shared by many of my colleagues. Some, indeed, despite being actively engaged in formulating object-relations theory, held a view opposite to mine—namely, that psychoanalysis is not concerned with the real experiences a person has had, or is having, in the external world, but only with his private internal world of thought, fantasy and feeling. To a biologist this contrast of internal with external, of organism with environment, made no sense. If we were to understand our patients' present difficulties, I felt sure that it was just as necessary for our discipline to include the study of the way children are really treated by their parents and its effects on them as it is to study the internal representations of parents that the children or adults we treat now have—indeed that the principal focus of psychoanalytic science should be to understand how the one interacts with the other, how a person's internal world of urges, desires, feelings, representations, expectations, hypotheses and fantasies interacts with his external world, comprising the idiosyncratic sequence of events to which he has been and is being exposed, often by happenings wholly outside his control. Believing that progress would be possible only if we have far more systematic knowledge about the effects on a child of the experience he has within his family, I concentrated my attention on that area.

There were several reasons why I decided to start my research by studying the effects on young children of their being removed from home to a strange situation with strange people, such as a residential nursery or hospital, rather than attempting the broader field of parent–child interaction in general. Reasons most relevant to my present theme are, first, that in my child guidance work I had been struck by the relatively high incidence of prolonged disruptions of a child's relationship with his mother-figure in the histories of severely disturbed children (Bowlby, 1940, 1944) and, second, that by 1948 there were already a number of other reports of similar findings, e.g. Bender and Yarnell (1941) and Goldfarb (1943). A third reason was that there could rarely be debate whether a particular child had or had not been exposed to such disruption. In this respect the variable under study contrasts strongly with variations in the ways in which parents treat, or have treated, their children, about which valid information is often very difficult to obtain.

Traditionally, clinical research starts with patients who seem to have certain problems in common and seeks to trace the causes of their problems retrospectively; but the limitations of this strategy are severe in regard to both sampling and validity of data. An alternative strategy, which is free of these defects and which I adopted, is to start with a putative causal agent and to trace its effects prospectively, as is habitually done in medical research, for example when the effects of a particular virus or bacterium are studied. My first idea was to follow up a group of children who, during their early years, had undergone a prolonged separation from the mother-figure and who had subsequently returned home. In the course of this work, however, it became evident that a more productive strategy would be to select children who were about to undergo such an experience and to observe them before, during and after it. One great advantage of this approach is that the reliability of the data obtained can be checked in the usual way by employing two independent observers and comparing the fruits of their observations.

The results of our prospective studies, pioneered by James Robertson (1952, 1953) and amplified by Christoph Heinicke (1956; Heinicke & Westheimer, 1966), are now well known. In particular, it was Robertson's early observations that led us to generalize the sequence of responses commonly seen when a young child is cared for by strange people in strange surroundings as, first, protest and an attempt to recover mother, secondly, despair of doing so and depression and, finally, emotional detachment from her. In addition, we drew attention to the child's acute fear after his return home lest he be sent away again (Robertson & Bowlby, 1952).

Although it was clear that many variables play a part in determining how a child responds to an event of the kind described, we felt confident that the most weighty is the loss of his mother-figure. Although these findings had a number of practical applications, what concerns us here are the theoretical problems they raise. Why should a young child be so distressed by the loss of his mother? Why after return home should he become so apprehensive lest he lose her again? What psychological processes account for his distress and for the phenomenon of detachment? Might answers to these questions, I asked myself, throw light on the kinds of behaviour conceptualized clinically as dependency, separation anxiety, depression and defence, to the explanation of which so much psychoanalytic theory is directed? My confidence that they might was strengthened by the experiences I was having treating patients analytically. Similarities in the ways in which adult patients respond to separation and loss and the ways young children respond to a separation of the kind we were studying were too obvious to ignore. For example, I was familiar with individuals, often described as dependent or hysterical, who tend always to make intense demands on others and to be anxious and angry when they are not met, and also with individuals, who might nowadays be described as narcissistic or exhibiting a false self, whose capacity to make close affectional relationships seems to be blocked. In all likelihood, I thought, these similarities were no accident but reflected a true identity of response overriding all differences of age.

It was with this varied collection of observations, clinical experiences and inferences in mind that I concluded that the first task for theory was to understand the nature of the child's tie to his mother.

At that time, in the early 1950s, there was no agreement on how to account for this tie. The dominant theory, advanced by Freud and widely held, was that a child becomes interested in his mother because she feeds him. Two kinds of drive are postulated—primary and secondary. Food is thought of as primary; the personal relationship, referred to as dependency, as secondary. This theory did not seem to me to fit the facts. For example, were it true, an infant of a year or two should take readily to whomever feeds him, and this clearly was not the case. An alternative theory, advanced by Melanie Klein (1948) and held by analysts of the object relations school, is also closely linked to food, though it postulates the primary drive as one directed towards possessing a breast. In due course, it is thought, the infant learns that attached to the breast is a mother. This again is a secondary drive theory of personal relations, and again the relationship is referred to as dependency. Variations in development were then attributed to events occurring during the earliest months and limited to the feeding relationship, with much emphasis on breasts and orality. Once again, I thought, the theory failed to fit the facts: variations in development seemed to me to be influenced far more by the mother's general attitude towards her child and how she treats him than by what happens simply during his feeding.

But, if the prevailing theories were inadequate, what were the alternatives?

During the summer of 1951, a friend mentioned to me the work of Konrad Lorenz (1935) on the following response of ducklings and goslings. It showed that in some animal species a strong bond to an individual mother-figure could develop without the intermediary of food, that it could develop rapidly during a sensitive phase early in life and that it tended to endure. This provided an alternative model for consideration and one that had a number of features that seemed possibly to fit the human case. Thereafter, the more I learned of ethological principles and of the behaviour of mother–infant pairs of other species, especially non-human primates, and the more I reflected on our observations of the enormous difference it makes to how a child behaves according to whether his mother–figure is present or absent, the more disposed I became to apply ethological principles to our problem. As a result I advanced the view that the human infant comes into the world genetically biased to develop a set of behavioural patterns that, given an appropriate environment, will result in his keeping more or less close proximity to the person who cares for him; and, further, that this tendency to maintain proximity serves the functions of protecting the mobile infant and growing child from a number of dangers, amongst which in man's environment of evolutionary adeptedness the danger of predation is likely to have been paramount. The various forms of behaviour that serve to maintain a child in proximity to his mother could then conveniently be grouped together under the term attachment behaviour.

From this standpoint it became possible to see separation anxiety in a new light. It has long been recognized by clinicians that a particularly common form of anxiety is anxiety about losing, or becoming separated from, someone loved. Why 'mere separation' should cause anxiety, however, has been a mystery. Freud wrestled with the problem and advanced a number of hypotheses (Freud, 1926d; Strachey, 1959). Every other leading analyst has done the same. With no agreed means of evaluating them, many divergent schools of thought have proliferated, and much fruitless debate has been engendered.

The problem lies, I believe, in an unexamined assumption, made not only by psychoanalysts but by more traditional psychiatrists as well, that fear is aroused in a mentally healthy person only in situations that everyone would perceive as intrinsically painful or dangerous, or that are perceived so by a person only because of his having become conditioned to them. Since fear of separation and loss does not fit this formula, analysts have concluded that what is feared is really some other situation; whilst traditionally minded psychiatrists have supposed that the patient's anxiety must derive from some biochemical or endocrine derangement.

The difficulties disappear, however, when a comparative approach is adopted. For it then becomes evident that man, like other animals, responds with fear to certain situations, not because they carry a *high* risk of pain or danger, but because they signal an *increase* of risk. Thus, just as animals of many species, including man, are disposed to respond with fear to sudden movement or a marked change in the level of sound or light because to do so has survival value, so are many species, including man, disposed to respond to separation from a potentially care-giving figure, and for the same reasons. Once seen in this perspective, the problem is solved.

A concept of great clinical value that has emerged from ethologically oriented studies of the mother–child relationships is that of a mother, or mother substitute, providing a child with a secure base from which he can explore. By the last months of the first year of life an infant brought up in an ordinary affectionate home is very clear whom he prefers to care for him, a preference especially evident should he be tired, frightened or sick. Whoever that may be, and it is usually his mother, is then able by her very presence, or ready accessibility, to create the conditions that enable her child to explore his world in a confident way. At the time of his second birthday, for example, a healthy child whose mother is resting on a garden seat will make a series of excursions away from her, each time returning to her before making the next excursion. On some occasions when he returns he simply smiles and makes his number; on others he leans against her knee; on yet others he wants to climb on her lap. But never does he stay for long unless he is frightened or tired or thinks she is about to leave. Anderson (1972), who made a study of this sort in a London park, observed that during the second and third years it is very rare for a child to go further than two hundred feet before returning. Should he lose sight of his mother, however, exploration is forgotten. His top priority then is to regain her, in an older child by searching and in a younger one by howling.

Now it is evident that there is no way of explaining this type of behaviour in terms of a build-up of psychic energy, which is then discharged. An alternative model available to us but not to Freud is to think of the proximity-keeping of a child as being mediated by a set of behavioural systems organized cybernetically. Activation of any such system occurs on the receipt of certain signals, of internal and/or external origin, and its cessation on the receipt of other signals, also of internal and/or external origin. In the case of attachment behaviour we can postulate that among conditions that activate it are pain, fatigue and anything frightening, whilst the conditions necessary to terminate it depend on the intensity of its arousal. At low intensity they may be simply sight or sound of the mother-figure, especially effective being a signal from her acknowledging his presence. At higher intensity termination may require his touching or clinging to her. At highest intensity, when he is distressed and anxious, nothing but a prolonged cuddle will do. We can then postulate that the behaviour that takes him away from his mother into the wide world, which is conveniently termed exploratory behaviour, is incompatible with attachment behaviour and has a lower priority. It is thus only when attachment behaviour is relatively inactive that exploration occurs.

As an individual grows older, it should be noted, his life continues to be organized in the same kind of way, though his excursions become steadily longer in terms both of time and space. On first entering school they will last for hours or days. During adolescence they may last for weeks or months, and new attachment figures are likely to be sought. Throughout adult life the availability of a responsive attachment figure remains the source of a person's feeling secure. All of us, from the cradle to the grave, it seems, are happiest when life is organized as a series of excursions, long or short, from the secure base provided by our attachment figure(s).

In terms of the theoretical model proposed, the pronounced changes in the organization of attachment behaviour that occur during individual development are regarded as being due, in part, to the threshold for its activation being raised (perhaps through changes in endocrine levels) and, in part, to the control systems becoming increasingly sophisticated, in particular by their coming to incorporate representational models of the environment and important people in it and also of the self as object and agent (Bowlby, 1973, Chapter 14).

The development during ontogeny of a set of systems of the kind described in humans, as well as in individuals of many other species, is attributed to the action of natural selection, namely to individuals well endowed with the potential to develop such systems, having survived and bred more successfully than those less well endowed—in other words, to Darwinian evolution. Since a disposition to show attachment behaviour in certain circumstances is regarded as an intrinsic part of human nature, reference to it as 'dependency' is not only misleading but seriously inappropriate because of the word's pejorative overtones.

It will be noticed that once attachment behaviour, and other forms of biologically determined behaviour, are conceived of in terms of control theory, the problem of the purposiveness of behaviour is solved without abandoning the concept of causation. Furthermore, the distinction between causation and function, sadly neglected in traditional psychoanalytic theory, becomes explicit. Activation and termination are caused when a system constructed in a particular way receives information of particular sorts. Of the various consequences to which activation leads, the one postulated as its biological function is the one that, evidence suggests, has led to the system having evolved during phylogeny (Bowlby, 1969, Chapter 8). In the case of attachment behaviour the function postulated is that of diminishing risk of the individual coming to harm.

At this level of analysis the question of whether an individual is aware of what he is doing, let alone why he is doing it, has no relevance, in fact no more relevance than has the question of whether an individual is aware that he is breathing and, if so, realizes why he should be doing so. Biological systems serving vital functions, whether at a behavioural or a physiological level, must be capable of operating automatically. Nevertheless, in the case of a human child, awareness of what he is doing, and more particularly awareness of the conditions that will terminate his behaviour, soon emerges, certainly by the end of his first year, and is a factor of great importance. For, once it is clear that a child is aware of the conditions that will terminate his behaviour, we begin speaking of intention, of his desire to achieve a certain goal, of his being satisfied when he does so and frustrated when he fails, of satisfaction bringing pleasure and frustration the reverse.

At this point we need to emphasize the sharp distinction between conditions necessary to terminate a certain form of behaviour, commonly referred to as its goal, and the biological function the behaviour serves. In the case of attachment behaviour in childhood, whereas we commonly expect both mother and child to be aware of the conditions necessary to terminate it, for example a certain degree of proximity, we do not expect awareness of function. The same holds in the case of eating and sexual behaviour. Most of us are aware that eating food will assuage our hunger, and we find pleasure in eating; but only the sophisticated are concerned with its nutritional function. Similarly, sexual desire can be assuaged without awareness of reproductive function. In both cases all but the sophisticated are concerned only with an urge to behave in a certain way and with the pleasure anticipated and received on reaching the terminating conditions (or goal), not with the biological function that the behaviour may serve. Often, in fact, when we feel impelled to act in a certain way that is readily explicable in terms of biological function, we concoct 'reasons' for doing so that bear little or no relation to the causes of our behaviour. For example, a child or adult who, in order to reduce risk, is biologically disposed to respond to strange sounds in the dark by seeking his attachment figure gives as his reason that he is afraid of ghosts. This is analogous to the 'reasons' for his behaviour concocted by someone who is, without knowing it, acting on a posthypnotic suggestion.

The distinction I have drawn between the function served by a certain form of behaviour and our knowledge of, and our striving to reach, the conditions that will terminate that behaviour is one of the criteria that distinguishes the biological realm from the psychological. Another is the distinction between, on the one hand, the behavioural system, postulated as a biological given together with some (though not all) of the conditions that activate and terminate it and, on the other, our awareness of the urge to reach a certain goal and our effort to find the means to do so.

Earlier I remarked that, in order to understand individual development, it is as necessary to consider the environment in which each individual develops as the genetic potentials with which he is endowed. The theoretical framework best suited to this purpose is that of developmental pathways proposed by the biologist, C. H. Waddington (1957).

Within this framework human personality is conceived of as a structure that develops unceasingly along one or another of an array of possible and discrete pathways. All pathways are thought to start close together so that, at conception, an individual has access to a large range of pathways, along any one of which he might travel. The one chosen, it is held, turns at each and every stage on an interaction between the organism as it has developed up to that moment and the environment in which it finds itself. Thus, at conception development turns on interaction between the newly formed genome and the intrauterine environment; at birth it turns on interaction between the biological constitution of the neonate, including his germinal mental structure, and the family, or non-family, into which he is born; and at each age successively it turns on the personality structures then present and the family and, later, the wider social environment then current.

At conception the total array of pathways potentially open to an individual is determined by the make-up of the genome. As development proceeds and structures progressively differentiate, the number of pathways that remain open diminishes.

A principal variable in the development of each individual personality I believe to be the pathway along which his attachment behaviour comes to be organized and, further, that that pathway is determined in high degree by the way his parent-figures treat him, not only during his infancy, but throughout his childhood and adolescence as well. In the second and third volumes of *Attachment and Loss* evidence in support of this position is reviewed and must on this occasion be taken as read (Bowlby, 1973, Chapters 33ff; 1980, Chapters 10–13, 18–21).

A principal means by which such experiences influence personality development is held to be through their effects on how a person construes the world about him and on how he expects persons to whom he might become attached to behave, both of which are derivatives of the representational models of his parents that he has built up during his childhood. Evidence suggests that these models tend to persist relatively unmodified at an unconscious level and to be far more accurate reflections of how his parents have really treated him than traditional opinion has supposed.

Within this framework aberrations of behaviour and neurotic symptoms are conceived as being due to the interactions that have occurred and that may still be occurring between an individual's personality as it has so far developed and the situation in which that individual now finds himself.

Let us pause here for a moment. In thus far sketching the conceptual framework I favour, I have doubtless said enough for you to see a number of points at which it differs from the traditional one. For example, the theory of motivation advanced differs radically from Freud's theory of psychic energy and drive, and the theory of developmental pathways differs in similar degree from his theories of libidinal phases, fixation and regression. Furthermore, the concept of attachment behaviour sees it as distinct from and of a status equal to that of eating and sexual behaviour, and as a characteristic present throughout life. Where lie the origins of these differences?

During the formative period of Freud's thought he was deeply interested in biology and concerned to formulate psychological theory in terms consistent with current biological thinking. This led him to explore the ideas of Darwin and other evolutionists of the period. At that time—the turn of the century—Darwin's theory of variation and natural selection as the agents of evolution was far from being the dominant theory it is today. On the contrary, Lamarck's theories regarding the inheritance of acquired characteristics and the influence that an animal's 'inner feeling of need' was thought to have on its structure were popular. So also was Haeckel's biogenetic law, which, claiming that ontogeny recapitulates phylogeny, overlooks the fact that selection pressures operate at all phases of the life cycle and that new species often spring from the immature forms of earlier ones (neoteny). Freud, we know, was deeply influenced by both Lamarck and Haeckel, and he commends their ideas repeatedly to his students.[3] The outcome was that much of his metapsychology and all his developmental psychology came to be founded on principles long since abandoned by biologists.

If, therefore, psychoanalysis is to become the natural science based on sound biological principles that Freud intended, there are compelling reasons for drastic changes in some at least of its basic assumptions. The framework I am advancing, based on Neo-

Darwinian principles and current work in developmental psychology and human information processing, is one such attempt.

Although psychoanalysis is avowedly a developmental discipline, it is nowhere weaker, I believe, than in its concepts of development. Many of the most influential of them, for example that of libidinal phases, stem straight from Haeckel. Thus, in his *Introductory Lectures* (1916–17), Freud emphasizes that the development of both ego and libido are to be understood as 'abbreviated recapitulations of the development which all mankind passed through from its primeval days' (p. 354), whilst the development of the libido is also seen in terms of phylogeny and the various forms taken by the genital apparatus in animals. In a case study published at about the same time, he attributes a person's ideas of 'observing parental intercourse, of being seduced in childhood and of being threatened with castration . . . [to] an inherited endowment, a phylogenetic heritage'; and he claims also that the Oedipus complex is among the 'phylogenetically inherited schemata' (1918b, pp. 97 and 119). All these ideas are repeated in his final works (e.g. Freud 1939a, p. 99).

Now it may be that few analysts today would subscribe to Freud's original formulations; yet there can be no doubt of their pervasive influence, not only on what is taught, but on the prevailing assumptions of how our understanding of emotional and social development is best furthered. Thus, pride of place continues to be given to reconstructions based on what is observed and inferred during treatment sessions, coupled with a persisting, if weakening, reluctance to give serious attention to the enormously important work now going on in the field of developmental psychology. Since in many previous publications I have drawn attention to the relevance of this work, I need say only that I believe that all the developmental concepts of psycholoanalysis will have to be re-examined and that most of them will in due course be replaced by concepts now current among those who are studying the development of affectional bonds in infants and young children by means of direct observation. The understandable reserve with which many clinicians have viewed this type of work in the past would, I believe, be dispelled were they to become familiar with the observations and ideas of such present leaders in the field as, for example, Mary Ainsworth (1977), John and Elizabeth Newson (Newson, 1977) and Colwyn Trevarthen (1979).

Ignorant though many analytic theorists appear still to be of the value or even the very existence of these studies, there is, I am glad to say, an increasing number of analytic therapists who draw on them in their treatment of patients. Let us turn, therefore, to the clinical field and consider the account given by a Californian analyst of his treatment of a woman patient, many of whose problems he attributes, I believe rightly, to events following her parents' divorce and the long period during her fifth and sixth years when she was in an institution. This account[4] not only illustrates the kinds of distressing personal problems to which experiences of these sorts give rise, including intense ambivalence, but it serves also to pose questions of how issues of defense and affect are answered within the conceptual framework I am proposing.

The problems for which Mrs G came for analysis were that she felt irritable and depressed and filled, as she put it, with hate and evil. In addition she found herself frigid with her husband, emotionally detached, and wondering whether she was capable of loving anyone.

Mrs G was three years old when her parents divorced. Her father had left home, and her mother, who began working long hours, had little time for her daughter. A year later, when Mrs G was four, her mother placed her in an orphanage, where she remained for eighteen long months. Thereafter, although she was back with her mother, family relationships continued to be disturbed and unhappy. As a result Mrs G left home during her 'teens and, before she was 21, had already been married and divorced twice. Her present husband was her third.

In the early phases of the analysis Mrs G was extremely reluctant to recall the painful events of her childhood; and when she did so, she broke down into tears and sobbing. Nevertheless, her analyst encouraged her to reflect on them further and to do so in minute detail since he believed this would help her. At the same time he paid at least equal attention to her relationship with himself in which, as would be expected, all the interpersonal difficulties she had had in other close relationships recurred.

Amongst much else in her childhood that was painful, Mrs G recalled how sad she had felt on being parted from her pets when she was sent away to the orphanage. Sometimes she dreamed about her time there with feelings of being overwhelmed. She recalled feeling very small among the many children, how there were no toys, the harsh treatment meted out and how she had sometimes misbehaved deliberately in order to get smacked [which at least meant she was given some attention—J.B.]

After four years of analysis Mrs G's financial difficulties led to the decision to end treatment in six months' time. Inevitably, the emotional conflicts she had in her relationship with her analyst became more acute. She now dreamed and day-dreamed more openly of him. From the first she had realized that parting would be painful. Separations had always made her angry, and, as she put it now, 'anger makes me sad because it means the end. ... I'm afraid you'll leave me or kick me out or put me away.' The analyst reminded her of how she had felt when sent to the orphanage. Struggling to think of herself as self-sufficient, she exclaimed: 'I'm clinging on to me. ... I'm taking care of me all by myself.'

A few months later, as termination approached, she linked how she felt about her analyst with how she had felt earlier about her mother: 'I don't want to release my mother—I don't want to let her go—she's not going to get rid of me.' By this stage of her analysis her active yearning for love and care had returned, together with her anger at those who had denied it her.

The radical change that had occurred in this woman was confirmed in other episodes. For example, during the early days of the analysis, her cat had died, but she had felt indifferent about it. As she had then explained: 'If I let it hurt me, I'd be saddened by everything. One will trigger off the rest.' But now, towards the end of the analysis, when another cat died, she wept.

Although therapy had restored this patient's feeling life and had resulted in her becoming able to make improved relationships, including that with her mother, a follow-up five years later showed, as would be expected, that she remained vulnerable to situations that arouse anxiety and sadness, such as separation and loss.

Let us examine the change that had occurred in this woman, whose condition might be described clinically as schizoid (Fairbairn, 1940), or as false self (Winnicott, 1960, 1974) or as narcissistic (Kohut, 1971). Before the analysis she had felt emotionally detached and had wondered whether she was capable of loving anyone; a loss left her feeling indifferent. Now she had become aware how deeply she longed for love and care, and how angry she felt at not being given it; and a loss led to tears. Thus, in situations where they were missing before, responses laden with deep affect now appeared.

To account for such a change, traditional explanations tend to use a hydraulic metaphor: affect has been dammed up and has now been discharged. The dam is regarded as a defense against an excessive quantity of excitation that is in danger of overwhelming the ego. Other explanations invoke processes postulated to occur in earliest infancy, for example fixation in a phase of narcissism or a split in the ego resulting from the projection of a death instinct.

An explanation of this woman's condition that I believe to be much closer to our present knowledge of the early development of affectional bonds and consistent with what we know about human information processing runs as follows: As a result of the intense pain caused her during her early years by the prolonged and probably repeated frustration of her attachment behaviour, experienced as frustration of her urgent desire for love and care, the behavioural system(s) governing her attachment behaviour had become deactivated and had remained so despite her wishes to the contrary. As a result the desires, thoughts and feelings that are part and parcel of attachment behaviour were absent from her awareness. The deactivation itself can be understood as being due to the selective exclusion from processing of any information that, when processed, would lead to activation of the system.[5]

The selective exclusion postulated, which, as recent experimental work shows, is well within the capabilities of our cognitive apparatus (Dixon, 1971; Erdelyi, 1974) and which I term defensive exclusion (Bowlby, 1980, Chapter 4) requires constant cognitive activity at an unconscious level. The fact that the behavioural systems remain intact and capable in principle of being activated, and so may on occasion show brief or incipient activation, can account for all those phenomena that led Freud to his ideas about a dynamic unconscious and repression. In fact the defensive exclusion that I postulate is no more than repression under another name, a name more in keeping with the conceptual framework adopted here.

The process of therapeutic change in this patient can then be understood as being due to the patient, thanks to the relatively secure base provided by the analyst, developing sufficient courage to permit some of the information hitherto excluded to go forward for processing (Bowlby, 1980, Chapter 20). This includes both information stemming from the present situation—for example evidence of the analyst's genuine concern to help his patient and the conflicting thoughts, feelings and behaviours that that arouses—and also information stored in memory, for example memories of the very painful events of childhood and the thoughts, feelings and behaviour aroused by them. As a rule information from the two sources is recovered as a chain in which information from the present, especially the transference, alternates with information from the past, with each link leading on to the next. Once the relevant information becomes accepted, of course, attachment behaviour is reactivated, together with the urges and desires, thoughts and feelings that go with it. In traditional terms, the unconscious has been made conscious and the repressed urges and affects released.

Not infrequently, as with this patient, an analyst has the task of drawing a patient's attention to memories he believes to be of importance and encouraging her to reflect on them instead of turning her back on them. In doing this an analyst is guided, of course, by whatever theories of personality development and psychopathology he may espouse. This is a point at which analysts of different schools diverge. For some the events thought to be important might refer to feeding and weaning and phantasies about them during the earliest months of life; for others to toilet training or witnessing the primal scene during the second year; for others again to oedipal situations and wishes during the third or fourth. In the case of Mrs G, the analyst drew on his knowledge of responses of young children to events surrounding a prolonged separation from mother during several of the early years.

It is well recognized that not every child who has been in an institution for eighteen months during his fifth and sixth years develops psychologically along the kind of pathway followed by

Mrs G. In her case other factors almost certainly entered in. In considering what they might have been, I am influenced by remarks Mrs G made during the final phases of her analysis, for example her fear lest her analyst should 'kick her out' or 'put her away' and her memory of how determined she had been that her mother should not 'get rid' of her. This suggests that as a method of disciplining her daughter, mother may have repeatedly used threats to send her back to the institution, threats we know from other evidence are far from rare and that not only have a terrifying effect on a young child but are also likely to generate intense hatred in him (Bowlby, 1973, Chapters 15, 17). The better an analyst's knowledge of childhood conditions likely to lead to disturbed development, the better can he understand and help his patients.

Inevitably, a patient's spontaneous or guided recollections of his childhood are of only suggestive value as evidence bearing on theories of personality development. What a patient tells us about his childhood, and especially what an analyst subsequently reports his patient to have said, are probably influenced as much or more by the analyst's preconceptions as by anything the patient may in fact have said or done; this is why I regard the systematic study by direct observation of children developing within different patterns of family care as indispensable for progress. Yet I also believe that observations made during therapy still have considerable research potential, although that potential will not be realized unless studies are conducted along far more systematic lines than have hitherto been usual.

The research strength of the therapeutic situation lies not in what it tells us about the patient's past, but in what it tells us about disturbances of personality functioning in the present, especially, I would claim, disturbances in a person's capacities to make secure attachments and the conditions in which these disturbances become ameliorated. The case of Mrs G can be used as an introduction to a research proposal, since there is much, both in the personality disturbance she presents and in the course of her analysis, that we have reason to believe is fairly typical.

Drawing on case reports already in the literature, it would be possible to make a number of generalizations, which could then be treated as predictions to be tested in further therapeutic work with patients showing similar clinical features. All such predictions, which would be conditional on the particular pattern of therapy to be followed,[6] could be couched in terms of what can be observed at first hand. They would include statements about how a patient would be expected to behave towards the analyst, the topics he would be expected to talk about or, in particular, avoid talking about, the affect he would be expected to show or not to show, and in what situations. Of special interest would be changes in behaviour, topic and affect that would be expected to occur in relation to certain types of current event, both those occuring in the patient's everyday life and those occurring within the analysis. Events of the latter sort would include how the analyst behaves, what he says and how he says it, with particular reference to interruptions in the analysis due to holidays, sickness or other circumstances. Tape-recording sessions to avoid biased reporting would, of course, be necessary.

By following the procedures proposed, it would be possible over a period of time to gather comparable bodies of data from two sources. One body of data would be gathered by means of direct observation of the development and patterning of affectional bonds during infancy and childhood in children experiencing different types of care. The other would be gathered, also by direct observation, of changes in the patterning of affectional bonds during the course of a certain type of therapy. Provided that the conceptual frameworks used in making both sets of observations and the questions each set addresses are the same, findings could be compared and developmental hypotheses tested.

This is but one way in which psychoanalysis as a body of knowledge about personality development and psychopathology might move towards becoming the natural science Freud always intended it to be.

What type of natural science have I in mind then? Let me specify.

At one time it was common to identify scientific thought with the hypothetico-deductive method advocated by Popper (1963) with its strong emphasis on falsifiability. This model, however, has been called sharply in question by several other philosophers of science, e.g. Kuhn (1970, 1974) and Harré (1970) and is now widely regarded as giving an inadequate and one-sided account of how scientific work proceeds. I am therefore not advocating Popper's model. Nor am I advocating the methods adopted by the physical sciences, which, it is now recognized, are far from being as representative of scientific method as was once supposed, and with which unfortunately scientific method is still sometimes identified.[7] In emphasizing the special status of physics, the biologist Carl Pantin (1968) points out that physicists have made their striking advances by excluding from consideration all but the simplest phenomena. Biologists, by contrast, are wrestling with phenomena of vastly greater complexity and perforce have had to employ different methods of investigation and to rest content with criteria of acceptability that though stringent, are less rigorous than those of the physicist. Suffice it to say, therefore, that the procedures that I believe psychoanalysts will be wise to employ and the criteria to which our science should strive to conform are close to those adopted by our neighbours in the biological sciences.

The conceptual framework I have sketched serves, I believe, to accommodate a substantial proportion of the data that psychoanalysis has selected as within its domain. The framework has the advantage of being compatible with evolutionary biology and neurophysiology and promises greater economy and internal consistency than do traditional ones. Nevertheless, what its strengths and weaknesses will prove to be cannot be known without extensive testing of its powers to solve problems not yet studied, which include for example those of sexual development and deviation, and a far more intensive examination than has yet been possible of its usefulness in solving the problems already given attention.

There is still at least one central and difficult issue I have not touched upon and that calls for a final comment. However much the knowledge of personality development and psychopathology derived from a scientific approach may help us in understanding another human being—and I believe it to be indispensable, especially for grasping what the constraints have been on a person's development and how the restrictions he now experiences on his freedom of thought, feeling and action originated—it is still a far cry from understanding the unique personal experience of life each one of us has. For that we need a very different perspective, one that, inspired by empathy and respect, enables us to experience each person as a unique individual living his life through time and exercising such freedoms as he has in his own unique world. Fortunately these two perspectives, deriving as they do from different realms of discourse, do not conflict—a truth that sensitive physicians have long demonstrated. As I have emphasized elsewhere (Bowlby, 1979), each perspective is appropriate in its own sphere while being wholly out of place in the other. Put briefly, I believe our task as psychoanalysts is, when researchers, to render unto science the things that are scientific and, when clinicians, to render unto the persons the things that are personal.

NOTES

1. See the critiques of Rubinstein (1976), Frank (1979) and Meissner (1979).

2. Almost all the ideas considered in this lecture have been discussed at greater length in the three volumes of *Attachment and Loss* (Bowlby, 1969, 1973, 1980).

3. For Freud's adherence to Lamarckian ideas see Volume 3, Chapter 10, of Ernest Jones's Biography (Jones, 1957). For the influence of Haeckel's biogenetic law see James Strachey's long editorial footnote to his translation of Freud's *Moses and Monotheism* (Strachey, 1964, p. 102) and especially Frank Sulloway's recent enquiry into the origins of Freud's metapsychology (Sulloway, 1979).

4. The account given here is derived from the contribution by Thomas Mintz to a symposium organized by the American Psychoanalytic Association on the effects on adults of object loss during the first five years of life (Mintz, 1976).

5. The term 'deactivation' was introduced by Peterfreund (1971) to refer to a system that, though still intact, is being rendered incapable of activation over a relatively long period. In this respect the condition differs profoundly from that of a system that happens to be inactive at a particular moment. It will be noticed that the aetiology of the clinical condition proposed here is the same as that proposed by Winnicott (1974), who attributes it to early environmental failure in the form of 'not good enough mothering'.

6. The technique of analysis adopted by Mintz appears to have much in common with that adopted in the United Kingdom by Donald Winnicott; see the account by Guntrip (1975).

7. For example, two clinicians who dispute the applicability of the methods of natural science to our discipline, Home (1966) and Will (1980), both make this mistake. Their arguments centre on the inapplicability of the methods adopted by the physical sciences: neither mentions biology.

CHAPTER EIGHT

The Freudian left
and the theory
of cultural revolution

Christopher Lasch

B oth the strengths of the new left's critique of domination and its underlying weaknesses reveal themselves, with particular sharpness and clarity, in the attraction of the new left to an intellectual tradition seemingly resistant to radical reinterpretation, yet essential, it turned out, to the new theory of revolution—the theory of cultural revolution—that haunted the imagination of the 1960s.

What brought about this improbable alliance of psychoanalysis and cultural radicalism, of Freud and Marx? We seem to have here a remarkable instance of the attraction of opposites. Freud puts more stress on human limitations than on human potential; he has no faith in social progress; and he insists that civilization is founded on repression. There isn't much here, at first glance, that would commend itself to reformers or revolutionaries—and, in the last analysis, the theorists of the Freudian left in one way or another have had to get around or explain away the deterministic, tragic side of Freud's thought, which has more in common with St. Augustine and Calvin than with Marx. Why then did the left bother with psychoanalysis in the first place?

The reasons lie in the political events of the 1920s and early 1930s. The failure of a socialist revolution to materialize out of the chaos of World War I, when all the objective conditions in central and western Europe seemed conducive to a turn to the left, prompted investigations into the subjective conditions impeding social and political progress. The rise of fascism seemed to provide additional evidence of deep-seated psychological resistance to liberating change. It raised doubts about the inevitability of historical progress and about the adequacy of Marxist orthodoxy, which could find nothing more illuminating to say about fascism than that it represented the last phase of a decadent capitalism. The solidification of the Stalinist regime in the Soviet Union provided a further challenge to the myth of progress. Opponents of Stalinism had to ask themselves why the Russian revolution, like so many revolutions in the past, had appeared to end in a regression to authoritarian rule. A kind of repetition-compulsion seemed to be at work in history: each attempt to get rid of authoritarianism succeeded only in reconstituting it on a new basis. Revolutions had evidently failed to attack authoritarianism at its psychological source. They had brought new classes to power without changing the underlying structure of power itself. They had modified institutions without breaking the pattern of domination and submission that underlay those institutions. In order to understand the self-defeating quality of past revolutions and to lay the psychological groundwork for a new kind of revolution that would put an end to domination once and for all, it was evidently imperative to understand the psychology of power; and psychoanalysis, it seemed, had more to say on this subject than any other theory of the mind.

For those who sought to grasp the underlying resistance to change that revealed itself even in movements ostensibly devoted to change, the attraction of Freud's work lay in its attack on the illusion of psychic autonomy. Men need masters because they are not masters of themselves: this became the central contention of the Freudian left. Freud's theory, on this view, provides the deepest glimpses into the divided self. It shows how society enters and deforms the individual psyche—not through indoctrination or cultural 'conditioning' but through the deeper mechanisms of repression and sublimation. The conviction that unites thinkers as diverse as Herbert Marcuse, R. D. Laing and Jacques Lacan is that psychoanalysis traces the origin of intrapsychic conflict to the conditions under which social authority recreates itself in the unconscious mind, and specifically to the institution of the patriarchal family, which crushes the revolt of the son against the father and saddles the son with a guilty conscience and makes him grow up to become a tyrant in his own right.

Much of this ground had been covered already, in the 1930s and 1940s, by Wilhelm Reich, who might be called—except for the inappropriateness of patriarchal imagery in this context—the founding father of the Freudian left. At times the work of radical Freudians in our own time looks like a rehash of Reich. But even Reich had not gone far enough to suit his followers. According to Norman O. Brown (1959), 'Reich was right in arguing that to fulfill its own therapeutic promise, psychoanalysis has to envisage a social transformation. Reich was wrong in limiting the social transformation involved to the liberation of adult genital sexuality'. Postwar thinkers agreed that the problem went deeper. The transformation of the polymorphous perversity of the infant into genital sexuality already reflected the triumph of the performance principle, as Marcuse (1962) called it, over the pleasure principle. A social revolution that aimed to break the cycle of domination and rebellion could not stop with the creation of a more permissive sexual morality. A so-called sexual revolution that confined itself to genital pleasure could easily lend itself to new forms of domination, as Marcuse (1964) tried to show in his theory of 'repressive desublimation'. The events of the 1960s and 1970s have provided further support for his contention that a society organized around consumption can easily absorb movements demanding sexual freedom, enlisting them into the propaganda of commodities so as to surround consumption with an aura of libidinal gratification. As feminists have pointed out, the new sexual freedom has brought about no important changes in the distribution of power or in the sexual exploitation of women.

The cultural revolution, then—the program of deep structural change envisioned by the radical Freudian left—went far beyond a mere 'sexual revolution'. Its task, as these theorists saw it, was not to set aside more opportunities for erotic indulgence, as a momentary release from the demands of alienated labour, but to eroticize work itself. The point was not to enlarge the domain of leisure but to abolish the very distinction between work and leisure, to make work into play, and to get rid of the aggressive, domineering attitude towards nature that informs the present organization of work. It was partly in order to explain the origins of that attitude that theorists of the new left turned to Freud. In other words, they turned to Freud for very good reasons. Unfortunately they brought with them a set of assumptions that owed more to the socialistic theory of the family (as Max Weber once called it) than to the founder of psychoanalysis.[1] Their attempt to base a general theory of culture on psychoanalysis, or to read psychoanalysis itself as a general theory of culture, led them further and further away from the critical core of psychoanalysis, its interpretation of clinical data. What began as a fruitful confrontation between psychoanalysis and Marxism ended in a reassimilation of psychoanalytic ideas to an older socialist critique of the patriarchal family—a critique that is becoming increasingly irrelevant to the conditions of advanced industrial society, misleading at best, downright dangerous at worst.

Although it is difficult to generalize about the various schools of thought on the Freudian left—followers of Marcuse, followers of Brown, Laingians, Lacanians, radical feminists, socialist feminists—they all share the central premise that the patriarchal family is the root of organized oppression. It is important to remember that this idea has a long history that antedates Freud and has continued to develop independently of Freud. From the beginning, it had pronounced feminist and socialist overtones. Bachofen's study of mother-right, Lewis Henry Morgan's study of archaic kinship terminology, Engels's analysis of the connections between the family, private property, and the state all appeared to call into question the universality of monogamy and to trace its rise to the subjugation of women. The myth of matriarchal origins has remained attractive to feminists ever since, long after its abandonment by anthropologists. But even without the corollary of a matriarchal stage of social development allegedly antedating the patriarchal stage, the idea that oppression originates in the family continues to find widespread acceptance on the left, in large part because it seems to explain the rise and persistence of Faustian, acquisitive, aggressive, domineering character traits. Not just the radical left, but the political culture of liberalism has been deeply coloured by a revolt against the discredited patriarchal authority of priests and poets and divinely anointed kings, and the critique of the family represents one of the most enduring ideological expressions of this revolt. Indeed, the imagery of revolutionary brotherhood, which has been bound up with modern state-building since the time of the French revolution, derives its emotional energy from the tension between the overthrow and reconstitution of patriarchal authority. Given the number of modern states that have originated in revolutions, it is not surprising that so many modern thinkers have associated the origin of civilization itself with an act of rebellion against the father, followed by the reimposition of his authority in new forms.

Freud's own theory of the primal horde incorporates much of this revolutionary imagery as well as the formal theories of nineteenth-century anthropologists. It is easy to see the attraction of this Freudian creation myth for the new left. It not only implicates the family in the origins of a repressive civilization, but for the first time it spells out the psychological linkages between them: linkages between political history and the family. The sons overthrow the father but internalize his authority and reimpose it on women and children. The original revolution thus becomes the prototype of failed revolutions ever since. The uprising of the rebellious sons momentarily breaks 'the chain of domination', according to Marcuse; 'then the new freedom is again suppressed— this time by their own authority and action'. Once established, the 'rhythm of liberation and domination' repeats itself throughout history—as in the life and death of Jesus, which Marcuse interprets as a struggle against the patriarchal laws in the name of love, a struggle betrayed by Christ's disciples when they deify the son beside the father and codify his teachings in oppressive new laws (Marcuse, 1962).

Dorothy Dinnerstein, like Marcuse, takes Freud's theory of the primal horde as a 'landmark account of the vacillation at the heart of rebellion', although she extends it by arguing that the sons submit to the father not only because of their ambivalence but because 'patriarchy remains a [psychological] refuge' from the more terrifying domination of the mother.[2] Juliet Mitchell (1974) likewise finds in *Moses and Monotheism* (Freud, 1939a) the 'story of the origins of patriarchy'. 'The brothers identify with the father they have killed. . . . The father thus becomes far more powerful in death than in life; it is in death that he institutes human history. The theory of the primal horde appeals to the new left—even with the qualification that it is 'speculative' and 'symbolic'—because it links the social to the psychological in a particularly vivid way and seems to show how the Oedipus complex, and with it the whole apparatus of patriarchal domination, transmits itself from one generation to the next.[3] The Freudian myth or theory traces the Oedipus complex back to the dawn of history and helps to define the need for a cultural revolution that transcends a mere change in power or institutions and breaks the cycle of rebellion and submission.

The case against the patriarchal family does not, of course, rest exclusively or even primarily on the theory of the primal horde, but I stress this issue in the hope of clarifying some of the psychological assumptions behind this whole train of thought. As Brown (1959) himself has pointed out, Freud's speculations about group psychology, both in his essay of that name and in *Moses and Monotheism* (Freud, 1939a), rest on a model of mental conflict that Freud had already discarded in the more strictly psychological writings of his last phase, starting with *Beyond the Pleasure Principle* (Freud, 1920g) in 1920. Freud's increasing awareness of a more deeply buried layer of mental life underlying the oedipal stage, his revision of the instinct theory, and his new psychology of women pointed to conclusions incompatible with many of the generalizations he continued to advance in his sociological writings. For one thing, this new line of analysis suggested that sexual pleasure is not the only object of repression. For another, it suggested that the agency of repression is not simply 'reality'. Accordingly the outcome of the Oedipus complex—the theory of which Freud now made explicit for the first time—cannot be seen simply as the submission of the pleasure principle to a reality principle imposed on the child by the father. It is not just that parental commands and prohibitions, toilet-training practices and threats of castration play a less important role in the child's development than Freud had previously thought. The entire conceptual scheme that opposes pleasure and reality, equating the former with the unconscious and the latter with conscious adherence to parental morality, has to give way to a different model of the mind.

In many ways the most important feature of Freud's structural model is the theory of the superego, which reflects his new understanding that the repressive agency is itself largely unconscious and that its demands go far beyond what is demanded by the reality-principle. Far from serving as the agency of reality, the superego derives at least some of its severity from aggressive energies in the id. The statement that it represents a 'pure culture of the death instinct', moreover, seems to imply an archaic origin of the superego and even to qualify the view that it represents the 'heir of the Oedipus complex' (Freud, 1923b). The same discoveries that led Freud for the first time to give formal expression to the theory of the Oedipus complex seem to diminish the absolutely decisive and determining importance he assigned to it. At the very least they indicate that the Oedipus complex, in men as well as in women, has to be regarded as the culmination of a long series of earlier developments that help to predetermine its outcome. Instead of saying that the Oedipus complex bequeaths to the child a punitive superego based on the fear of castration, we might say that castration anxiety itself is merely a later form of separation anxiety that the archaic and vindictive superego derives from the fear of retaliation by the mother, and that, if anything, the Oedipal experience tempers the punitive superego of infancy by adding to it a more impersonal principle of authority, one that is more 'independent of its emotional origins', as Freud (1925j) puts it, more inclined to appeal to universal ethical norms and somewhat less likely, therefore, to associate itself with unconscious fantasies of persecution (Strouse, 1974). We might speculate further that the Oedipal superego rests as much on the wish to make amends as on the fear of reprisals, though even here it is clear that feelings of gratitude—the most important emotional basis of what is called conscience—first arise in connection with the mother (Klein, 1957).

In any case, patriarchal domination has to be seen as a secondary formation. This seems to be the unmistakable implication of Freud's later work and of much of the work subsequently produced by Kleinians, ego psychologists and object-relations theorists, too quickly dismissed by the Freudian left as uncritical celebrants of the 'mature', integrated ego. It is not hard to understand why most writers on the left, with the exception of Brown and some of the psychoanalytic feminists, have shown so little interest in the implications of Freud's structural theory. Even Marcuse, who claims to take the later Freud as his starting point, makes little use of these ideas. The reason is clear: they undercut the idea that repression originates in the subjection of the pleasure principle to the patriarchal compulsion to work. Jacques Lacan is even more explicit in his championship of the early Freud, and for something of the same reason: he can find no warrant in Freud's later works for the assumption that desire is inherently subversive and revolutionary and therefore has to be suppressed in the 'name of the father.' In the work of Lacan's followers—notably Deleuze and Guattari in their *Anti-Oedipus* (1977)—the Reichian theory of sexual revolution often re-emerges in all its crudity, dressed up with Gallic pretentiousness as a theory of 'schizoanalysis' that claims to go far beyond not only Freud but Lacan himself. Naturally Deleuze and Guattari see the oedipal theory as Freud's greatest single mistake. Other writers on the left, correctly sensing that Freud's ideas are more important than his personal prejudices, have seen him as the first theorist of patriarchal psychodynamics, even as an unwitting critic of patriarchy. Deleuze and Guattari, on the other hand, unable to distinguish between theory and ideology, have regressed to the vulgar stereotype of Freud as an apologist for patriarchal domination. Thus the platitudes of the old left, seemingly relegated once and for all to the bargain basement of social criticism, reappear in chic salons as the latest Paris fashions.[4]

There would be no point in discussing shopworn platitudes about sexual revolution in the same company with more sophisticated theories of cultural revolution if they did not share the central belief that mankind would be better off in a fatherless society. Even if patriarchal domination is viewed as a secondary formation, it remains the principal focus—the principal target—of the investigations undertaken by the Freudian left. The rise of Freudian feminism has fixed attention more firmly than ever on this issue.[5] Although most feminists continue to regard Freud purely and simply as a propagandist for patriarchy, whose ideas have nothing to contribute to an understanding of the oppression of women, a few of them have begun to see that psychoanalysis becomes valuable to feminism precisely by showing that male domination does not rest on brute force alone but has deeper psychological roots. If psychoanalysis indicates that paternal despotism itself rests on an earlier despotism of the mother, this additional insight, it would seem, merely strengthens the case for abolishing the sexual division of labour that assigns early childcare exclusively to women. Such is the argument advanced by Dorothy Dinnerstein in *The Mermaid and the Minotaur* (1976), a book conceived as an extension of Brown's *Life against Death* (1959), and in somewhat different form by Nancy Chodorow in *The Reproduction of Mothering*.[6]

Without quarrelling with the specific contention that men and women should cooperate more fully in the work of nurture, I should like to suggest that the same evidence by which Freudian feminists try to support it—namely, the evidence that reveals the importance of the pre-oedipal mother—undermines the more general contention that all forms of oppression lead back to the patriarchal family. Freudian feminists advocate more than an expanded role for men in child care. In company with other feminists, and with the Freudian left as a whole, they demand the abolition of the family, on the grounds not only that it oppresses women but that it produces an acquisitive, aggressive, authoritarian type of personality. In their eyes the family provides the psychological underpinning of the 'nightmare of infinitely expanding technological progress', as Brown (1959) calls it. Because technological progress seems to have reached a dangerous dead end, it becomes imperative not merely to understand the psychology of power but to identify an alternative to the 'patricentric' personality in the form of a narcissistic, Dionysian or androgynous personality type. Now that Promethean man apparently stands on the brink of self-destruction, Narcissus looks like a more likely survivor.[7] What some critics condemn as a massive cultural and psychological regression looks to theorists of cultural revolution like a long-overdue 'feminization of American society', as one of them calls it (Engel, 1980). If the 'basic feminine sense of self is connected to the world' while the basic masculine sense of self is separate, Nancy Chodorow (1978) argues, modern society obviously has no future as long as men hold the upper hand. Hence the Freudian feminists' 'challenge to traditional psychoanalytic definitions of autonomy and morality' and their attempt 'to articulate conceptions of autonomy that are premised not simply on separation, but also on the experiences of mutuality, relatedness, and the recognition of an other as a full subject' (Engel, 1980).

But the effort to uphold narcissism as a theoretical alternative to possessive individualism rests on shaky ground. The psychoanalytic evidence cited to support the case for narcissism actually weakens it. Consider the work of Janine Chasseguet-Smirgel, much in vogue with feminists.[8] She makes a sharp distinction between the superego and the ego ideal, the heir of primary narcissism, which seeks to close the gap between infantile omnipotence and the reality of dependence on the mother. Seeking reunion with the mother yet continually thwarted in this search, the ego ideal can become the basis of later identifications founded on a loving symbiosis with the world rather than on fear of punishment. According to one feminist, this argument weakens the 'ideal of the radically autonomous and individuated man' and holds out the 'possibility of [psychological development and cultural] creation that is "engendered" rather than fabricated' (Engel, 1980). Maybe so; but the significance of Chasseguet-Smirgel's work for social theory lies in its vivid description of cultural conditions that encourage a regressive rather than a developmental or evolutionary solution to the problem of separation—and these are precisely the cultural conditions that prevail today. 'In order to be again united with the ego', she writes, the ego ideal 'can choose either the shortest route, the most regressive one, or the evolutionary one.' Desire feeds on obstacles, and frustration may impel the child into the Oedipus complex, in which the desire for symbiosis associates itself with the newly conceived fantasy of incestuous reunion with the mother. On the other hand, 'if the mother, [say,] has deceived her son by making him believe that with his (pregenital) infantile sexuality he is a perfect partner for her ... his ego ideal, instead of cathecting a genital father and his penis, remains attached to a pregenital model' (Chasseguet-Smirgel, 1976b).

According to Chasseguet-Smirgel, the attempt 'to re-establish the fusion between the ego and its ideal by evading development' dramatically reveals itself in certain forms of group psychology.

Whereas Freud saw the group essentially as a revival of the primal horde, with the leader as a father-figure and the group as a band of brothers, Chasseguet-Smirgel argues that many groups find their dominant fantasy in collective reunion with the mother. The Nazi movement, for example, 'was directed more toward the mother goddess ... than God the Father. In such groups, one witnesses the complete erasure of the father and the paternal universe, as well as all of the elements pertaining to the Oedipus complex'. Group psychology in the modern world rests more often on the need for illusion than on the need for leadership, and modern ideology serves to promote the mass illusion of omnipotence. Groups tend to choose as their leaders not the man of action, the domineering father-figure, but the master illusionist skilled in propaganda and the histrionic arts, who gives each member of the group the 'opportunity to think that he neither needs to grow up like, nor identify with, his father'.

Chasseguet-Smirgel (1976b) concludes her paper on the ego ideal with a discussion of religion and science. She argues that mysticism and drug cults, like ideology, follow the short cut to Nirvana, in contrast to religion, which stresses the obstacles to Salvation. In Christianity, the father still reigned alongside the son. The 'absolute reign of the son,' the ideal upheld by modern charismatic sects (and also the ideal, it will be recalled, upheld by Marcuse), 'implies [a painless] union with the mother.' This analysis, incidentally, helps to explain why the death of God has not made men more self-reliant and autonomous. On the contrary, the collapse of religious illusions has only prepared the way for more insidious illusions, and science itself, instead of serving as an agency of general enlightenment, helps to reactivate infantile appetites and the infantile need for illusions by impressing itself on people's lives as a never-ending series of technological miracles, wonder-working drugs and cures, and electronic conveniences that obviate the need for human effort. Among the 'external forces which stimulate the old wish to bring the ego and the ego ideal together by the shortest route', and which contribute to the 'changes in pathology we observe today', Chasseguet-Smirgel (1976b) reserves the most important place for 'those factors which tend to take progress in science as a confirmation of the possible and immediate reuniting of the ego and the ego ideal'.

Other external influences encouraging psychic regression come readily to mind: the stimulation of appetites by advertising; the confusion of public discourse; the waning belief in the rationality or intelligibility of moral standards; the decline of the father's role in child-rearing and moral instruction; the emotional estrangement of men and women, which may encourage mothers to make husbands out of their sons. These developments, I would argue, not only impel the ego ideal to seek the shortest route to the oceanic feeling of infancy, they have the further effect of intensifying the archaic elements of the superego itself, partly as a defense against intensified instinctual appetites, partly in default of a more mature and better integrated superego. If the best hope of psychic autonomy lies in a 'dual reign' of the superego and ego ideal, as one feminist puts it, we seem to live in the midst of social conditions that deform both of these agencies and make it harder than ever for people to grow up gracefully.[9] To characterize these conditions as a culture of narcissism may obscure the positive contributions of primary narcissism to emotional development. If so, I would gladly characterize them in some other terms—say, as a culture of the uninhibited ego ideal. I have no intention of upholding a rigidly patriarchal scheme of psychic development or of down-grading the feminine values—if we insist on calling them feminine values—of mutuality and union with others. I wish only to call attention to the irony that those values may have come closer to realization in the patriarchal societies of the past than in our own society.

The point, I think, comes down to this: that although it is no longer difficult to imagine a society without the father, it is a serious mistake, perhaps a dangerous mistake, to confuse it with Utopia. The Freudian left, which took shape in opposition to the old left with its economic determinism and its naive faith in material progress, has identified many of the central problems of our society and many of its central needs: in particular, the need to curb the spirit of acquisition and domination, the need for a more nurturant attitude towards nature, the need for a new relation between men and women. By directing so much of its criticism against the patriarchal family, however, the new left has confused the issue. It has deflected criticism for the real problem to a pseudo-problem, from the corporation and the state to the family. The worst features of our society derive not from the despotism of the authoritarian father, much eroded in any case, but from the regressive psychology of industrialism, which reduces the citizen to a consumer and bombards him with images of immediate and total gratification.

Psychoanalysis has a great deal to say about that psychology, and more generally about the connections between social structure and personality structure. What it has to say, however, does not support the notion that liberation consists in the repudiation of family ties or the introduction of a new system of collective childrearing. Freud cannot be called in at the last minute to shore up an older critique of patriarchal authority that has long outlived whatever usefulness it may once have had. The value of his ideas for social theory lies in their radical challenge to received ideologies of every kind. We are still very far from having assimilated the implications of psychoanalysis for social and political theory. A first step would be to see that instead of authorizing the 'appropriation' of Freudian insights for the defense of pre-established political positions, psychoanalysis really points to the need to rethink every position and to formulate a new one—a new vision of the good society and of democratic citizenship. In this respect, Freud's legacy represents a far more radical body of knowledge than most radicals have ever understood.

NOTES

1. Weber (1961) points out that 'The socialistic theory proceeds from the assumption of various evolutionary stages in the marriage institution. According to this view the original condition was one of spontaneous sex promiscuity within the horde ... corresponding to the complete absence of private property. ... The second evolutionary stage according to this socialistic theory is group marriage [followed by] the "mother right", as a fundamental transition stage. ... Under this arrangement, ... the distinction of chieftainship was fixed exclusively in the woman, and she was the leader in economic affairs, especially those of the household community. ... Finally, the transition to patriarchal law ... and legitimate monogamy is in socialistic thinking connected with the origin of private property and the endeavor of the man to secure legitimate heirs. Herein takes place the

great lapse into sin; from here on monogamous marriage and prostitution go hand in hand.'

2.   See Dorothy Dinnerstein (1976). The theory of the primal horde, according to Dinnerstein, explains the 'central lure of patriarchal despotism—the opportunity for self-deceit that has so far allowed every big revolution against tyranny to give birth to a new tyranny' (Deleuze & Guattari, 1977).

3.   For warnings about the 'speculative' and 'symbolic' character of Freud's theory of the origins of civilization, see Mitchell (1974) and Marcuse (1964).

4.   In keeping with the regressive impulse behind their work, Deleuze and Guattari insist that Freud was right when he assumed that children are seduced by their parents and wrong to shift the blame to the child by deciding that seduction occurs only in the child's fantasy. 'Guilt is an idea projected by the father before it is an inner feeling experienced by the son. The first error of psychoanalysis is in acting as if things began with the child. This leads psychoanalysis to develop an absurd theory of fantasy, in terms of which the father, the mother, and their real actions and passions must first be misunderstood as "fantasies" of the child' (Deleuze & Guattari, 1977).

5.   For still another defense of 'this image of revolt springing from mutual recognition and nurturant activity which may guide us in our struggle against instrumental rationality toward a society without the father' (Benjamin, 1978).

6.   Earlier feminists denounced Freud as an apologist for male supremacy. Either they refused to have anything to do with psychoanalysis at all or, like Karen Horney, Clara Thompson and other Freudian 'revisionists', they sought to counter Freud's 'biological determinism' by introducing a corrective emphasis on culture. Recent feminist interpretations of Freud tend to reject such simplifications. Feminists may continue to dismiss psychoanalysis or to endorse more 'scientific', experimental, behavioural psychologies instead. See, for example, Naomi Weisstein (1970), 'Kinder, Küche, Kirche as scientific law: psychology constructs the female', in Robin Morgan, ed., *Sisterhood Is Powerful*, but such positions have now come under heavy criticism, and thoughtful feminists find it more difficult than before to content themselves with a reply to Freud that takes the form of a 'simple ideological opposite', as Stephanie Engel (1980) puts it.

Instead of dismissing or denaturing Freud, feminists therefore seek 'to reappropriate what is powerful and coherent in psychoanalytic theory by writing women and feminine experience back into the center of the vision' (Engel, 1980).

The interpretive strategy that emerges in recent work by Engel, Mitchell, Chodorow, Dinnerstein and Jessica Benjamin depends on accepting Freudian theory, in its general outlines, as an accurate account of psychic development under the 'patriarchal' conditions that have heretofore prevailed (which assign childrearing exclusively to the care of women and subordinate the work of nurture to the masculine projects of conquest and domination), while holding out the possibility that a radically different system of work and nurture would produce a radically different personality structure. Psychoanalysis reveals its 'patriarchal' bias, on this view, not in Freud's *obiter dicta* on female inferiority (expressions of personal opinion that should not be allowed to obscure what is useful in his scientific work), but in its inability to imagine any path of psychological maturation that does not presuppose a radical rejection of the mother, fearful submission to the father, and the internalization of his authority in the form of a guilty conscience. Psychoanalysis is thus compromised by its uncritical acceptance of the 'ideal of the guilty, self-controlled and realistic bourgeois man' (Engel, 1980).

The new psychoanalytic feminism seeks, in effect, to carry on the critique of 'instrumental rationality' initiated by Max Horkheimer, Marcuse and Brown, and to feminize it by showing that instrumental values vitiate 'critical theory' itself, which equates psychological autonomy with bourgeois individualism and the patriarchal family. This line of argument, linking feminism to the critique of enlightenment, becomes most explicit in Jessica Benjamin's (1978) article in which she argues that Freud, Horkheimer and their misguided followers assume that 'freedom consists of isolation' and that 'denial of the need for the other' represents the only 'route to independence'. The 'objectifying and instrumentalizing attitude which is so pronounced in western patriarchy ... implies not merely the subjugation but the *repudiation* of the mother by the father. It is in this sense that ours has been a society dominated by the father and that, insofar as instrumental rationality prevails, we are [still] far from fatherless'. The alternative to this patriarchal 'dependency among equals' allegedly lies in what Benjamin refers to, rather sketchily, as 'women's kinship and friendship networks', 'sisterhood', 'mutual recognition and nurturant activity', and so on—slogans that play a prominent part in neo-feminist thought but leave the reader wondering how the values they allude to could be institutionalized, except in a totalitarian setting (in which the child-rearing functions of the family had been completely absorbed by the state) that would deprive them of any substance.

7.   For a celebration of the 'death of daddy' and the emergence of a 'post-Promethean world of narcissistic pleasure', see Henry Malcolm (1971).

8.   The two essays by Chasseguet-Smirgel that are repeatedly cited by feminists are 'Freud and female sexuality' (1976a) and 'Some thoughts

on the ego-ideal' (1976b); see also 'Perversion, idealization and sublimation' (1974).

9.   Engel (1980) says, 'The super-ego, heir to the Oedipus complex,
insists on reality and the separation of the child from the mother,
whereas the ego-ideal, heir to the state of primary narcissism,
restores the promise of the imagination, of desire, and the fantasy of
re-fusion. The exclusive reign of the ego-ideal, the infantile fantasy of
narcissistic triumph, forms the basis of illusion, of blind adherence to
ideology, and of the perpetual desire Lasch cites as characteristic of
narcissists. Yet the desire to reconcile ego and ego-ideal, the drive to
return to the undifferentiated infantile state of primary narcissism,
helps to provide the content and drive for the imagination as well as
for the emotions that are the heart of our creative life. Thus an
alternative to Lasch's vision [and, more generally, to the whole Freudian model of emotional development, with its alleged overemphasis on
the superego] is the insistence that neither agency of morality should
overpower the other—this challenge to the moral hegemony of the
super-ego would not destroy its power but would instead usher in a
dual reign'.

CHAPTER NINE

Psychoanalysis and the natural sciences: the brain–behaviour connection from Freud to the present

Karl H. Pribram

The issues

John Bowlby (Chapter 7, this volume) points out that 'From 1895, when Freud made his first attempt to sketch a theoretical framework for psychoanalysis, until 1938, the year before he died, Freud was determined that his new discipline should conform to the requirements of a natural science. Thus in the opening sentence to his *Project* (Freud, 1887–1902) he writes: "The intention is to furnish a psychology that shall be a natural science . . ."; whilst in the *Outline* (Freud, 1940a) we find a passage in which he asserts that once the concept of psychical processes

I gratefully acknowledge the help with the concepts in physics which I received from discussions with my son John K. Pribram, Illy Prigogine, Elizabeth Rauscher and especially Geoffrey Chew, David Bohm and Basil Hiley. Of course, I am solely responsible for the views set forth in this essay, for I may have interpreted their remarks in ways that they themselves would find inappropriate.

being unconscious is granted, "psychology is enabled to take its place as a natural science like any other."'

Bowlby goes on to point out that 'nevertheless, despite Freud's unwavering intention, the scientific status of psychoanalysis remains equivocal'. Still, as noted by Marie Jahoda (1972) in a provocative address to the British Psychological Society some years back, 'Freud won't go away' despite the disenchantment with many of his views by the psychological community. Jahoda suggested that this is due to the fact that Freud's ideas have continued to capture our interest because he raised critical questions. She also noted that neither psychoanalysis nor social and clinical psychologists have as yet adequately answered these questions.

Perhaps the problem lies in the limited focus that has come to characterize these sciences. Freud and Bowlby are correct in their aim: after an initial descriptive phase, answers to questions must be framed in a larger context if they are to *remain* scientific. By this I mean that observations must not only be reliably confirmed (descriptions do not vary overly much from time to time and place to place), but the observations must become validated by tightly coupled relationships to observations made with alternative techniques. Only then are the observations truly shareable and shared. This is the way not only of common science but of common sense (where observations in the visual and auditory modes are validated against each other and against the tactile).

Freud was of course the epitome of a natural scientist at his best. Validation of observations came naturally to a member of the *Fin de Siècle* Viennese intellectual community. Allan Janik and Stephen Toulmin, in *Wittgenstein's Vienna* (1973), declare that this community presented in microcosm most of the important ideas that were to shape the course of history in the twentieth century. Validation was sought not only within the natural sciences but with the broad sweep of philosophical thought. It is significant, therefore, that Freud took several courses with Brentano, the philosopher of Act Psychology and 'intentional inexistence' (intentionality), who has often been coupled with William James as a forbearer of American Realism. There is reason to believe (see, e.g., Raymond Fancher, 1971) that psychoanalysis is indeed indebted to this tutelage.

In addition to Brentano, there was, of course, Wittgenstein and, more important to Freud, Ernst Mach and Morris Schlick, who planted in the soil known as the Viennese Circle seeds that, in the hands of Gustav Bergman, Rudolph Carnap, Herbert Feigel and Hans Reichenbach, would sprout the formal gardens of positivist and linguistic philosophy.

Freud himself was an avowed Machian. He attempted to place the neurology and psychiatry which he had learned from Meynert, Charcot and Hughlings Jackson (whose works he translated from English to French) into the positivist framework that Mach believed could unify the natural sciences. To read Freud's work in this context makes it possible to take the seminal issues with which he dealt and examine them from the standpoint of developments in the natural sciences during the intervening century. The theoretical frames that Freud developed can usefully be grouped into two major categories: the clinical and the metapsychological (Gill, 1975). I will deal in this chapter only with the metapsychology, which Freud defines as the set of mechanisms that operate to produce both normal and clinical manifestations. These mechanisms were conceived by Freud as both neural and social and are therefore at the heart of the brain/mind issue. Taken in this light, the problems raised in the psychoanalytic metapsychology are as pertinent today as they were in the nineteenth century. And I believe we have in the laboratory and in theoretical work made some considerable progress in the last 100 years. It is my purpose to address these problems once again and to compare Freud's treatment of them with currently tenable views. I begin with the most fundamental of these—the concept of energy.

Energy

In this section I wish to make a case for 'dematerializing' energy and to neutralize it with respect to psychological processes as well. The natural science definition of energy is given in terms of a potential to perform, or an actual performance of work. In turn, work is defined as the production of a constructive change in the system or the maintenance of a system in the face of destructive influences. A system is any configuration of events whose totality is more simply described as a unit than as a summation of its components. Constructive is synonymous with systematic; destructive with breakdown into components. There is a precise relationship between material systems (masses) and energy, a relationship summarized by Einstein's famous equation: energy equals mass times the speed of light squared ($E=mc^2$).

Further, Einstein, A. Lorentz and H. Minkowski applied this equation to quantum mechanics, where they made explicit the relationship between momentum on the one hand and space and time on the other. This relationship is given as $M=X^2-t^2c^2$ (in which $X=x,y,z$), the three components of space and the component of time, t, are related once again by the velocity of light squared. Because of the fact that no material object can exceed transmission at greater than the speed of light, Einstein's theory of special relativity denies physical matter access to the coordinate system M (a Minkowski enfolded conceptual space). Many quantum and relativity physicists have for this and additional reasons (such as the observer effect which produces Heisenberg uncertainty and Bohr complementarity) tantalizingly suggested that these higher dimensionalities might be identified as psychic or psychological (see, e.g., Wigner, 1969). Such identification poses the danger of a panpsychism with which they feel uncomfortable. The dilemma is resolved if we simply view all such higher-order abstractions as neutral with respect to the mind/matter duality, especially since so much of the representation of these abstract 'spaces' is mathematical. Though mathematics is a psychological process, what is so startling is that it can describe the material world so effectively. But that does not mean that *all* mathematics necessarily describes matter. The example just given suggests that extramaterial (though not necessarily therefore psychic) 'entities' may be so described.

Note that according to this view the speed of light and therefore light itself may also be considered neutral with respect to the material/mental duality. Light is massless though its path (though not its speed) is altered by masses (i.e. by gravitational forces). Light is, in fact, conceived as 'pure' electromagnetic energy, a conception consonant with the view that it is neutral with respect to matter. That the pattern (or path) of a form of energy should change when in proximity to matter does not disconfirm such a view. The bending of light can be conceived to take place much as the bending of water or air waves by the configuration of obstacles. This is, in fact, the approach taken by Bohm, Hiley and Stuart (1970) in their analysis of the two slit experiment and their inferences regarding the quantum potential.

There is a tendency in psychology, including psychoanalytic psychology (where it is identified in English as cathexis), to use the concept 'energy' in a less well-defined fashion. As McFarland (1971) has pointed out, this is not necessary: behaving organisms expend energy in doing work. There is no reason to restrict the energy concept to non-living systems: behavioural systems certainly are capable of doing work, and the measurement of the quantity of energy expenditure should not be different for living than for non-living systems.

What, then, are we to make of 'psychic' energy? Could I not substitute 'psychological' for 'psychic' energy? And then equate 'behavioural' and 'psychic'? Aside from the fact that psychological processes must be inferred from observed behaviour and the two are therefore at different levels of discourse, not many of my behaviouristic friends would be happy with the deeper meaning of this syllogism; nor probably would those of you who are psychoanalytically minded. Why? Why shouldn't we as scientists *infer* psychological processes from the behaviour of organisms? Everyone else does.

Skinner (1971) has clearly stated the reasons for the behaviourist bias: psychological language, i.e. mental terminology, carries along with it much connotative excess baggage, which makes it tedious and awkward to discern precise meanings. But this did not prevent Newton and other physical scientists from borrowing terms such as 'energy', 'force' and 'field' from popular discourse and successfully using them precisely in a scientific context. In fact, 'energy' and 'force' were primarily *psychological* concepts until the advent of Galileo, Kepler and Newton, much as colour, flavour and charm are primarily psychological concepts today—yet for nuclear physicists these terms are precise attributions that qualitatively describe hadrons and quarks.

My proposal is this: let $E = mc^2$ be the equation that relates space occupying matter to neutral (with respect to the mental/material dichotomy) 'moments' of potential energy and to time (via the speed of light). Then let us explore the possibility that potentials describing energy and time can be related by way of behavioural analysis to psychological, i.e. mental aspects in a similar fashion. To do this we must first agree that energy per se is neither material nor mental but can readily be transformed into 'matter' and 'mind' and that the transfer functions that describe the transformations can be precisely stated. We must also agree to the scientific definition of energy as a measure of a potential or actual performance of work.

Entropy

This section continues the exploration of energy-related concepts. Entropy, a measure of the efficiency with which work is accomplished, is such a concept. Inefficiency begets heat, as when we burn fuel or generate atomic power. According to the Einstein equation heat, which is infrared 'light', introduces the time arrow into the material world. This allows changes to occur, changes that can be measured in terms of the amount of order or disorder which characterizes matter. For example, when waves are generated in water or air, the waves per se do not produce a new substance; rather, they *additionally organize* the medium (water, air). These second-order organizations need also to be conceptualized because they can produce or absorb additional work. The analysis of how efficiently they do this is the province of thermodynamics, and the concept that captures the essence of these additional organizations is called entropy.

The first law of thermodynamics states that every energic reaction begets an equal and opposite reaction, i.e. the total quantity of energy within a system remains constant. It is the law of constancy which is one of Freud's two major postulates upon which he builds his metapsychology. (The other is the neuron doctrine from which he derives the organizational structure that deploys energy.) Given that the sum-total of the quantity of energy in a system remains constant, how then can the work done by transforming liquid water to steam be accounted for? The answer lies in the second law: systems can be efficient in their work, or they can be inefficient. When systems are inefficient, a great deal of heat is generated; efficient energy use minimizes heat loss (thus 'thermodynamics'). Where Einstein's equation relates energy to those organizations we identify as *matter* via light, thermodynamics relates energy to additional types of order via heat. These additional types of order are called *entropy*—although the term is used in the negative, i.e. to describe the absence of such alternate orders. Thus negentropy becomes a measure of order.

An important ontological question (a question of origin) is posed by the observation made above that waves and other such organizations arise secondarily in material organizations. The question is whether such negentropic orders could arise *independently* of matter. In Clerk Maxwell's day, when an 'ether' was postulated to fill the universe, the answer might have been simply given. The Michaelson–Morley experiment, which failed to demonstrate any ethereal drag on the earth's rotation, did away with the 'ether'. But the universe is filled with evidences of electromagnetic energy; furthermore, light and heat radiate through this energy-filled 'field'. Bohm and Hiley (see e.g. Philippides, Dewdney and Hiley, 1979) have recently proposed that, in fact, a vacuum is not a void but a plenum densely filled with potential energy—the quantum potential—and have drawn out in sophisticated fashion the consequences for micro-physics of this proposal. So perhaps the relationship of *negentropy* to energy can be conceived of to parallel that of *matter* to energy rather than to be intrinsically dependent on it. This would mean that electromagnetic energy per se could become patterned, and this is not a completely unfamiliar occurrence. Our radio and television programmes depend on just such patterns. We speak of such programmes as communicating 'information' and Brillouin (1961) and others have detailed the correspondences between information and negentropy.

Thus entropy as well as energy can be considered neutral to the material/mental duality. But just as in the case of energy, negentropic organization does depend on matter and/or mind to manifest—to realize. Prior to manifestation, such organizations are potential only: in short, it takes matter and/or experience (such as, e.g., thinking) to manifest the potential energy and entropy as work. Manifestations occur especially at the boundaries of material systems and at interfaces between them.

The second law of thermodynamics states that in non-living material systems, negentropy tends over the long haul to decrease, entropy (i.e. disorder) to increase. Schrodinger (1944) has pointed out that living systems are characterized by opposing the second law: life begets order, at least temporarily. Prigogine (1980) has recently provided specific equations by which disorder is dissipated in living systems by virtue of the fact that they are characterized by temporary stabilities, even though they are not in equilibrium (i.e. they do not show the constancy relationship of the first law). Further, Eigen (1977) has suggested that the chemical evolution, which occurred even before biological evolution, is based on mechanisms that controvert the overall tendency of physical systems to degenerate entropically. Thus, counterentropic (information enhancing) processes characterize the living world, its precursors and many of its constructions, its capacity for phenomenal (i.e. mental) experiencing and its cultures. As is the case for energy, entropy does not easily fall into either pole of the material/mental duality. Energy and entropy are inferred, and their existence is therefore paradoxically prior to matter and mind.

Error processing vs. information processing

The relationship between thermodynamic theory and information measurement theory has been detailed by Brillouin (1961), Prigogine (1980), and Weiszacker (1974), among others. In technical, scientific usage, information is a measure of the organization of a system on the basis of possible alternative aspects of that organization. Thus a switch is a binary logic element; it can be either off or on—and a measure of the amount of potential information (this is also called uncertainty) describes the number of alternatives (two) provided by the switch. Computers are composed of switches and therefore can be utilized as information processing systems. Norbert Wiener (1948) and his colleagues, Warren McCulloch, Walter

Pitts and Jerome Letvin (see McCulloch & Pitts, 1943), compared the construction of computer binary logic with that of the nervous system.

This comparison revealed that many parts of the nervous system operate in an entirely different fashion. Although the nerve impulses generated in axons give the appearance of simple switches, neurons in aggregate are spontaneously active and become organized into 'oscillators' and 'homeostats'. Oscillators behave like clocks in helping to synchronize the activities of the nervous system. Homeostats, often regulated by clocks, are characterized by feedback loops in which the consequence of the action corrects, when necessary, the process that produced the action. Homeostatic controls of the body's chemistry are of this nature; thermostats are familiar examples of such mechanisms, which are constructed primarily to maintain constancy.

For many years feedback control mechanisms and information processing devices were considered together under the heading 'cybernetics' without clear distinction. For example, in *Plans and the Structure of Behaviour* (Miller, Galanter & Pribram, 1960) my colleagues and I developed Test–Operate–Test–Exit (TOTE) feedback units which, when hierarchically organized, were conceived, in an unexplained fashion, to become information-processing programmes. In their classical ethological contribution, von Holst and Mittelstaedt (1950) developed the principle of reafference, which also failed to make the distinction between feedback and information processes. These early proposals failed to account for the active generative nature of organisms, their exploratory and creative aspects. Mittelstaedt (1968) and Pribram (1971) took heed of this failure, and others, as for instance Mackay (1966), Ashby (1963), and Teuber (1964), began seriously to search for a model that would allow for generative feedforward processing as well as feedback maintenance of constancy.

My particular solution to this problem, presented in *Languages of the Brain* (Pribram, 1971), was the development of a processing unit composed of *two* feedback units *connected in parallel*. This is essentially the mechanism used as an adjustable thermostat. The small wheel on top of the device adjusts the gap between two pieces of metal. This gap is at the same time also determined by the expansion (or contraction) of these pieces of metal due to the amount of heat in the room.

The paralleling of control has interesting consequences. In neurology and common discourse we call such controls 'voluntary'. For instance, Helmholtz pointed out that if we voluntarily move our eyes about, the world remains still. But if we move our eyeball with a finger, the visual world jumps. It is as if, in the normal course of seeing, the visual scene falls upon a 'screen', and our neural apparatus moves that 'screen' at the same moment and at the same rate as it moves our eyeball. In fact, Brindley and Merton (1960) have shown that when the eye muscles are artificially paralysed, the world moves when an attempt is made to move the eye—as if the 'screen' had been set in motion while the eyes remained paralysed. Teuber (1960) has labelled this 'screen-moving' mechanism a 'corollary discharge': of course, no actual screen need be involved—only a signal that computes a corrective neural process simultaneous with or just ahead of the signal that produces the movement of the eyeball. Initiation of the movement can be attributed to the oscillatory nature of the components of the feedforward mechanism, which, when they become synchronized, 'clock' the initiation. A prime example of this 'clocking' is the ability to awaken spontaneously at a preset time. Thus, feedforward organizations are not unique to vision—cerebellar control of voluntary actions of all sorts seems to work in a similar fashion (Ruch, 1951; Pribram, 1971). In fact, the technique of biofeedback, which has become so popular in efforts to regulate ordinarily autonomous internal homeostatic processes, apparently depends on producing a doubling of feedbacks: to the ordinarily operating internal homeostatic feedback an external feedback is added (Pribram, 1976). When the two feedbacks work in parallel, *voluntary* control is achieved over a previously automatically stabilized process.

What, then, is the difference between the signals that operate 'closed' feedback loops and those that involve corollary discharges and 'open' feedforward loops or helixes? A feedback process is constructed to maintain constancy, to be repetitive, redundant. Ashby (1963) has noted that feedback controls involve the processing of redundancy, *not* information in the usual Shannonian sense. Shannon in his original essay (Shannon & Weaver, 1949) describes feedback signals as 'bad' information—i.e. as indicative of *errors* rather than of alternatives. In short, there are two very different mechanisms to be distinguished: mechanisms that maintain constancy through error processing and mechanisms that process alternatives, i.e. 'good' information. There is, therefore, a distinction to be made between error processing and information processing. Error processing depends on feedback, closed-loop mechanism; information processing depends on a higher order feedforward open loop (helical) mechanism that subsumes *alternative* feedback loops *connected in parallel* and thus transcends (brings under 'voluntary' control) the operation of any single feedback (Figure 1).

As noted, feedback processes operate primarily to maintain constancy: neurophysiologically they have been shown to be load-adjusting mechanisms. Changes in environmental load demand changes in the amount of work necessary to maintain, in the face of changing environments, posture, sensory adaptations and the homeostatic regulations of the internal environment. Recall that

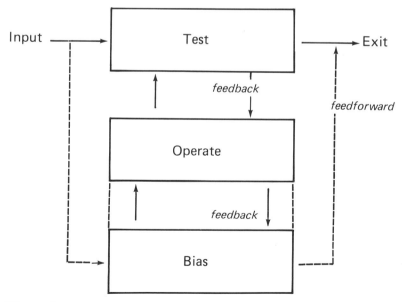

Figure 1

'amount of work' is a measure of energy, not entropy. Thus error (or load) processing feedback mechanisms are related to the first law of thermodynamics—the law of constancy, the law of amount of energy.

By contrast, feedforward mechanisms, because they involve alternatives (alternative feedback loops connected in parallel), are truly information processing mechanisms in the technical sense. Note that since feedforwards are composed of feedbacks, feedforwards are hierarchical to feedbacks. But note also that the composition of feedforwards *must* be in parallel: Ross Ashby (1960) has shown that simply multilinking feedback units with one another leads to hyperstability and thus to almost total resistance to change (i.e. the system cannot learn). As Ashby also noted, however, when they are joined in parallel, adaptive change is facilitated. Parallel control operations can be readily bootstrapped into lists so that structural programming by way of list structures becomes possible. (A list structure is a set of parallel alternatives that can be addressed serially, as in most current computer programmes, or simultaneously, as in content-addressable programming [Spinelli, 1970; Pribram, 1971].) Programming is concerned with the efficiency with which work can be accomplished: a good programme solves a difficult problem more rapidly at less cost and with less effort than a poor programme. Programming—i.e. information processing—thus concerns the second law of thermodynamics, the law of entropy.

Primary vs. secondary processes

The psychoanalytic concept of cathexis is an energy-related concept. In his 'Project for a scientific psychology' Freud (1950a) defines biological energy as Q, a quantity probably of chemical origin, a portion of which, Q_n, can 'occupy' a neuron. This Q, in German *'Besetzte Potential'*, was translated into English as 'Cathexis' (see Pribram & Gill, 1976). Cathexis can be shifted about by producing action currents that are propagated along the axons of neurons but the shifts are impeded by resistances that characterize the junctions between neurons. Thus a qualitative

Ohm's law, Current=Voltage (Q_n)/Resistance of neuron function consonant with the electrochemical nature of the nervous system underlies Freud's conception of energy. (The psychoanalytic model has often been erroneously stated to be hydraulic because the hydraulic metaphor was often used in the nineteenth century by electrical engineers to describe electrical processes.) The law of energic constancy which provides Freud's first postulate is therefore modified by the operation of a second major postulate upon which to build the metapsychology: Freud, the observer of the agnosias (he is responsible for naming them) uses this Ohm's 'law' of neural function to organize gnostic, cognitive processes by way of a brain system that can transcend the order provided by the law of constancy. Cognition negates the entropic tendencies (to agnosia, disorder) inherent in physical systems.

One might ask whether this parallel between the foundations of the psychoanalytic metapsychology and those of thermodynamics are coincidental; to me, it seems unlikely that the seminal work of Holtzman in thermodynamics was unknown to Freud and his colleagues, who were intent on creating a physicalistic psychobiology in the image of Mach and Helmholtz.

Intentional or not, the parallel exists. Freud, in the 'Project' (1950a), clearly distinguishes two processes: one is reactive, the other more complexly organized and proactive. The reactive process can involve muscles, glands or other neurons. Whenever energy is transferred to one of these tissues, a reaction ensues: muscles to environment back to organism; glands back to a sensitive nervous system; neurons back to neurons, in junctional loops. These are the *primary* processes: discharge into the environment; the creation of an accruing chemical quantity which Freud calls the generation of 'unpleasure'—the basis of the pleasure principle; the formation of associative pathways.

Primary processes become organized into secondary, cognitive processes by virtue of (1) mechanisms that inhibit or delay the primary process; (2) reality testing procedures that compare the inputs from the senses with those from the primary processes; and (3) the evaluation, by means of these two mechanisms, of the consequences of actions.

By now you also are sure to see the parallel between feedback-controlled error processing and Freud's primary processing systems on the one hand, and feedforward information processing and secondary, cognitive processing on the other. Over the past decades there have been several suggestions (e.g. Holt, 1962; Peterfreund, 1971) that psychoanalysis abandon the energy concept in favour of more current information–processing formulations. My feeling, based on the above analysis, is that this would be unfortunate. Experimental psychology has just recently begun to distinguish simple associative mechanisms from more complexly organized truly cognitive processes (see, e.g., Anderson and Bower's, 1973, horizontally vs. vertically, hierarchically organized associative nets, and Hilgard's, 1977, work on dissociative processes). The experimental analysis of the neural mechanisms involved in motivation and emotion reviewed in the next section clearly argues for the importance of primary transformations of energy in the behavioural economy of living systems. At the same time these energy-related processes can readily be distinguished from secondary negentropic ones, which are dealt with in the final section under the heading of cognitive competence and the problem of limited span. The results of these experiments, especially those on attention span, make up an imposing body of knowledge which allows considerable refinement of the model presented in the 'Project' (Freud, 1950a) while remaining firmly within its scope.

Motivation and emotion
as energy-related primary processes

Ordinarily when a person works consistently we infer that he is motivated to do so and perhaps interested in what he is doing. Whenever his application is inconsistent or inconstant, we note that he is emotionally unstable, either because he is easily aroused, overly 'distractable' or 'blocked'—i.e. he is either easily interrupted or has some 'hang-up'. Thus motivation and emotion are concepts that relate directly to the quantitative aspects of energy defined as the potential or actual performance of work. In a sense, therefore, behaviourally or experientially derived concepts often encompassed by terms such as 'psychological' or 'psychic energy' are appropriately applied to these motivational and emotional aspects of behaviour and experience, especially as they involve biological 'drives' (Freud's *Triebfeder*) and the metabolic processes they represent. However, in keeping with the theme set forth in this presentation, the energy per se is not 'psychic' but neutral. We infer its existence from the biological and psychological work potentially or actually accomplished. Psychological work becomes manifest in changes in the complexity of organization (i.e. in the structure of redundancy) and in the reduction of errors.

Neurobehavioural research has extensively seconded the relationship between biological energy metabolism on the one hand and the basic aspects of motivation and emotion on the other (see, e.g., Grossman, 1967, for review). More interestingly, such research has also allowed a biological distinction to be made between motivation and emotion.

Let us begin with oral behaviour. Digestion of food and water practically ceases when a particular brain system is interrupted or chemically antagonized, e.g. the nigrostriatal dopaminergic system of fibres coursing lateral to the hypothalamic nuclei (Teitelbaum, 1955). By contrast, after disrupting another system (the ventromedial region of the hypothalamus), ingestion of food and water is slow to terminate, and the animal is difficult to satiate (Meyer, 1963). Other factors, such as filling the stomach, intestinal hormones, etc., appear to modulate these primitive 'go' and 'stop' brain mechanisms, which are in reciprocal homeostatic balance. But more important in the present context is the fact that the 'go' and 'stop' systems are involved in a greater range of activities than oral behaviour. Thus the basal ganglia, in which the nigrostriatal 'go' fibres terminate, are well known to be critically involved in postural set, and by means of electrical excitation my colleagues and I have shown (Spinelli & Pribram, 1966; 1967; Lassonde, Ptito & Pribram, 1981) that receptive field properties of cells in the sensory systems are altered as well: perceptual and postural readiness as well as motivation to eat and drink are controlled by these 'attitudinal' brain systems.

Similarly, when the medial hypothalamic 'satiety' mechanism is electrically stimulated, not only do eating and drinking cease, but all behaviour is temporarily stopped. The animal alerts as if by some external distraction. The amount of alerting when of external origin has been shown to be related to the structure of the redundancy of the stimulus and not to the amount of information that it conveys (Smets, 1973). Similarly, when internal stimulation is increased, the animal first becomes alerted, showing interest and exploratory behaviour. Then, with a greater increase, it shows distractibility, withdrawal and finally uncontrollable lashing out, the 'sham rage' described in earlier investigations of this region of the brain. Just as the nigral origin of the 'go' system has basal ganglia (striatal) components in the forebrain, so does the medial hypothalmic 'stop' system: the nucleus accumbens and septal region on the orbital surface of the frontal lobe and the amygdala on the medial surface of the pole of the temporal lobe.

A model of energy-related mechanisms can be drived from these studies by accepting Brobeck's suggestion (1948) that the energy metabolism of the organism is anchored by temperature homeostasis. Both eating and muscle contractions tend to increase body temperature; breathing and drinking tend to decrease it. In keeping with this suggestion we found (Chin, Pribram, Drake & Green, 1976) that temperature discrimination is disrupted by electrical stimulation of the temporal pole and amygdala as well as the adjacent orbital region of the frontal lobe, not by stimulations of the parietal region where most somatosensory stimuli are processed. Others as well have found that parietal resections do not disrupt temperature discrimination.

In the spinal cord, temperature pathways are intimately interwoven with those of pain. From the experimental results described above for the hypothalamus and the many others that show an interference with aggressive and avoidance behaviour after amygdalectomy, septal lesions and resections of the surrounding temporal and frontal lobe structures (see, e.g., Pribram & Weiskrantz, 1957; Barrett, 1969; Bagshaw & Pribram, 1965), one may conclude that the pain pathways also contribute heavily to the 'stop' system. In fact, the discovery of the endorphins has supported the Melzack–Wall suggestion (1965) that pain is subject to gating, making the regulation of pain a homeostatic process. Pain and temperature thus form the core of a quantitative dimension of experience which I have called the 'protocritic' (Pribram, 1977). The term protocritic was derived from Henry Head (1920) who distinguished between a quantitative 'protopathic' and a qualitative 'epicritic' dimension (characterized by 'local sign'—i.e. by being located in time and space). It is the epicritic aspects of experience which are processed in systems that reach the cortex of the parietal lobe and other portions of the posterior cerebral convexity. 'Protocritic' (since the quantitative dimension is not restricted to pathology) processing involves the limbic forebrain (amygdala, accumbens, septal nuclei and the related cortical formations [Pribram & Kruger, 1954]) and the anterior frontal cortex, which, on the basis of much other research as well, can be considered as the intrinsic or 'association' cortex for these limbic structures (Pribram, 1954, 1958, 1959). It is this relationship of frontal cortex to the protocritic dimension that made frontal rather than parietal cortex the necessary choice for intervention in cases of intractable suffering.

Freud in the 'Project' (1950a) delineated a primary brain system (*Primär Gehirn*—his ψ system) which has many of the protocritic processing attributes of the nigrostriatal and frontolimbic forebrain systems I have here described as the substrate of a motivation/emotion mechanism. Freud, on the basis of the work of Magendie (1822) in Paris and of Karplus and Kreidl (1909) in Vienna was cognisant of metabolic 'drive' stimuli [*Triebfeder*] which were regulated by 'key' neurons to maintain the constancy of the internal environment of the organism (Magendie's 'milieu interieur', 1822; Cannon's homeostasis, 1929). Freud anchored his core mechanisms around an adrenalin-like secretion by the mechanism of the 'key' neurons: 'according to our theory, it would, to put it plainly, be a *'sympathetic ganglion'* (Freud, 1887–1902, p. 203). Pain was related to this system in the fact that the sympathetic system is triggered by actual noxious stimulation or threat thereof. Whenever the sympathetic system coped by maintaining constancy, the organism felt comfortable; whenever the limits of constancy were exceeded, the organism experienced pain and discomfort. When the limits of constancy were suddenly breached, affect was said to be generated; slower failures were experienced as 'unpleasure' (the basis of the pleasure principle) by virtue of the adrenalin-like secretions of the key neurons.

It is here that the model presented in the project gave Freud a great deal of trouble, much as it does today in any discussion that is based on an assumed buildup of 'unpleasure' or of 'psychic energy'. For Freud conscious experience is based on qualitative i.e.

organized, patterned neural processes, and he had a precise mechanism to account for it. The pleasure–unpleasure dimension, being quantitative and not patterned, should be inaccessible to consciousness. But we do experience pleasure and malaise (and also hunger, thirst, zest, nausea, appetite, lethargy, love, etc.). Freud wrestled throughout his life with the problem of how a quantitative energetic mechanism could result in qualitative conscious feelings. For a long time, he settled for a single-dimension 'pleasure–unpleasure' which reflected the quantitative homeostatic cycle—the action with equal and opposite reaction of the constancy principle, the first law of thermodynamics. He was terribly dissatisfied with this solution and attempted many alternatives. But not until the essays in *The Origins of Psychoanalysis* (Freud, 1887–1902) did he finally hit upon the correct solution: of course, to become available to consciousness, these processes must display patterns, despite the fact that they do not display local signs. The coordinates of the dimensions to these patterns need still to be established; they are not simply time and space. Much current research is devoted to analysing the complexity of neurochemical systems and their relationship to one another in the regulation of motivation and emotion and the feelings associated with these processes. This is perhaps the most active and promising field of research in the brain sciences. The basic homeostatic mechanisms reflected in the operations of various forebrain mechanisms become cognitively 'labelled' not only according to the relationships among internal states, but also with respect to the environmental situation (Freud's exigencies) in which they become manifest (Schachter & Singer, 1962). It is this cognitive discriminative component that makes the feelings conscious in the psychoanalytic sense (Matte-Blanco, 1975).

Cognitive competence and the problem of limited span: getting things done efficiently

The central concept in current studies on behavioural efficiency relates to the observation that it takes effort to overcome limitations in processing span. Living systems show a variety of limitations in *span*: in memory span (e.g. Miller, 1956; Simon, 1974;

Pribram, 1980a,b); in attention span (Broadbent, 1977; Kahneman, 1973; Pribram & McGuinness, 1975); and in executing what is intended (Miller, Galanter & Pribram, 1960). William James (1901) originally developed the theme that overcoming the limitations of span distinguishes conscious experience and willed action from automatic behaviour. Constructively overcoming automaticity involves the expenditure of energy; a person may be considered highly motivated but incompetent. Only when automaticity is overcome efficiently is there an expenditure of 'will' or 'effort' as the term is used by William James and in this essay. Effort can thus be thought of loosely as an expression of 'psychic entropy' rather than 'psychic energy', provided that once again we keep in mind that energy and entropy are simply inferences neutral to the mind/matter duality. In short, we will use 'effort' or 'will' as terms that relate to the efficiency with which limitations in span (due to constraints imposed by neurobehavioural or environmental organizations) are overcome.

Daniel Kahneman (1973) has reviewed a large body of behavioural evidence regarding the limitations in span. In his review he equates attention, arousal, effort and the capacity to process—as do most experimental psychologists working on these problems. When, however, biological and especially brain variables are included in the experiments, a clear distinction between several of these concepts can be made, and others are found incomplete and/or inaccurately described. Take, for instance, the idea that limitations on span are due to some fixed processing capacity that cannot be altered. True, there is a 'magical number' (Miller, 1956) of 'items' that can be processed more or less simultaneously, but true also is the fact that by grouping, chunking and contextualizing, what constitutes an 'item' can be radically changed in the direction of including many of the original 'items'. Experiments on the processing channels in the brain—channels made up of the sensory-motor pathways—show that as much as 98% by actual fibre count can be dispensed with, without significant impairment in discrimination behaviour (Galambos, Norton & Frommer, 1967). This is convincing evidence in favour of a sizeable pool of reserve capacity—thus limitations on span must be due to some factor(s) other than fixed capacity. A better candidate would be the efficiency or competence with which the sensory-motor channels are used; the way signals within them become grouped, chunked, and parsed. In a set of simple experiments some years ago, I demonstrated that the anterior frontal cortex of primates is critical to the development of such competence: by inserting pauses in a stream of items, a cognitive prosthesis was provided to monkeys with frontal resections so that they could perform tasks that they had hitherto failed to master. The prosthesis works much as do the pauses we use to distinguish words and phrases:

Deerseatoatsanddoeseatoatsandlittlelambseativy

is hard to decipher. Competencies are attained by appropriate pauses and punctuation and other forms of contextualizing a stream of items (Pribram, 1980c).

One major form of contextualizing is through reinforcing contingencies. Behaviour is shaped by punctuating and emphasizing certain consequences as if by placing an apostrophe at the end of a particular sequence of acts. Thus the sequence becomes fitted to a context—it becomes con-sequent. The process of reinforcement makes sequences of actions con-sequential. Reinforcers increase (or, if deterrents, decrease) the probability of recurrence of the behavioural sequence (in keeping with Skinner's behaviouristic definition—e.g. 1969). As might be expected, reinforcing (and deterring) contingencies (contexts) are relatively ineffective in guiding behaviour after lesions of the primate frontal cortex (as e.g. after frontal leucotomy, Pribram, 1959).

Additional experimentation showed that this deficiency in relating reinforcing contingencies to behaviour leads to a failure in arranging the behaviour according to the likelihood, the probability of occurrence, of the reinforcing contingency. Time estimation is not impaired—a steady stream of behaviour (or of withholding behaviour) occurs, until the occasion for reinforcement arrives. Most normal primates, whether human or nonhuman, tend, when reinforcements occur regularly, to take a respite after being reinforced and to gradually resume work in a crescendo that culminates (studying all night) just before the punctuating contingency (the exam). Not so after resection of their frontal cortex. The contextual boundaries that determine behaviour in probabilistic situations have become loosened (Pribram, 1969).

This is not the only aspect of efficient processing that has been related to brain function, however. Electrical stimulation as well as lesion studies have shown that the anterior frontal cortex and that of the posterior convexity are reciprocally related in influencing the receptive field of the cells in the primary sensory projection systems. Further, when the posterior cortex of the convexity (the intrinsic 'association' cortex, which lies between the extrinsic sensory and motor projection systems) is bilaterally resected, monkeys fail to sample as many alternatives as do their controls (including those with frontal lesions [Pribram, 1959]). Recall that Shannon's measurement of the amount of information processed depends on the probability with which a potential alternative is sampled. It is the cortex of the posterior convexity that determines the sample size being processed while the frontal cortex determines the deployment of probability distributions (based reinforcing contingencies) across that sample. In short, competence in processing is dependent on a sampling parameter established by the posterior convexity, and a probability variable based on chunking, grouping and parsing due to the operation of the frontal cortex.[1]

Conclusion

As we have seen in this chapter, Freud deals with primary energic mechanisms in terms of motivations (which he calls wishes) and emotions (unpleasure and affect) based on associative memory structures and feedback organizations. We are now in a position to ask whether the entropic, secondary cognitive processes as described in 'The project' (Freud, 1950a) bear any resemblance to the sampling parameter and probability deployment processes briefly described here. Specifically, we need to question whether the sampling parameter operates in a fashion similar to reality testing and whether the controls on the *probability variable, the parsing, chunking, and contextualizing* are in any way foreshadowed by some similar executive operations in the 'Project'. The answer to both questions is 'yes'. There is evidence from my laboratory that provides experimental data concerning these cognitive controls. Basic are studies that show that the primary

PERSONAL REALITY

PRIMARY PROCESSES

Energy, Work Related
Getting Things Done *Somehow*
and/or Being Hung-Up
Wishes, Dispositions

BIAS TO RISK

Emotions   Motivations

Affects   Memory Store

(Nigrostriatal
Systems)

(Limbic, i.e.
Accumbens/Septal
and Amygdala
Systems)

SECONDARY PROCESSES

Cognitive, Entropy Related
Getting Things Done *Efficiently*
Ego, Executive

BIAS TO CAUTION

Probability   Image and
Structures   Information Processing

Contextualizing   Choice Among
Chunking   Alternatives
                   Processing Proportions
                         and Ratios

(Frontal System)   (Posterior Convexity)

160

CONSCIOUSNESS

LOGIC/RATIONALITY

EXTRAPERSONAL SENSORY REALITY	PERSONAL REALITY	EXTRAPERSONAL MOTOR
Phenomenal	Protocritic	Behavioural
Epicritic	Intensive	Epicritic
Extensive	Context Determining	Extensive
Local Sign		Local Sign
Holonomic		Invariant
Spectral		Object Constancies
Correlational		Actions
Distributed		Communications

161

process emotion/motivation systems bias the organism to risk and that this bias is countered by a bias to caution which is imposed by the secondary, cognitive systems, those that deal with overcoming limited span. Next, it can be shown that working conjointly, these brain/behaviour systems operate to construct personal reality; that when the systems are damaged, agnosias and neglect syndromes result. There is also a still higher-order interaction: that between the systems involved in personal reality with those that construct extrapersonal or sensory reality to result in *consciousness*. Specifically, this relates to the various definitions of consciousness that arise in psychoanalysis, medicine and philosophy. A clarification of the conscious/unconscious distinction as used in psychoanalysis results. Finally, I want to mention another set of high-order interactions, those between the 'personal' systems and the *motor* systems of the brain that generate *behaviour*. Evidence can be presented to suggest that these interactions give rise to the natural *languages* in man and also in such language-like cultural structures as music and mathematics.

As noted at the outset, the intent of this chapter is to suggest that a neuropsychological theory as extensive as that presented by Freud in the 'Project' (1950a) can be constructed on current evidence. The parallels that are drawn between the two theories indicate a reservoir of nineteenth-century and twentieth-century knowledge that is common to both. It is additions to this common reservoir that will lead to modifications of the theory and any practice that is based on the theory. The reservoir also provides a frame within which psychology, psychiatry and psychoanalysis can conform to the natural sciences—the goal towards which Freud worked so hard.

NOTE

1. The importance of the chunking process, the resulting size of the chunk and the contextual boundaries that are set was illuminated by a conversation with Professor Robert Audley during the dinner following the inaugural lecture. Audley pointed out how even a simple problem can be wrongly answered by neglecting its context and using

habitual algorithms. As an example, he referred to the answer to the question, 'If I have two children and one of them is a boy, what is the probability that the other child is also male?' Most numerate people will vigorously defend their answer that the probability is one-half, based on their emphasis on the independence of successive births and their ingrained defence against the gambler's fallacy. They miss the import of the context 'one of them is a boy', which does not identify whether the boy is the younger or the older child. Thus the only outcomes under consideration are (boy, boy), (boy, girl) and (girl, boy), which are clearly equiprobable. Hence, if one child is a boy, the probability that the other is a boy is one-third!

CHAPTER TEN

The role of illusion
in the psychoanalytic cure

John Klauber

C ure by truth and by illusion are closely interwoven at the heart of psychoanalysis. The technique of psychoanalysis depends crucially on a phenomenon evoked by an act of psychic prestidigitation. That the technique depended on such an act was not consciously realized by Freud at first, though the adoption of the hypnotist's setting of the couch, with the analyst sitting out of the patient's view, accompanied at first by pressing the patient's head to evoke memories, suggests that he may have had some subliminal awareness of it. After all, quasimagical techniques were in the air: hypnotism itself, and experiments in the occult. Pierre Janet had already introduced himself consciously into his patients' hallucinations and acted a role there (quoted in Ellenberger, 1970). The act of psychic prestidigitation to which I am referring is the evocation by the setting of psychoanalysis of the phenomenon of transference, which Jung already described in 1907, to Freud's satisfaction, as the alpha and omega of psychoanalytic treatment. This is the area in which truth and illusion mingle inextricably, and the area where the constant attempt to extricate one from the other has increasingly become the main focus of therapy.

I ought to sketch out a brief description of transference. As used in psychoanalytic treatment, the transference refers to the displacement of conflictual wishes from an earlier relationship into the relationship with the analyst. Perhaps all our relationships have an important element of transference. But the analytical set-up of free association and the couch, designed to diminish the pull of reality, causes the transference elements to be experienced more sharply. To give examples: a migrant from a less developed community who has guiltily settled in England cannot resist the fantasy that the analyst is a cart-driver with a whip and thinks he can smell garlic on his breath; a woman athlete abandoned by her mother at eighteen months but warmly loved and encouraged by her grandmother finds her portly, middle-aged male analyst almost irresistible sexually; a man whose seductive actress–mother was always leaving him as a child is constantly afraid that the analyst will throw him out; a man with a phobia of eating in childhood and a tendency to indulge himself in adult life cannot rid himself of the strange compulsive thought 'Do analysts eat?'

The earliest (Breuer & Freud, 1893–95) recognized and unexpected form of transference was the falling in love of a woman patient (Anna O) with a male therapist—with Breuer, in fact, and then Freud. (Freud does not report the analysis of a male patient until 1909). It became apparent that this guilty falling in love had its precursor in the patient's wishes in childhood in relation to her father, and her fears of punishment by her mother—that is, in the normal culmination of the sexual development of the earliest years in the Oedipus complex. But by the early 1900s this would already have appeared to be a simplistic statement of the complexities of relationship that go to make the transference. Freud came to see that the transference uses a multiplicity of childhood relationships and often expresses them indirectly via other relationships, that it 'uses reality very skilfully' and that defences against the transference wishes are as important as the wishes themselves. The patient can thus be seen as repeating his past conflicts in a new and intensely felt relationship with the analyst, where they can be studied and resolved as their incongruity becomes manifest. By 1912 Freud was stating that the battles of analysis were fought out more and more during its course on the field of transference. Today, all psychoanalysts take up the manifestations of transference from the start.

I will give one brief example to illustrate how transference reveals itself from the beginning and can be interpreted. A man who was successful in a quite different profession decided he wanted to train as a psychoanalyst. During the interview he remarked that his experiences in a recent climbing expedition had convinced him that people were often called brave when in fact they were suicidal. What he was telling me about his life situation was that in giving up his career for a climbing expedition in psychoanalysis, he did not know whether he was being brave or suicidal, and he was appealing to me quite realistically as a psychoanalyst to help him determine which it was. But behind this, in the transference, as it turned out, he was putting me in the position of his elder brother, who had lured him on towards false ideals and squashed him whenever he tried to express his true personality. He was now watching me to see whether I would lure him on to false ideals or allow him to express his personality. Both could be represented by training to be a psychoanalyst, and true and illusory ideals were intertwined in a complex way in the aspiration.

Transference arises as a result of conflict, and in this example you can clearly see the resistance to becoming a psychoanalyst as well as the desire for it. Now transference is classically described as a resistance to analysis. It is a resistance because it is a way of behaving instead of remembering. But it immediately strikes one as a little pejorative to call transference a resistance when the whole analytical set-up is designed to induce it. After all, the development of transference manifestations, and particularly, as the analysis proceeds, the development of the neurotic conflict itself in relation to the analyst—that exacerbated form of transference known as transference neurosis—means that the patient is showing the analyst his illness in the only way he can, and experiencing it and watching it at the same time. The development of transference, distressing as some of the forms in which it shows itself may occasionally be, is an invitation to the analyst to help the patient discriminate the illusory from the real at an increasingly complex psychological depth and is for this reason a therapeutic experience. It was also noted long ago by Freud that as the neurotic conflict concentrates itself in the transference-neurosis, the patient's difficulties in his outside life are reduced.

It might be truer to say that, therapeutic as the transference experience is, there is an element in both patient and analyst—which resists it. Whatever varied motives the analyst's sitting behind the couch serves—and its main conscious *raison d'être* is to activate Freud's Magic Lantern for the manifestation of transference—it is also true that the analyst's calm, mirror-like attitude serves to protect him from the patient's emotions. In earlier days some analysts even wore white coats. I suspect that psychoanalytic theory sees the transference as primarily a resistance precisely because it is irresistible, and because both patient and analyst have such difficulty in relinquishing the relationship formed in the context of transference. Indeed, the danger of being carried away by emotion is a constant threat to both analyst and patient in their intimate relationship, and the jokes that are made about analysis—not to mention occasional unfortunate occurrences—testify to it. The prototype of such jokes is the male analyst who refuses a request by a woman patient with the words, 'I shouldn't even be on the couch with you'.

Almost every patient enters analysis reluctantly. His reluctance is articulated on two limbs. One is his fear of surrendering to the attraction of pure feeling, the other is his fear of being deprived of feeling. Two characters in Shaw's *Major Barbara* present the problem well: Todger Fairmile, the music-hall wrestler of whom Barbara reports that he 'wrestled against the Jap till his arm was going to break, but he wrestled against his salvation till his heart was going to break', and Barbara's father, Andrew Undershaft, who has known suffering as a foundling and an East-ender who understands the fear of losing feeling and quietly says to her, 'You have learnt something, that always feels at first as though you had lost something'.

Psychoanalysis began with the appreciation of the therapeutic effectiveness of discharging emotion—with the relief of hysterical symptoms of the cathartic method. Perhaps this has been in some respects undervalued since interpretation and understanding gained pride of place over the release of repressed memories. Of course, for several decades the aim of interpretation was regarded as the facilitation of this release, an aspiration that failed to recognize the evident truth that it remained largely an unrealizable ideal. But authors like Ernst Kris (1956a,b) have made us a little wary even of the ideal, making it clear that the sudden release of repressed memories has a traumatic quality. It results in the idealization of analysis, with the longing for another magic moment, and therefore may be regarded, at least in theory, as a sign of insufficiently subtle analysis of the defences holding the memories out of consciousness. If the defences are adequately analysed, the memories are not experienced by the patient as repressed. Freud had already recognized that this type of recall was a sign that the analysis was nearing completion. Modern analysis rests more on reconstruction and particularly reconstruction from the transference, with less insistence on direct confirmation by memory. In Bernfeld's (1932) words 'it does not so much reconstruct events as build a model of the mind'. The ideal model of analysis had already in Freud's day undergone a shift of emphasis from the direct emotional results of recall in favour of the growth of the synthetic functions of the personality.

In place of the English psychological jargon (which is supposed to represent Freud's direct and simple German) 'Where Id was there shall Ego be' (1933), I would prefer to translate '*Wo Es war soll Ich werden*' as 'What was It must become Me'. But it would be just as true to say of our patients, all of whom suffer predominantly from inhibitions, that their ideal of therapy is the converse—that 'What was Me should become It'. This is what the transference experience gives them.

I am now approaching the crux of my discussion. This is the nature and value of the therapeutic madness called transference induced by psychoanalysis. People will immediately object that I exaggerate if I call it madness. I agree that I exaggerate. The transference is marked by a striking invasion of the patient's normal sense of reality, and it displays confusional and, even in normal subjects, occasionally delusional features. But analysis would be impossible unless sanity were constantly regained. However, I do not wish to describe the forces that remain in control. I wish to describe the therapeutic value of the surrender to transference. Perhaps illusion would be a more suitable word than madness, especially if you will accept a tentative definition of illusion as a false belief accompanied by uncertainty as to whether it should be given credence. An illusion is produced by the break-through of unconscious emotion without consciousness surrendering to it completely. An illusion is a waking dream but somewhat less convincing.

There can be few cultures that have failed to recognize that dreams are valuable. In one way or another it has always been realized that they tell us something that we did not previously know about our feelings, and we hasten to communicate our dreams to those with whom we are intimate and get their reaction. The dream of the transference illusion confuses an old relationship with a new one. It therefore makes a comparison. The transference illusion is not simply a false perception or a false belief. It is the manifestation of the similarity of the subjective experience aroused by an event in the past and in the present. The illusion therefore represents a new piece of understanding, expressing itself, not in the language of logical thought, but in that of artistic creativity.

We do not normally explain the patient's illusions as comparisons. In the theory and practice of psychoanalysis we are preoccupied with the patient's epidiascope with which he projects his stock of emotional slides onto the analyst, whom we still try essentially to represent as a blank screen, though this has been modified in the last thirty years by the analysis of what is inexactly called the analyst's countertransference, that is to say, his response. I do not wish to question the general validity of this approach, which has become the back-bone of psychoanalytic technique. And the strength of the patient's illness, determined by the strength of his unresolved feelings, determines the inevitability of this projection. The transference illusion reduces his peripheral thoughts and his reactions to individual experiences to a common emotional bedrock.

Now when we know our feelings, we feel more real. Of course, coming to know our feelings is a process of discrimination. But it is the illusion in psychoanalysis that first brings the patient in touch with the reality of his feelings. I think that this is a very important reason why patients are so reluctant after analysis to acknowledge the illusory content of their transference. Dionysius is a frightening god. They would much rather explain how in reality their analyst was exactly as they perceived him. And I think that in over-stressing the value of interpretation, as in my opinion many analysts do (though Ferenczi, Bálint and Winnicott belonged to a different stream), psychoanalysts betray the same fear as their patients of the clarifying emotional power of illusion. The illusion, then, makes the patient feel more real and puts more emotion at his disposal. It has done him a valuable service, because we need access to illusions and dreams to live. Freud pointed out, for instance, that falling in love shows many of the characteristics of mental abnormality. We cannot live by reality alone. We need the illusions that touch reality 'With a celestial light'. That is why religion is so important in all societies, not excluding, however much we may object to religion, the esoteric forms that often pervade scientific societies. Its illusions give us the emotional courage to live beyond reality. It directs our faith, which Tolstoy (1903) defined as 'the force whereby we live'. In psychoanalysis the transference helps the patient not only to discriminate, but to imagine.

With this little hymn to the irrational, I am introducing my next point about the value of the transference experience. The feelings that are mustered by the analytic set-up, and experienced in relation to the analyst, are frustrated by him. What the analyst largely does is to interpret. Although he will also show his human feelings and understanding in a wider context than that of pure interpretation, his analytic skill—and, I suspect, his clinical success—can be measured by the degree to which his humanity is co-ordinated with his analytic function. Because the patient is forced by the analyst's interpretations to learn instead of to feel, he has to use the emotion aroused by analysis elsewhere.

I will quote what a woman in her thirties, speaking of a quite new phase of tenderness between herself and her lover of many years' standing, said to me, as I noted it down immediately after the session. 'I don't know whether I love him more because I love you. I don't know whether I substitute him for you. I think that because I trust you I can love him'. She then said, 'Love comes through knowing oneself. It may refer to God or to another person. But it is truth'.

What was truth and what was illusion in her attitude, and how were they related? Did she love me, or did she only love a mother or a father from early childhood as her memories of them came nearer to consciousness in the analysis and were projected onto me? Was the new tenderness in her relationship with her lover based on a transference of her feelings for an analyst whom she was idealizing and who was responding to her idealization? Or did a new absence of fear of her relationship with me (which was also a feature of that phase of analysis) release tender feelings for me which she could no longer control, so that she could only solve the problem of her frustration by displacing them onto her lover?

If loving me enabled her to love him more, then it may well have been, as she suspected, that he received what was really meant for me. Indeed, in part, it must have been so, because she not infrequently confused us. But if she loved him more because she trusted me, then her trusting me enabled her to make a generalization to the effect that 'men with certain characteristics can, after all, be trusted'. This would imply no confusion. This new trust would have removed her fear of him, and therefore her hostility, and thus allowed her for the first time to love him without ambivalence.

One of the problems of truth and illusion in transference love was broached by Freud (1915a) when, in a paper remarkable in its time for its capacity to deal coolly with a scandalous subject—but open to criticism today—he asked if it was 'genuine'. He concluded that it was as genuine as any. If it had clear sources in the infantile, so does all falling in love. That transference love was often used as a resistance against being analysed was neither here nor there, except for the technical difficulty of handling it. And he warned analysts that a woman patient would not take more kindly to her love being scorned than any other woman.

Freud did not discuss in any detail the difficulties that might arise if patients fell 'genuinely' in love with their analysts. For him it was the unavoidable consequence of a medical situation and had to be accepted as such. This assumed, of course, in Freud's simile, that the analyst could be relied on not to behave like the joker in the dog race for a garland of sausages who spoilt the race by throwing a single sausage onto the track. The woman would be free to use her newly won capacity for love in the service of her ordinary life. That is perhaps the situation that my patient was describing. That is to say, the transference illusion is of value not only as a technical aid to the resolution of the conflict that gives rise to it, but because the illusion can be carried on into life to give a new impetus to relationships and ideals with a less direct relationship to the original conflict.

The primary therapeutic illusion that enables the patient to equate one love object with another is that time does not exist. It is a similar therapeutic illusion to that which enabled the Narrator of *A la Recherche du Temps Perdu* (Proust, 1981) to know that he would become a great writer when he rescued the essence of an experience 'from the order of time' by equating the sensation of the uneveness of the paving stones in the courtyard of the Princesse de Guermantes on his way to her Matinée with the unevenness of the paving stones in St Mark's Baptistry in Venice, and the tinkle of the spoon against the plate when he entered the Library with the sound of the hammer against the wheels of the railway train stopped near a little wood. The patient, like Proust, has the illusion as the result of 'involuntary memory' that his experience exists outside time, and Freud and psychoanalysts in general (not to mention some idealist philosophers of history) have become the victims and the beneficiaries of the same illusion. The concept that experiences can be repeated is used in psychoanalysis as though Heraclitus had never lived. For instance, Freud defined happiness as the fulfilment of a childhood wish. But a childhood wish is never exactly fulfilled—only the transformed derivative of a childhood wish, and I believe that it brings joy and satisfaction rather than happiness. In fact, although Freud defines the Unconscious as being timeless—in spite of the many unconscious biological clocks that we have in our body—the recognition of the similarity of an emotional experience in time is immediately followed by an activation of the secondary process, which evaluates the experience and sets new ideals. It is what Proust called 'the miracle of an analogy' that liberates, and allows each memory, in the words of Howard Moss (1963), to be 'transfigured by the velocity of the future'.

I think that this is central to the concept of psychoanalytic cure. The experience of timelessness is a mystical experience of profound value, and an essential prerequisite of cure, but it is not the cure itself. Nor does the cure consist only in the secondary evaluation of the primary emotional experience. The cure consists in the fact that the patient's comparison and differentiation of the experience makes possible a new development in which he can again lose the power of discrimination in terms of a new unconscious synthesis of reality and illusion.

It is the continuity of this process that is at the centre of the patient's development, and it begins more than it ends with the analysis. During the time patient and analyst are together, a way of looking at the analytic experiences is unconsciously agreed between them. This area of common understanding, which enables the analysis to proceed, is, by the fact that two separate personalities are involved, of necessity limited. In my view, the patient can only develop his own analysis fully when he is free from the analyst, and from what has been called in an unpublished contribution by W. Zusman 'the modelling myth'.

It is therefore precisely his secondary criticism of his original analytic experiences and their interpretation that enables his real development as an individual, and not as a disciple, to take place. This is, of course, easier for the ordinary run of patients to accomplish than it is for those patients who are also psychoanalytic trainees and will have to continue to associate with their former analysts.

I think that it was of this development that my patient spoke when she said that knowing oneself could be equated with love and that this love did not possess an inherent direction, but might be for God, or for another person. I think that when she spoke of God she referred to a *logos*, an ordering principle that comes from self-scrutiny, leading to self-knowledge. I think she spoke of something like Proust's 'miracle of an analogy'. I think she meant that as one discriminates one's feelings better, they can also be experienced more sharply and therefore allow one to love another person, or an ideal, wholeheartedly. I think she spoke of the inner world and its possibilities that only self-knowledge can create, free from dependency on other mortals. She was speaking of her own inner order, and I have been attempting to translate what she described into a theory of psychoanalytic therapy. In psychoanalysis the *logos*, the Word, is inevitably made Flesh by the transference. This is another therapeutic illusion. But in a successful analysis the Flesh again becomes the Word.

CHAPTER ELEVEN

Perversion and the universal law

Janine Chasseguet-Smirgel

M an has always endeavoured to go beyond the narrow limits of his condition. I consider that perversion is one of the essential ways and means he applies in order to push forward the frontiers of what is possible and to unsettle reality. I see perversions not just as disorders of a sexual nature affecting a relatively small number of people (whose role and importance in the socio-cultural field can never, however, be overestimated) but—and this is one of the theses I wish to uphold—as a dimension of the human psyche in general, a temptation in the mind common to us all.

My studies and my clinical experience have led me to believe that there is a 'perverse core' latent within each one of us that is capable of being activated under certain circumstances. I hope to give you an insight into what I see as the wider implications of something that, at first sight, is merely a deviation—often a picturesque deviation—of sexual behaviour, recalling, for example, that perversion and perverse behaviour are particularly present at those times in the history of mankind that precede or go with major social and political upheavals: the Fall of the Roman Empire, as we know, coincided with a widespread decadence of behaviour. It has become a banality to connect the advent of Nazism with dissolute sexual behaviour, to the extent that several films show the proliferation of transvestite cabarets just before Hitler's assumption of power. I am thinking, in particular of 'Cabaret', 'The Serpent's Egg', and also 'Damned'. In this last, Visconti imagines that the main character indulges in incest with his mother, dresses up as Marlene Dietrich in 'Blue Angel', and rapes a little girl who, as a result, commits suicide. This is a hint of Matriosha's rape and suicide in 'The Devils' (Dostoevsky, 1873). Dostoevsky's Stavroguine belongs to a party of Russian nihilists. As a matter of fact, Dostoevsky was really describing the Netchaiev Group. As to the works of the Marquis de Sade (to which Dosteovsky refers, by the way, when Chatov accuses Stavroguine of being a debauchee), they are contemporary with the French Revolution, and the author's life is closely entangled with its significant developments.

A first hypothesis then comes to mind: should we not associate historical ruptures, which give an inkling of the advent of a new world, with the confusion between sexes and generations, peculiar to perversion, as if the hope for a new social and political reality went hand in hand with an attempt at destroying sexual reality and truth?

Now, in my opinion, the oedipal tragedy arises largely from the *chronological time-lag* that exists between the emergence of the boy's desire for his mother and the attainment of his full genital capacity. This time-lag is the result of pre-maturation in the human being, who is at birth less fully developed than are animals. It could even be at the root of the universal taboo of incest, where that which is forbidden is substituted for infantile impotence. (I refer here to certain concepts put forward by Béla Grunberger in 1966).

The bedrock of reality is created by the difference between the sexes and the difference between generations: the inevitable period of time separating a boy from his mother (for whom he is an inadequate sexual partner) and from his father (whose potent adult sexual organ he does not possess). When the child comes to recognize the complementary nature of his parents' genitality, he is reduced to feelings of his own smallness and inadequacy. Recognition of the difference between the sexes is thus bound up with recognition of the difference between the generations.

The *perverse temptation* leads one to accept pregenital desire and satisfactions (attainable by the small boy) as being equal, or even superior, to genital desires and satisfactions (attainable only by the father). Erosion of the double difference between the sexes and the generations is the pervert's objective. He is generally helped to reach it by his mother who, by her seductive attitude towards him and her corresponding rejection of his father, fosters in him the illusion that he has neither to grow up nor to reach maturity taking his father as a model in order to be her satisfactory partner.

The anal-sadistic universe and perversion

Regression to the anal-sadistic phase brings about the erosion of the double difference between the sexes and the generations—of all differences, in fact—and this regression seems to me to be consubstantial with perversion.

In some of my other works I have had occasion to turn to the author best placed to reveal the very essence of anality and sadism, the Marquis de Sade himself. In particular I have made a study of the Sadian setting; but I shall not return to that aspect today. Instead, I should like to examine in some detail the outcome of the process that goes on in the place I have likened to the digestive tract.

Sexual intercourse is naturally the theme present throughout this work. In Sade, it is always a group activity in which protagonists—building up extremely complex positions that are then unmade and transformed—are men and women, children and old people, virgins and whores, nuns and bawds, mothers and sons, fathers and daughters, brothers and sisters, uncles and nephews, noblemen and rabble: 'All will be higgledy-piggledy, all will wallow, on the flagstones, on the earth, and, like animals, will interchange, will mix, will commit incest, adultery and sodomy', such is one precept in the 'Code of Laws' of 'The 120 Days ...' (Sade, 1966, p. 56).[1] Sometimes the differences between sexes and ages would be abolished in an obvious way: one of the 'ceremonies' in the 'The 120 Days ...' takes the form of marriages arranged between children: 'Both were extraordinarily arrayed in the most formal dress, but also reversedly, that is to say, the little boy was costumed as a girl, the little girl wore boy's clothes' (ibid., p. 148). And likewise: 'That evening, the Bishop, in the guise of a woman, marries Antinoüs, whose rôle is that of a husband, and then, as a man he weds Celadon, whose rôle is that of a girl'. Antinoüs and Celadon are both children. Again, Noirceuil says to Juliette: 'For a long time I have been beset by a most extraordinary fantasy, Juliette, and I have been looking forward to your return, as you are the only person in the world with whom I can indulge it. I wish to get married twice in the same day: at ten in the morning I shall dress as a woman and marry a man; at noon, I shall dress as a man and marry a male homosexual in the guise of a woman. And in addition to this . . . I want a woman to do the same thing: and what woman other than you could indulge this fantasy? You must dress up as a man and marry a female homosexual at the same service in which I, as a woman, will be marrying a man; and then, you as a woman, will marry another female homosexual dressed as a man, while I, having put on clothes befitting my sex, will wed, as a man, a male homosexual dressed up as a girl' (Sade, 1967, 'Story of Juliette', 9, p. 569).

A permutation of the erotogenic zones and their functions also takes place and has the effect of making them interchangeable. *Mixture* could be considered the heading under which the whole of Sade's fantasy world is placed.

It is clear that, for Sade, incest is not in any way connected with the assuagement of a deep longing for the oedipal object, but with the abolition of 'children' as a category and 'parents' as a category. Expressed in more general terms, the pleasure connected with transgression is sustained by the fantasy that, in breaking down the barriers that separate man from woman, child from adult, mother from son, daughter from father, brother from sister, the erotogenic zones from each other and, in the case of murder, the molecules in the body from each other, it has *destroyed reality, thereby creating a new one, that of the anal universe where all differences are abolished.*

This, in essence, is the universe of the *sacrilege*, since every-thing—especially all that is taboo, forbidden or sacred—is devoured by an enormous grinding machine (the digestive tract) disintegrating the molecules in order to reduce the mass thus obtained to excrement. The erotogenic zones and different parts of the body become interchangeable and are metamorphosed by a kind of diabolical surgery.

In *'The New Justine'* (ibid.), there are, in fact, two sadistic surgeons, Rombeau and Rodin. Rodin will kill his daughter by taking out her womb. This is a demiurgic fantasy, of which I shall have more to say later. *The Sadian hero puts himself in the position of God and becomes, through a process of destruction, the creator of a new kind of reality.*

Here, I think it appropriate to quote a number of Sadian assertions on murder. At first sight, they would appear to be based on commonplace materialistic arguments. But on giving the matter more thought, we discover they are central to the understanding of Sade, sadism and perversion in general. Rombeau, discussing murder with Rodin, talks of 'these portions of disorganized matter we throw into the crucible of Nature, afford her the pleasure of *creating anew, under different forms*' (ibid., p. 263).

Now we have Bressac, talking to Justine: 'The power of destruction is not given to man; the most he can do is to *vary the forms*, but he hasn't the power to annihilate them. *Now all forms are equal in the eyes of Nature*; nothing is lost in the gigantic *cauldron* in which her variations are produced; every piece of matter that falls into it constantly springs forth *in other guises. And of what significance is it to her creative hand if this piece of flesh, which today conforms to the shape of a two-legged creature, is tomorrow brought forth as a thousand different insects?*' (ibid., p. 202).

Sade endlessly reiterates these ideas, and you can find dozens of examples in his work.

I think this recurring theme of the *changing of forms*—of man's ability not to annihilate things but to dissolve and metamorphose them—after breaking down the molecules, means that *all things* must revert to chaos, the original chaos that may be identified with excrement.

The materialistic reasoning of Sade when he speaks of the equality of man with an oyster, the equality of all human beings, the equality of Good and Evil, the equality of death and life and his denial of the body–soul dualism—ideas inherent in his 'philosophi-cal' arguments—reveals but one basic intention: *to reduce the universe to faeces*, or rather to annihilate the universe of dif-ferences (the genital universe) and put in its place the anal uni-verse in which all particles are equal and interchangeable.

The disharmony coming from prematuration in man and the distress and sense of helplessness that goes with it causes the human young to be dependent on the object for his survival.

Now this state of helplessness, distress and dependence is openly denied by Sade. Here, for instance, is a fragment of Bressac's conversation with Justine, before he slays his own mother: '... The creature I am destroying is my mother; so it is from this standpoint that we shall examine murder. ... The child is born; the mother feeds it. In performing this service for the child, we may be sure she (the mother) is directed by a natural feeling that prompts her to get rid of a secretion that might otherwise prove dangerous for her. Thus it is not the mother who is doing the child a service when she feeds him: on the contrary, it is the child who is performing a service for his mother. ... What! Must I owe a person something for doing me a favour I could perfectly well do without, something that fulfills a need in him alone? So it is clear that on every occasion in life a child finds himself in a position to dispose of his mother, he should do so without the slightest scruple; he should even do so purposefully, because he cannot but hate such a woman, and revenge is the fruit of hate, and murder, the means of revenge. So let him pitilessly slay this creature to whom he wrongfully imag-ines he owes so much; let him, without consideration, tear apart this breast that has suckled him' (ibid., pp. 209–210).

We have seen how Sade endlessly repeats the idea that Nature might be a *crucible*, a melting-pot, that is, the pot in which the chemical fusion of substances takes place. The Sadian hero identi-fies with her, a cruel and almighty mother, taking over the role of the originator of all creation, that of God himself. For this destruc-tion represents the creation of a new dimension, that of indifferen-tiation, confusion and chaos.

The Sadian hero actually becomes the grinding machine, the cauldron in which the universe will be dissolved. 'Would that some mechanic might discover a machine that would pulverize the world, he alone would deserve gratitude from Nature, since

Nature's hand is impatient to recreate a work ... that has failed at the first attempt' (the monk Clement, to Justine, ibid., p. 402).

And: 'One day, as I beheld the Etna, whose breast spewed forth flames, I wished I could become this famous volcano.—"Mouth of Hell", I cried, as I considered it, "if, like you, I could flood all the towns round about me, what tears I could cause to be shed!"' (Jerôme, another monk, ibid., p. 45).

Taking over the role of Creator by bringing about the anal universe implies the dethronement of the Creator. Many pages, especially in 'Justine' and 'Juliette', are concerned with atheistic professions of faith accompanied by insults and blasphemies towards God: 'God is shallow and ridiculous. ... We have nothing but contempt for this God you are foolish enough to believe in. ... He is a creature of the imagination' ('The New Justine', ibid., p. 130). 'Oh! Justine, how I loathe and detest this idea of God!'

God is an 'idiot', a 'baby's rattle', an 'unworthy phantom', a 'powerless, sterile illusion', a 'bizarre and disgusting idol', a 'bloody fool', a 'deified knave', a 'cunning impostor', a 'fool', a 'base character', and so on.

But, following the logic of the principle that requires everything to return to a state of confusion, God himself must undergo a transmutation and become faecal matter. When Bressac tries to convince Justine of 'the deception and stupidity' of religion (ibid., p. 179), he comes to a point when he tells her: '. . . This great God, the Creator of all we see, will deign to descend 10 or 12 million times every morning in the form of a piece of dough, to be digested by the faithful and soon to be transformed in their intestines into the vilest excrement ... and man will eat and defecate his God, because his God is good, and He is omnipotent' (ibid., p. 190).

For the Sadian hero it is a matter of reaching a state of complete merging, involving the modification of the order of Creation, the suppression of any notion of organization, structure, or division. It implies doing violence to Nature, eradicating the essence of things, and thus instituting the *absolute mixture*.

Let us not forget that 'The 120 Days ...' is considered to be 'a catalogue of perversions', and that perversions are intimately connected with actual sadism, as the need to abolish the (genital) universe of differences and thus subvert reality *means that perversion is inevitably sadistic.*

In fact, the abolition of differences prevents psychic suffering at all levels: feelings of inadequacy, castration, loss, absence and death no longer exist.

I should like to show how this universe is contrary in every detail to the one described in that text on which our Judaeo-Christian civilization is based.

The forbidden mixture: hybris and hybrid

First of all, I should like to remind you of some well-known passages from the Bible which, in *The Manual of Instruction in the Israelite Religion*, edited by the Grand Rabbi Deutsch (1976), are quoted as examples of the 'forbidden mixture'. Let us take first the famous commandment: 'Thou shalt not seethe a kid in his mother's milk'. This commandment is repeated several times in the Tora (Exodus XXIII–19; Exodus XXIV–26; Deuteronomy XIV–21).

Psychoanalysts usually read into this a formulation of the law against incest (the mother and the child being united by the same substance, milk). But an article called 'Prohibitions against simultaneous consumption of milk and flesh in orthodox Jewish Law' by Woolf (1945) goes a step further than this first approximation and puts forward hypotheses that are, in my opinion, more complete and more convincing. The author, basing his argument on a series of documents, points out that seething the kid in his mother's milk formed part of the worship of Astarte: '. . . That seething the kid in his mother's milk means placing the child back in its mother's belly, giving it into the full and undivided possession of the mother. The son belongs to the mother'. *The Biblical Commandment would represent an attempt to destroy the matriarchal law.* Consequently, the quality of *isolation* that characterizes ritual Jewish eating habits would be the result of the struggle of Jewish monotheism against the paganism all around it, a struggle not only of an external nature, but of an intrapsychic one as well. This hypothesis confronts us with the fact that 'the mixture' (milk and meat) implies *the exclusion of the father*, in favour of the union between the mother and the child.

In Leviticus XIX, verse 19, the Almighty says: 'Ye shall keep my statutes. Thou shalt not let thy cattle gender with a diverse kind; thou shalt not sow thy field with mingled seed; neither shall a garment mingled of linen and wool come upon thee'.

In Leviticus, chapter XVIII, verses 6–18, the Almighty lists the commandments more closely connected with incest. However, I should point out that the aim of all these commandments is to prevent the breaking down of the barriers that ensure that the essential nature of things is preserved:

6. None of you shall approach to any that is near of kin to him, to uncover their nakedness: I am the Lord.

7. The nakedness of thy father, or the nakedness of thy mother, shalt thou not uncover: she is thy mother; thou shalt not uncover her nakedness.

8. The nakedness of thy father's wife shalt thou not uncover: it is thy father's nakedness.

9. The nakedness of thy sister, the daughter of thy father, or daughter of thy mother, whether she be born at home, or born abroad, even their nakedness thou shalt not uncover.

10. The nakedness of thy son's daughter, or of thy daughter's daughter, even their nakedness thou shalt not uncover: for theirs is thine own nakedness.

11. The nakedness of thy father's wife's daughter, begotten of thy father, she is thy sister, thou shalt not uncover her nakedness.

12. Thou shalt not uncover the nakedness of thy father's sister: she is thy father's near kinswoman.

13. Thou shalt not uncover the nakedness of thy mother's sister: for she is thy mother's near kinswoman.

14. Thou shalt not uncover the nakedness of thy father's brother, thou shalt not approach to his wife: she is thine aunt.

15. Thou shalt not uncover the nakedness of thy daughter in law: she is thy son's wife: thou shalt not uncover her nakedness.

16. Thou shalt not uncover the nakedness of thy brother's wife: it is thy brother's nakedness.

17. Thou shalt not uncover the nakedness of a woman and her daughter, neither shalt thou take her son's daughter, or her

daughter's daughter, to uncover her nakedness: for they are her near kinswomen: it is wickedness.

18. Neither shalt though take a wife to her sister, to vex her, to uncover her nakedness, beside the other in her life time.

Verses 20–23 forbid adultery, the sacrifice of children to Moloch, homosexuality, intercourse of a man or a woman with an animal. We notice that this catalogue of commandments (a *negative catalogue*) corresponds almost exactly to the catalogue of transgressions (a positive catalogue) contained in the work of the Marquis de Sade, specifically '*The 120 Days ...*'. Let us take, for example, 'Passion', number 20 of the 3rd part (the 'Passions' are numbered after the fashion of verses in the Bible). We find here the coalescence of several Biblical prohibitions: 'In order to combine incest, adultery, sodomy and sacrilege he emboggers his married daughter with a host'.

We notice that Biblical prohibitions are based on a principle of division and separation. In pathology this quality appears as an *isolation* mechanism at the root of obsessional neurosis. We know that in this kind of neurosis anal-sadistic regression has replaced genitality, but that anal driving forces are subject to very intense defence techniques. Freud (1926d) associates isolation with the taboo of touching and bodily contact, whether it be aggressive or tender, with the object. In passing, I should like to put forward the idea that isolation in obsessional neurosis is a more generalized mechanism that tries to fight off the anal-sadistic desire for muddle and confusion. In this sense, it would take the form of a reaction-formation against the typically perverse ideas of indivisiveness and amalgam (the reduction of objects to faeces).

If we turn now to Genesis, we see that it is entirely based on principles of distinction, separation and differentiation:

In the beginning God created the Heaven and the Earth. And the Earth was without form and void ...

(God will bring order into this original chaos and divide it up): And God divided the Light from the Darkness ...

God said: 'Let there be a Firmament in the midst of the waters and let it divide the waters from the waters'.

And God made the Firmament and divided the waters which

were under the Firmament from the waters which were above
the Firmament ...

And God said: 'Let the earth bring forth grass, the herb yielding seed and the fruit tree yielding fruit after his kind, whose
seed is in itself, upon the earth': and it was so. And the earth
brought forth grass and herb yielding seed after his kind, and the
tree yielding fruit, whose seed was in itself, after his kind.

In the passage that follows, the adverbial phrase, 'after their
kind', is repeated like a leitmotiv. Now in this differentiation
between the species we see again an absence of intermingling or,
more precisely, an absence of hybridization. The commandment
not 'to sow thy field with mingled seed' is also translated as 'hybrid
seed'. The close connexion between the hybridization of seed,
materials or animals is clearly defined in Maîmonides' explanation of the Jews being forbidden to use lemons from trees that have
been grafted. This was to prevent the orgiastic practices that went
on when neighbouring people carried out the grafting: during the
ritual a couple would have sexual intercourse that was 'against
nature' (Eliade, 1956, p. 28). The man who does not respect the law
of differentiation challenges God. He creates new combinations of
new shapes and new kinds. He takes the place of the Creator and
becomes a demiurge. Notice that the word *hybrid* comes from the
Greek *hybris*, which means violence, excess, extremeness, out-
rageousness. *Hybris* is for the Greeks, we know, the greatest sin.
'And ye shall be as gods', the serpent said to Eve (Genesis, chapter
III, verse 5).

In Greek, the original meaning of 'nomos', the law, is 'that which
is divided up into parts'. Thus we find that the principle of separation is the foundation of the law. This leads to derivations which
seem to have only a remote connexion with the word: 'musical
mode', for example, and 'song'. We may understand the connexion
better if we take the meaning of 'anomos', 'without laws', which
gives us 'without rhythm', and 'a tune that isn't a tune'. A further
meaning of 'nomos' (the accent being on the second syllable) is
'division of land', 'province', 'pasture', 'grazing land': i.e. direct
applications of the principle of separation. The word 'noun' comes
from the Latin 'nomen', which, in turn, comes from 'nomos'. Now
the noun is a part of speech that names a person or a thing, that is

to say takes it out of chaos and confusion and gives it definition. And in fact Genesis relates the Story of Creation not merely as a time of separating and dividing, but—and, in my opinion, this comes to the same thing—one of *naming*. In verse 5, it says: 'God called the light "Day" and the darkness He called "Night"'. When He made the firmament (verse 7), 'God called the firmament "Heaven"' (verse 8), etc. Anomy, on the other hand, implies confusion and lack of differentiation in values.

We know Freud compared obsessional neurosis with a private religion (Freud, 1907b). I should like to put forward the hypothesis here that perversion is the equivalent of *Devil religion*. Indeed, I am borrowing Freud's words on the subject:

> I have an idea shaping in my mind that in the perversions, of which hysteria is the negative, we may have before us a residue of a primaeval sexual cult which, in the Semitic East (Moloch, Astarte) was once, perhaps still is, a religion. . . . Perverse actions are always the same—with a meaning and made on some pattern which it will be possible to understand. I dream, therefore, of a primaeval Devil religion, whose rites are carried on secretly, and I understand the severe therapy of the witches' judges'. [Letter to Fliess, 24 Jan. 1897, p. 243]

The Devil has obvious anal characteristics, but I have dealt with the regressive anal-sadistic element in perversion sufficiently to go on to look at another aspect of the devil: as *the rival of God*. The devil is a fallen angel who revolted against God. He is also called Lucifer—a name that only appeared in the fourth century. Lucifer is a perfect example of *Hybris*, of man's desire to discredit the power of the Father–Creator and put himself in His place.

Now it is perfectly clear that the pervert in general, and Sade in particular, sets out, consciously or unconsciously, to make a mockery of the law by turning it 'upside down'. So that teachers, charged with '*bringing up*' the child, will be, on the contrary, the means of his initiation into debauchery. The culmination of the deviation of the role of educator comes in 'Philosophy in the boudoir' with the sub-title 'or Teachers of immorality—dialogues for the education of young ladies'. We know what the aim of the work was: the erotic initiation of a young virgin into group love-making, homosexuality, incest and crime.

In 'The New Justine', it is God Himself who is consulted on sexual pleasures. From the mouth of an effigy of God, there fall rolls of paper on which are written injunctions to carry out such and such debauchery. They shout abuse at God: 'Despicable image of the most ludicrous nonentity, you, who are only at home in a bawdy house and useless, except for regulating the pleasures of the ass'. In 'The 120 Days ...', 'The Code of Laws' lays down the rules of debauchery. The same sort of thing is found in the statutes of 'The Society of the Friends of Crime'.

Subversion of the law, the parody of a religion devoted to the worship of God, seeks to reverse the way leading from indistinctness to separation and demarcation. We are very close to the worshippers of Satan here, and religions of the devil. A black mass is a parody of the sacrifice of Christ. In it the cross is placed upside down, or facing the wall, the mass is said backwards and the Tetragrammaton is pronounced the wrong way round and is accompanied by sexual orgies. In every case there is a reversal of values leading to a return to primal chaos. In my opinion, this reversal of a system of values is only the first stage in an operation whose end is the destruction of all values.

Down through the ages, philosophies, ideologies, myths and rites have been founded on the belief that we originate from primordial matter from which every other kind of matter will be created. Therefore, the transmutation of one element into another should be possible. This theory is at the centre of the alchemical conception of the world. I can quote here but two examples that demonstrate a belief in the possibility of creating a new kind of reality out of original chaos. This belief is linked, sometimes quite openly, with perversion; as in the case of dionysiac rites involving intersexual disguises. 'Their aim is regression to primordial confusion', writes Mircea Eliade (1962, p. 141), 'and their goal is the symbolical restoration of "chaos", the state of unity without differentiation that preceded the Creation. This return to confusion manifests itself in a supreme act of regeneration and an enormous increase in power.

The second example is found in the Gospel of Thomas, which was popular among the first gnostics. According to it, Christ said: 'When you make two human beings into one, and when you make the inside as the outside, and the outside as the inside and the top as the bottom! And if you make the male and female into one so that the male is no longer male and the female no longer female, then you will enter into the Kingdom.'

My hypothesis is that perversion represents a similar reconstitution of Chaos, out of which there arises a new kind of reality, that of the anal universe; this will take the place of the psychosexual genital dimension, that of the Father. The world of division and separation presupposes a three-dimensional psyche: between mother and son, the Father–Creator, but in fact, reality itself, introduces a barrier, that of incest, which Jeremiah, in the Bible, describes in such a beautiful metaphor: 'Will ye not tremble at my presence, which have placed the sand for the bound of the sea by a perpetual decree, that it cannot pass it?' (Jeremiah, chapter 5, verse 22). This bound or barrier is the prototype of all bounds or barriers, and, consequently, of all differences.

I should like to point out that at a certain level the anal-sadistic universe of confusion and homogenization constitutes an imitation or parody of the genital universe of the father. In fact, one could say that it appears in the history of the development of the individual as a preliminary sketch, a rough draft of genitality. It is only later on in life that it becomes an imitation of it. Freud's article, 'On transformations of instinct, as exemplified in anal eroticism' (1917c), is quite clear on this subject. In it the anal-sadistic phase appears not as just a specific mode of pregenital organization, but as a sort of protogenitality or pseudo-genitality in which objects, erotogenic sources and pleasures are adapted to the child's potential; contrary to objects, erotogenic zones and gratifications of a genital nature. According to Freud, the faecal mass or 'stick' foreshadows the genital penis, the production of stools becomes a prototype of child-birth (the infantile sexual theory of giving birth through the anus), the daily separation from the faeces is a precursor of castration, excrement in the rectum anticipates genital coitus. So if, in the course of development, the anal-sadistic phase represents a sort of 'trial gallop' on the part of the child towards adult genitality, to try and replace genitality by the stage that normally precedes it is to defy reality. It is an attempt to substitute a world of sham and pretence for reality. 'The Planet of the Apes' takes the place of a human world.

It was not my intention to condemn perversion any more than it was my intention to sing its praises. I simply wished to put it in a more general context than that in which it is perhaps usually seen: that of man's attempts to escape from his condition. The pervert is trying to free himself from the paternal universe and the law. He wants to create a new kind of reality and to dethrone God the Father: 'Yes, we are gods', says one of the Marquis de Sade's heroes (Saint-Fond).

I have also implicitly tried to show that ethics and the conception of reality were based on the same underlying principle.

NOTE

1. Quotations from de Sade's *'The 120 days ...'* are taken from the English translation; other de Sade translations from the French are the work of the translator of the present chapter.

CHAPTER TWELVE

Memory as preparation: developmental and psychoanalytic perspectives

Albert J. Solnit

Introduction

Developmentally, children, adolescents and adults have changing resources for remembering their lives and preparing themselves for life in the present and immediate future. Physical, emotional and cognitive resources are in a complex and dynamic interactional balance, unique for each individual, throughout the maturational and developmental continuum. However, each healthy person continuously yearns for and seeks to feel coherent within himself and with his group as an individual with a unique history. Intuitively, each person wants to think and act with a sense of integrity and wholeness in which there is no disabling or painful awareness of a division between affect, cognition and behaviour.

Preparing a child for a potentially traumatic experience is also a way of preparing the memory of that child for becoming an adolescent and adult. The plan to influence memory before the fact acknowledges that challenging, frightening, threatening events do not become static memories. In fact, memories of such events attract other thoughts and recollections that become available as a support for or as an obstacle to healthy development. Thus, remembering is closely tied to preparing. Preparing includes anticipation, which is embedded in remembering even if the task is a new one, never before encountered. Clinical observations and follow-up studies will be presented in order to explore how preparing and remembering are mutually influential and regularly reflect the unfolding of developmental needs and capacities throughout the life cycle. Observations from the psychoanalytic and other clinical situations will be used as a basis for these formulations. Most of the emphasis will fall into the areas in which, as Anna Freud (1965) put it, '. . . psycho-analytic theories can be applied profitably to preventive work'.

From historical and biographical observations, a number of inferences can be made about the inner mental life of children and adults. These inferences can in turn be elaborated and used to inform the question of how each person uses anticipation and memory, for example, in the care of the body, especially in regard to illness or injury. A derivative assumption has been made, i.e. each person seeks to feel coherent with regard to his present and future by having a sense of his past as sequential, comprehensible and as an inner guide for what lies ahead. In yearning for and seeking coherence, narrative 'truth' often will fill in for historical truth (Spence, 1982). Young children, before they have the capacity for logical thought and sequential remembering, need the continuity of the physical and psychological presence of their affectionate parents, their primary love objects, to provide such a recourse. Thus, in this way as in many others, parents provide auxiliary ego functions for the immature child.

Initially, the subject is approached from outside, i.e. observations of manifest behaviour become the empirical data from which inferences are made, predominantly those suggested by psychoanalytic theories of trauma, object relations and the ego and its mechanisms of defence, especially in its repressive functions. Other theoretical propositions that are often useful include lines of development and autonomous ego functions. Next the subject will be approached from how childhood appears in the psychoanalytic treatment of adults and children. In this section the subject will be approached from the inside, i.e. clinical psychoanalytic observations are the empirical data.

From clinical observations
Adults

Rosa

I first met Rosa after she had been a hospital patient for more than three weeks. She was referred to as a middle-aged Italian woman with a fever of unknown origin. Rosa's fever chart suggested a Pel Ebstein fever profile, which, along with her weight loss and anaemia, were indicative of a lymphomatous malignancy. However, the physical examination, blood count and smear did not confirm this grave diagnosis. I was uncomfortable about Rosa's despondency and felt overwhelmed by her thick chart filled with repeated examinations and laboratory tests, none of which were conclusive. Meanwhile, Rosa was wasting away. As I approached her, she smiled weakly and asked where I was from. Before I could answer she said, 'I can tell, your parents came from Italy. Are you married? I didn't correct her first assumption, but did inform her that I was unmarried. She hoped I would help her feel better, not only so she could leave the hospital but also because she had a favourite niece that she thought I would like to meet. When she felt well she would invite me over to her house for a good supper and to meet her niece.

I told Rosa that after she felt better we could look into her plan. Encouraged by Rosa's personal interest in me, I told her how puzzled I was about the beginning of her illness—what really happened? Rosa said that it had started three months earlier, soon after her 50th birthday. She first thought it was her menopause because she had hot flushes and did not feel her usual energy. I asked what she had done about those difficulties. She explained that she and her husband had gone to see their doctor, and that she had asked for a tonic. I asked her what the tonic was, and she thought for a moment, then suddenly blushed. I asked if she were having a hot flush. She smiled warmly and said no, she had just remembered something that was personal and that she had forgotten all about it until just now as we were talking. Then she explained that the usual tonic had not helped, so her doctor gave her a special treatment. With embarrassment she described how the physician took blood out of her husband's arm and injected it into her backside (pointing to her buttock). She said it was silly to feel upset by that but it seemed so personal.

I then asked about where she and her husband had grown up, and the history unfolded. She and her husband had been born in Sicily and had emigrated to the United States when they were young adults. Both had been strong and healthy, except that while they were in Sicily her husband had fevers and could not gain weight. After coming to the United States his fevers had disappeared. Since then they had always lived in Brooklyn, New York, and had never returned to Sicily.

The fevers began within a month of the intramuscular injection of blood, and we were able to identify *Plasmodia Malariae* as the cause of Rosa's fever, weight loss and anaemia.[1] She responded well to treatment and returned home soon thereafter.

In this case, Rosa was better able to remember what had happened to her after she became interested in me as a person who looked familiar and eligible for her niece. The repression barrier activated by forbidden erotic feelings and fantasies had been lifted when she felt comfortably stimulated by my interest. She was able then to become active on her own behalf by injecting herself into my personal life without being rejected or too directly gratified. One could say that she entertained acceptable erotic fantasies about me and her niece.

In feeling accepted by me and with my encouragement, Rosa was able to recover a repressed (or suppressed) memory that led to an accurate diagnosis and a specific treatment that was effective in eradicating the malaria.

After her treatment Rosa was very friendly, but she seemed to have dropped her personal interest in me. Probably the return of health also enabled her to be more realistic. In a speculative vein, she also may have lost her interest in me because in diagnosing her illness I was associated with the guilt she felt about the exciting, forbidden fantasies of having her husband's 'bad' blood injected into her buttocks and with the resulting 'evil' illness that required hospitalization and treatment.

Enabling Rosa to remember was the key that unlocked the door behind which her illness was hidden. My appearance and interest stimulated Rosa's interest in me, which became a preparation for Rosa to remember the injection and for me to recall what I knew about malaria. In that sense, remembering was a joint patient–doctor process that allowed us to identify and treat her illness.

In this presentation several interviews have been condensed into one narrative account. This could not have happened if there had not been the time and the setting for Rosa to talk and remember her life in Sicily, about the move to the New World, about her six children, about her husband's work and his fear of retirement. She was also able to express her depressed feelings about being past the child-bearing period, which she explained were the best years of her life. Psychoanalytic propositions will enable the reader to have further speculations about Rosa's sexual yearnings and fantasies.

Children

Johnny

Working with child and mother were essential in preparing Johnny for his hospitalization, surgery and recovery. The mother's fears, stemming from her own past experiences as a hospital patient, indicated that she would need special help in order to be supportive to Johnny. Assistance to the mother enabled her to feel increased confidence and competence which was vital for Johnny's preparation for the immediate hospitalization and surgical care. At the same time, Johnny's mother was able to prepare herself to provide him with essential support for the future, including the availability of a coherent, useful memory of his own past experiences.

Johnny, age 2½ years, had suffered for 18 months from repeated upper respiratory infections with severe head colds, earaches and hearing loss. His speech was garbled; his behaviour restless, destructive, and demanding. He suffered nightly from wakefulness and frequently came into his parents' room as they slept. He was the only child of a 23-year-old mother and a 27-year-old father, who was employed as a salesman. Johnny's mother had gone back to work as a full-time telephone operator when he was 6 months old. Her work schedule was irregular, and during those years Johnny's home life in the overindulgent but quarrelsome atmosphere of his grandparents' flat was chaotic. When he was 2, however, his mother gave up her job, and the family obtained an apartment of their own.

Despite this background, Johnny was said to be an easy-going child until his hospitalization at 20 months of age for the removal of a large nevus from his right arm. He was in hospital for three days. Visiting by his parents was not allowed. When he returned home, he was tense and irritable, fearful of his mother's departures and unable to play at any activity for more than a moment or two. His mother was puzzled and uncertain in her attempts to reassure him. At times she expressed her anger at Johnny for his restless, irritating behaviour.

When Johnny came to the outpatient clinic in his third year, his irritability and restlessness made examination difficult. He was found to have obstructing, scarred, inflamed tonsils and adenoids, but was otherwise physically normal. He was given symptomatic therapy. Hearing loss was noted, though it varied, and at times his hearing seemed normal. After several unsuccessful attempts to cure the problem with antibiotics, tonsillectomy and adenoidectomy were recommended, especially because of the persistent hearing loss. Johnny's mother was asked if she could come and stay with him in the hospital throughout his stay. Because of her own past hospital experiences she was apprehensive about this plan but dutifully agreed. A week before admission Johnny and his mother returned to the hospital by appointment to prepare for the hospitalization. In a playroom setting Johnny was invited to play with toys and to talk to the playnurse with the mother present. The nurse used age-appropriate language and a doll and a toy doctor set to explain the hospitalization, anaesthesia, surgery and other care to Johnny and his mother. They were also shown where Johnny would stay. The mother was encouraged and shown how she could play and talk with her son about the hospitalization and operation. She was advised to start this two days before admission. Then in a separate interview she discussed with the social worker anxieties she had about her own previous hospitalization and operations. Johnny played with the nurse during the mother's interview with the social worker.

Since Johnny had fears about the use of the toilet and was not yet toilet-trained, the hospital staff was asked to avoid all manipulations around the anus, such as would be involved in rectal temperatures, enemas or anaesthesia. They were also asked to help Johnny's mother in taking an active role in caring for Johnny in hospital and to encourage her to speak freely about her own uncertainties and fears.

Upon admission, Johnny played happily in the playroom with the other children. He slept well the first night with his mother in her own bed beside him in the hospital room. The following day, the nurse, whom he knew, gave him a pre-operative injection before breakfast, again explaining why he could not have anything to eat or drink. Then she took him to the operating room, as he had been told would happen. He was still awake when he reached the operating room and struggled for a few seconds while being anaesthetized.

The operation was carried out successfully, and Johnny's mother was present when he regained consciousness. She was able to reassure him from time to time as he would awaken and then drift off again. The following morning it was with reluctance that he left the playroom in order to return home. Three days later Johnny visited the hospital for the routine throat examination and was encouraged to play with the toys. He showed no fear on returning and seemed to have suffered no ill effects. He enjoyed playing with hospital toys he recognized in the waiting area.

A developmental examination, given 9 months later, showed that Johnny had made more than 12 months' progress in language, motor control and social adaptation in the interval. A nursery school was recommended. He had in the meantime become interested in and cooperative about his toilet-training. A significant turning point in the relationship between mother and son had occurred during the hospitalization. In the hospital Johnny's mother had been able to gain satisfaction and confidence from her ability to take care of her son effectively. As his physical health improved, she became proud of his progress and was able to relate to him with increasing affection and approval.

Johnny's case illustrates how a potentially traumatic experience was successfully averted. Due to an earlier traumatic hospitalization there had been an initial developmental maladaptation, further complicated by a troubled mother–child relationship. Effective preparation for and the success of the second hospitalization and surgery resulted in development-promoting experiences for child and mother, which compensated for and redirected the earlier developmental difficulty and their impaired relationship.

The mother's earlier anger at Johnny for his restless, dissatisfied behaviour was in part traced to her own guilt about his first hospitalization. In the second hospitalization, the preparation of child and mother supported the protective presence of the mother throughout the child's hospitalization, which, in turn, promoted the undoing of the traumatic effects that the earlier experience had produced. The subsequent improvement in physical health played a significant role in improving the child's disposition and consequently the mother–child relationship (Solnit, 1960). Concretely, Johnny's hearing and speech improved, and he was able to be active in and cheerful about his nursery school programme and in his social experiences at home and in the neighbourhood.

In Johnny's case the present became a planned opportunity for a reworking of the past. At the same time it was preparation for the future. In an important sense, the second hospitalization provided Johnny with memories that could mitigate or modify and reduce the importance of what he remembered from his first hospitalization. A defeat was transformed into a victory! He resumed his progressive development, including an active interest in asserting control of his anal sphincter. Johnny was able to revise his past memories and his future anticipations through his present experiences.

As my colleague, Dr Peter Neubauer (personal communication, 1983) has wondered, to what extent is a shared experience— mother with child in hospital—already evidence of being prepared? Does it also imply for the young child, as we think it does, that there is no substitute for the physical and psychological presence of the mother? The mother's 'magical' omnipotence is operational only when she is with the young child, especially if the infant's or toddler's capacity for object constancy is not yet firmly established or has been acquired only recently? Also, in Johnny's case, he and his mother were being prepared for what had been traumatic in the past, a previously devastating experience, which was negatively familiar and associated with a setback in Johnny's development in terms of ego and drive regression. Thus the preparation included an awareness of the negative valence of the memory of similar experiences in the past. By taking this into account, the health team enabled Johnny and his mother to transform specific disrupting and upsetting memories into a more coherent recollection in which the negative valence faded in its relative significance as a marker for new or anticipated experiences.

In another instance, memories of past soothing could be recalled as preparation for anticipated or threatening pain in the present.

Larry

Larry, 4½ years old, was hospitalized for anaemia and weight loss. After careful examination and evaluation, he was taken to surgery for what was presumed to be a neuroblastoma. Although his parents had been in the hospital with him a great deal, there had been no explicit preparation for the hospitalization, anaesthesia or surgery. It was assumed that he was too young to understand.

Larry cried fearfully as he was placed on the gurney and asked the intern, Dr Eztin, to stay with him. The young physician had become quite fond of this reflective, frightened, charming child and his parents. Dr Eztin accompanied Larry to the operating room, where Larry asked at each point what was going to happen next. The intern answered as best he could. As the anaesthetist prepared to induce Larry, the child was panic-stricken, looked at the masked men and women around him, glanced at those sitting on the benches of the old-fashioned amphitheatre, and said to his doctor, 'What are they going to do to me?' Dr Eztin became anxious and self-conscious, but his concern for Larry enabled him to take the child's hand and haltingly explain that the doctors and nurses wanted to help him with the growth in his tummy that made him feel weak and sick. Larry interrupted crying, 'No! Why does the man want to blow away the funny stuff?' Dr Eztin explained, 'He wants to give you a smell medicine so you can sleep. Then it won't hurt while the doctor takes out the growth in your tummy'. Larry cried out, 'Dr Eztin, sing me the song Mummy sings when I go to sleep!' The young doctor gulped and began to hum Brahms' Lullaby. Larry quieted down, clutched his doctor's hand and gradually accepted the anaesthetic induction.

Larry died two months later of his fulminating malignancy. He had often asked his mother or his doctor to sing him a quiet song.

Larry was holding on to his yearning for and memory of what was a soothing, safe closeness to his mother at a time of overwhelming fear. He made a desperate effort to use the past as he faced a frightening, dangerous present. Dr Eztin responded intuitively to the child's need. Realizing that he had not been prepared for this challenge by his academic and clinical education, he dipped into his own past for those memories, those experiences that would answer Larry's need. Dr. Eztin reflected, 'Isn't it ironic that my mother is the one who prepared me for that situation?'

Later, in his own analysis, Dr Eztin came to recognize that there had been an unrequited longing in his own childhood that had led him to his response to Larry. At the age of 5½, Dr Eztin had passed two weeks in fear and loneliness while his father and mother remained at the hospital with his sister, awaiting a crisis in the life-threatening illness of their infant daughter. He remembered that his mother had been away at bedtime and that he had missed being tucked in and having a good-night story or lullaby. Eventually Dr Eztin also remembered how worried he had been because he felt he hadn't called his mother soon enough when his little sister had become ill while he was watching her in the perambulator. At that time he thought that if he were older or knew more, he could have saved her from the life-threatening illness. Eventually, his sister made a full recovery, and he became a paediatrician. In a crucial sense Larry's and Dr Eztin's pasts were mingled in life-threatening illnesses. One child died, and the other survived.

Christina

As Freud said, 'since every such construction is an incomplete one, since it covers only a small fragment of the forgotten events, we are free to suppose that the patient is not in fact disputing what has been said to him but is basing his contradiction upon the part that has not yet been uncovered' (1937d).

In the next case, there was a sudden accident. This required constructing the past, remembering experiences for which there could be no preparation.

Christina, 3½ years old, was run down by an automobile as she darted across the road to warmly greet close friends. She suffered multiple communuted fractures of the skull, bifrontal lacerations and contusions of the brain, scalp lacerations, a fracture of the upper extremity and multiple abrasions and contusions, necessitating a wide bifrontal craniectomy,[2] immediate and repeated transfusions, a tracheotomy, and placement in a paediatric intensive care unit. Chrissy's parents were familiar with the hospital; as their daughter's life moved from precarious uncertainty to recovery, one of them was in the hospital by her side at all times.

To be most helpful to Chrissy, the parents needed to know in understandable detail what guided the professionals in their general precautionary care and in their planned and deliberate treatment of the child. As a result of this collaboration by the parents, we became more sharply aware of the psychological risks of the intensive care unit, and Chrissy was saved from several well-intentioned errors of care and treatment that are more common than we like to realize in the complex multi-service environment of such a children's ward.

One cannot speak too highly of the extraordinary scientific and technical knowledge, skill and competence that saved Chrissy's life and made possible a complete recovery. At the same time, an intensive care unit, by virtue of its vigorous monitoring demands, tends to dehumanize the care of patients, especially young children. Because of the informed dedication and tact of Chrissy's parents, the intensive-care staff cooperated fully with one of them staying with Chrissy throughout the acute phase of the hospitalization.

The presence of Chrissy's parents elaborated and consolidated the excellence of her medical and nursing care by maintaining a close human contact; by facilitating non-verbal communication that enabled Chrissy to know, as she entered the world of the living and full consciousness, that there was a safe and reassuring continuity that spanned the crevice of a traumatic disruption in her life and the care that enabled her to resume it.

What led to a successful physical recovery could have been accompanied by severe psychological trauma, which our study of this child suggested would have included a severe speech and learning problem. There was a good deal of persuasive evidence that the parents' presence, their availability to counselling by a child psychoanalyst with paediatric training, and their guidance of Chrissy were critical factors in her complete rehabilitation. For example, it appeared that not only Chrissy's brain damage but also her extreme apprehensiveness were involved in her initial inability to verbalize. It may never be possible in reconstructing that psycho-neuro-physiological difficulty to elucidate how much Chrissy's recovery of her speech resulted from neurological healing and how much resulted from overcoming her fear that speaking would lead to catastrophic consequences[3] (i.e. she rushed joyously across the street and was struck by the automobile just as she was warmly greeting her good friends). It is not crucial to know how important the cortical brain factors and how important the psychological factors were in this impairment of function. Both were involved, and both required attention in her slow, at times arduous, but full recovery of speech. The parents were advised that it would help Chrissy to recover if they enabled her to understand, gradually and as she was interested, what had happened just before the accident, about the accident itself, and the ongoing treatment—to fill the gap in the story of her life by helping her construct and reconstruct her past so it was continuous and coherent, not necessarily complete in each detail.

Several years after, in reviewing the accident and Chrissy's recovery, her mother said in a letter to me

> ... we were advised and encouraged to do all we could to verbalize explanations to Christina, starting long before she fully recovered consciousness, as to what was happening to her, why

the bandage, why the cast, why the trache, catheter, etc., and then to explain, first simply, and soon in quite precise detail, the story of the accident, which has proved, we think, to be helpful not only in the short but also the long run, i.e. the last 2½ years. Christina has consistently shown the ability to handle questions from kids and others quite matter of factly about why she wears an attractive fiberglass helmet (a different one each day), has restrictions on activities, and how the accident happened. (She used to tell people, 'I have a soft head,' which was a little puzzling to people who did not know the details!) She has never been afraid of cars, nor of crossing the road. I don't know how unusual this adaptation is, but it certainly has been welcome.'

The mother's letter continued,

We had thought of explanations (regarding Chrissy's initial speech difficulty) along the following lines: (1) Since speech is the last faculty to be learned, it would naturally be the last to return. (2) We felt it was somehow related to those few frightening days for her when she was fully conscious but literally could not speak because of the trache. (She tried to make noises a couple of times, looked quite bewildered when nothing came out, and then stopped trying.) (3) Once the trache was removed, she *decided* in some sense to maintain control, by rather clearly refusing to try to talk, in this one area, when she had lost control over so many other areas of previous autonomy, i.e. bladder, bowel, feeding, etc. It was fascinating to us to observe how quickly and efficiently a child learns to communicate in sign language all of her essential needs. And it was significant that her first words (after 4½ weeks without any) were spoken in the middle of the night when her gestures could not be seen and when she had to wake me up with 'Mama, I want water.'

As Chrissy recovered and developed, she continued to fill in and rework her memory of the accident and its aftermath. What seemed apparent was her persistent effort to be able to explain it to herself by explaining it to others when they asked. The daily use of the attractive fiberglass bonnet-helmets called attention to her difference, so she had no need to initiate conversations about her 'head'. In a sense, the fiberglass helmet was a continuing, realistic reminder of what had to be remembered and reworked until it made sense to Chrissy at each phase of her development.

By the time Chrissy was 8 years old, she could explain factually what had happened to her when she was 3½ and why she wore attractive fiberglass helmets to protect her head which had a large part of the skull bone missing. Still, she suppressed most of the unpleasant aspects of her treatment and experiences concerning the accident and the recovery from it in the hospital.

However, her parents have supported her continued efforts to cope with or prepare for the present and future by sustaining the construction, revisions and continuity of the past as it is reshaped by the experiences and demands of the present and near future as well as by her progressive development.

With Chrissy's and her parents' permission, we have a vivid illustration of how she continues to use the ongoing constructions of the past in the service of and as preparation for the present and near future. As Freud (1937d) said, 'Instead of taking an example of this from an analysis (which would be easy to find out but lengthy to describe) I prefer to give an account of a small extra-analytical experience which presents a similar situation ... strikingly ...' (p. 263).

When she was 17 years of age, Chrissy was admitted to a prestigious university (actually to several) and began her matriculation there after spending a year abroad on her own. The following is part of an essay written by Chrissy as the autobiographical sketch required to complete her application to that university.

Her essay is entitled,

'Ten years in the life of a hard hat'.[4]

'I have a soft head.' This is my explanation to strangers of the decorated helmet that I wore from age three to age fourteen. When I was three years old I was hit by a car and suffered severe skull fractures to my forehead and the right side of my skull. During the brain surgery the surgeons had to remove the fractured bone, leaving a large gap in my skull. The doctors decided not to insert a metal or plastic plate, which was often done in similar cases, because there was not enough bone left in the forehead to make a firm anchor. Instead, they decided to see how much bone would grow back and await the development of new technology. To protect my brain in the meantime I wore a polo-style helmet, highly decorated with colorful stickers.

This experience of being different from the crowd had many effects on my personality and growth, some of which remained even after the helmet came off. As I reflect on the different ways that wearing a helmet has affected me, I realize that they cannot be neatly classified as positive or negative. Often they were a mixture of the two. Overall, I believe this experience was valuable and caused me to develop in ways different from, and in some ways faster than, many of my peers.

During the ten years with my helmet I seldom met children or adults I didn't know without some sort of comment (usually intended kindly) being thrown at me. The most common of these 'one-liners' were: 'Hey, girl, where's your motorbike?' 'Are they dropping bombs?' and 'Has World War III started already?' When I was young, I thought all of this was very humorous and even enjoyed the attention. As I got older, however, personal appearance became more important and I became self-conscious about being different in appearance; the comments became repetitive and irritating. If I was in a large group, I would sometimes 'hang back', trying to hide like a turtle under its shell, in anticipation of the comments which I knew would come.

Many people thought I was strange because I was different, and it was occasionally hard to make friends; I usually had a few good friends rather than hanging around with a large group. Although this was sometimes lonely, it taught me to be independent and to value my friendships highly.

When I reached school age, my parents decided that kindergarten, with its roughhousing and tree-climbing, was too dangerous for me, and I was put straight into the first grade. As a consequence, I have been one of the youngest students in my grade each year. Possibly as a result of this, I have almost always gotten along with people older than I and now often find that I enjoy them more than those exactly my age. *When I now look back on my 'helmet period', I realize that dealing with my situation caused me to have a greater independence, responsibility, and to have a more serious perspective than many children my age.* This could be another reason that I have always sought out older friends. I also learned to get along with adults very well, perhaps because they often gave me special treatment. My most enjoyable experience recently has been working at a day camp the last two summers. The camp staff was a diverse group of very interesting people, most older than I, and I especially enjoyed working with them in musical and dramatic projects and sharing some adult responsibility with them.

For several years immediately following the accident, my parents were very protective of me. All of the corners on our furniture were padded. I was not allowed to ride a tricycle, climb trees, or participate in other potentially dangerous activities. Sometimes this caused me to feel left out among my peers. As I got older, I was given more freedom in small steps; I didn't learn to ride a bicycle until the fifth grade. In junior high, I was permitted to do some limited skiing and also went on a rock-climbing trip with my grade.

Because of these restrictions, needless to say, I was not the greatest athlete of my class! To make matters worse, when I finally got up my courage to join a community soccer league, I was declared ineligible because the rulebook stated that players could not wear protective headgear.

Despite all the drawbacks of wearing a helmet, however, I did learn to take advantage of it in certain situations. E.g., I learned to exploit my situation at home. Whenever my younger brother and I got into a fight, I would take off my helmet and taunt, 'Ha, ha! You can't hit me now!' My use of the helmet as a weapon in these battles undoubtedly infuriated him.

My unusual situation also led me to have an interest in other people who were 'different'. As a child, I read many books about other children who were physically or mentally handicapped or had a fatal disease. My favourite book of this type was *Eric* by Doris Lund, the true story of a 17-year-old's struggle with leukemia. I also very much enjoyed John Gunther's *Death Be Not Proud*. In the eighth grade I began volunteer work in a recreational program for the handicapped and became a good friend of one of the participants, John, a blind and deaf man about 35 years old. Because John was blind he did not know about my helmet, but I felt that my own handicap produced a special bond with him.

Three years ago, I went to a distant general hospital where surgeons were developing a new technique in reconstructive surgery. In my case, it involved combining a rib and 'bone paste' ground from the hip bone with a plastic mesh which was screwed into my skull in such a way that I could actually grow a new forehead. Fortunately, my doctors at the time of the accident had been correct; ten years later, a completely new technique for replacing large amounts of missing bone had been developed. My parents had always told me that one day I would have an operation and would not have to wear my helmet anymore. For this reason I never had any doubts about going ahead with the surgery, in spite of its risks and uncertainty about its success.

Two weeks after the surgery, I was out of the hospital and finally became 'one of the crowd' for the first time that I could remember, except that I felt a little self-conscious about the wig I wore until my hair grew back. It was quite a shock for me to suddenly become a completely normal-looking teenager, and the adjustment was very slow. I would occasionally still catch myself feeling different and 'hanging back' in groups even though there was no longer a reason for it, and this still happens sometimes. But I am getting used to and enjoying the fact that people whom I have gotten to know after the surgery don't know about my helmet.

I feel that my years as a hard hat were very valuable. I learned that one can be different and still get along, and I think that this lesson helped me to resist peer pressure to conform, resulting in greater independence. I also learned to accept situations that can't be changed. However, it is possible that this has also made me less likely to try to change situations.

Life as 'the girl with the helmet' certainly had both good and bad aspects. I occasionally find myself missing my helmet when I'm feeling too 'normal' and want to be different again. (When I had to wear it, however, I would have often done anything to get rid of it!) I now look back on that time with a smile realizing that, on balance, it was very constructive. However, it is not something I would recommend for everybody!

From psychoanalytic observations

In psychoanalytic treatment we rely on approximations of memory. In recovering memories about childhood from the psychoanalytic treatment of an adult, we expect that there will be an emotional quality that is similar to or derivative of the original experience that enables the analysand to achieve a sense of conviction about the past through reexperiencing a past event or emotionally charged experiences. Usually, this remembering is an updated version of the past, displaced or transferred onto the analyst. Subsequently, through reconstructing the past, the discrepancy between the feelings about the analyst and the reality of the psychoanalytic treatment are worked out as part of the psychoanalytic treatment process. In this way a partial 'reliving of the past' becomes crucial for understanding the analysand's neurotic difficulties as well as his developmental characteristics, personality make-up and symptomatic difficulties for which the analysand has sought treatment.

The following account focusses on part of the psychoanalytic treatment of an adult who had been well known to us as a parent of a child treated at our Centre. The clinical psychoanalytic material provides an inside view of memory failure and how the treatment process enabled the analysand to use remembering to overcome maladaptive behaviour and as preparation for new situations.

Harry

Harry, 35, married and father of two children, sought treatment because of his repeated, unnecessary destructive disputes with his boss in a middle-sized engineering firm. Psychoanalytic treatment revealed that he also suffered from a chronic marital difficulty. He felt his wife did not respect him. There were frequent outbursts in which he sulked, felt put down and withdrew into spiteful, stony silences, to the detriment of the marital relationship and with negative effects on his two daughters, who felt rejected by him.

In the psychoanalytic treatment, two lines of memory were opened up which he had been living out neurotically but did not remember. The first was the recall of having been sick and confined to bed for six months at the age of 13. As he reconstructed the illness in his psychoanalytic treatment, he had been diagnosed as having a streptococcus infection, and the family doctor explained that he could damage his heart if he did not remain in bed quietly for six months. He then brought up a clear memory of his father sternly warning him not to move or he would damage himself. As we examined the clarity of this new screening memory, the patient gradually recalled that his mother and father had been very worried that he's be too restless in his sleep and had tied his hands and feet to the bed frame to keep him from moving. In the transference, he felt 'tied down' by the analysis. He recalled his anger at his parents and his fear of damaging himself. Later in the analysis we were able to reconstruct his deep conviction that he had made himself sick through masturbation associated with exciting phantasies of being overwhelmed by a strong woman, i.e., being forced to have sex with a woman.

Although this first line of recall was far from precise, it made sense to him and explained why he had been out of school for six months, a memory gap that had always puzzled him. It also led to his understanding why he was always trying to trap his boss into errors that led to anxious confrontations in which the patient felt put down, became compliant and felt relieved and depressed.

In the next two years the patient's relationship to his boss gradually changed. He was promoted several times, until he reached a managerial level that was highly satisfying and in which he now was the boss of a large number of employees. He felt he was especially skilled in helping young 'hell-raisers' when they entered the firm under his tutelage.

As he reached the end of his treatment, with improvement in his working capacities and satisfaction, he filled in further gaps in his memory. For the first time since adolescence, he recalled that when he returned to school after six months of illness, he used to play basketball after school despite his father's threatening prohibition. The father had indicated that since he had had the infection and might have weakened his heart, he should not engage in any vigorous competitive sports. He remembered that he had to play, not only for the fun of it (he dearly loved and was highly skilled in such sports), but also because he was so anxious about falling ill again that in a counter phobic way he had to face the danger of competitive sports to find out if he was all right. Furthermore, he could not resist the pleasure it gave him once he allowed himself to think of playing the game.

In the analysis it was clear that playing basketball was also equated with masturbation. As he would begin each game, he felt a mounting irresistible pleasure and tension with anxiety after which he felt relief that he had not died or fallen ill again. Once again he felt that he had passed through a dangerous situation. Subsequently, after graduating from high school and looking for work, he gave up sports and took what he felt would be a safe job which would not be too competitive. It was clear that he arranged for and accepted limits in his education and work that unconsciously he felt would offer safety and would avoid the danger of competition and greater satisfaction. In the analytic treatment it became clear that he felt that he had 'damaged' himself and might damage himself further if he was too amibitious or competitive.

The second line of remembering was the painful feeling that his father had preferred his older sister and that his mother, though more even in her affections, never took his side when the father and older sister seemed to gang up on him. This was reconstructed both in the transference (he was certain that the analyst preferred the woman patient that preceded him) and in clarifying his ongoing distortions of his relationship to his wife, when he would perceive his criticism and anger at her as her lack of respect for him. His sulkiness and stony silence were updated replicas of how he had acted when he felt let down by his father's preference for the sister and especially because mother did not seem to take his side. At those times he felt that no one really admired and cared for him.

As Harry recovered these memories and replaced unconsciously motivated destructive behaviour at work and at home with the conscious memories of traumas and sense of deprivation, his recollections became worked through. He came to understand how he arranged to have his difficulties at work and at home; that he had been making choices about his way of shaping his personal relationships that served unconscious motives. These motives represented a neurotic residue of past burdens of trauma and deprivation. In his psychoanalytic treatment and in his life experiences Harry learned that he could make other choices about his relationships once he was more aware of himself and how he behaved. Remembering liberated him. It enabled him to know the story of his life more coherently, though it did not provide him with a historically complete and accurate narrative about himself. Then, he was able to gain relief from his persistent destructive behaviour pattern at home and at work, especially at work.

In using the psychoanalytic treatment process, Harry uncovered the gaps in his memory and gained a more coherent view of himself in his current situation and as a preparation for future life experiences. As Freud had predicted in 1912, the patient said, 'Of course, I've always known about these matters, only I never thought about them'.

In Harry's case, Loewald (1978) would say, 'The movement from unconscious to conscious experience, from the instinctual life of the id to the reflective, purposeful life of the ego, means taking responsibility for one's own history, the history that has been lived and the history in the making'.

Discussion

Psychoanalysis has called attention to the many ways in which remembering is blocked or distorted and how 'forgetting' can become a painful or costly psychological burden. Preparing a child or adult for a planned or expected threatening event, or helping a child or adult cope with, remember and integrate an unexpected ovewhelming event, are similar ways of preventing the damaging, depleting effects of undesirable repression and its derivatives. The aim is to safeguard the individual's capacity to feel coherent. The psychoanalytic theory of trauma and the assumption of a protective barrier that has limits to what it can protect against are useful ways in which to approach this risk factor, i.e. the risk of incoherency in human development.

Throughout, two assumptions are taken for granted, though each deserves further systematic investigation. The first is that the repression barrier to the first four or five years of life, the infantile amnesia, is desirable and development-promoting in the healthy child. The second is that the undoing or prevention of repression is viewed as desirable after noxious or traumatic experiences *when there are better or more tolerable present and future alternatives*. Denial and repression may be the least detrimental alternatives if the present and future provide unlimited and unremitting deprivation, trauma and disruption—e.g. remembering might not be preventive if the child or adult is the victim of continuing or recurrent Holocaust conditions. Thus, this application of psychoanalytic theory as a preventive measure is applicable and useful in a non-Holocaust world, one of reasonable order, continuity and peace. Children and their parents need (and deserve) a world in which life can be worth living and remembering.

At nodal points of development—what we can term normal developmental crises—past familiar experiences become a basis for preparing for what lies ahead. Thus, preparing and remembering are interdependent. What has been negative, traumatic or overwhelming can become a negative preparation for subsequent or new experiences. Similarly, if remembering is realistic, a trial action that repeats the past and adds to it the integrative quality of an active memory includes a dimension of working through and working out unrealistic past attitudes and expectations that otherwise would ill prepare the child and adult for what happens next. Remembering can be anticipatory of active understanding and problem solving, a crucial aspect of preparing for what had happened—the reworking of memory—and for what will happen in an appropriate and adequate way. These responses to the past, present and immediate future range from perception to remembering and from remembering to anticipation in preparation for mastery. Thus, the mobilization of inner and outer resources (mentally, emotionally and socially) can lead from cognitive comprehension to the practice of trial actions of remembering and anticipating, which, in turn, can lead to mastery even when the event, e.g. surgery, is painful and threatening.

Remembering and preparing may be useless and even undesirable when the outcome is fatal or leads to a life that is not worth living. It should be underscored that remembering is selective, not always appropriate and almost never completely accurate from an objective point of view. Remembering as useful preparation is best before the fact. However, an unexpected, sudden demand for preparation—e.g. a severe auto accident—produces psychological trauma that can only be worked out after the fact. Both before and after the fact it is the selective use of remembering, including the dosage and the sequence, that can enable the individual to grasp and integrate the experience, i.e. to work with it, rather than to be overwhelmed, shattered and permanently burdened with memories that distort and crowd out the realities of the present.

Preparing a child for a potentially traumatic event is also a way of preparing the memory of that child. Such an effort to influence memory before the fact is an acknowledgement that challenging events do not leave a static residue but, in fact, become dynamic memories that attract other longings, feelings and recollections. These memories may serve defensive as well as adaptive functions and are the background for each person's search for a coherent sense of himself. This search expresses a basic psychological need that must be met if that person is to achieve a realistic view of himself. A person cannot feel confident and worthwhile if he feels separated into isolated parts that cannot be integrated. In the maturing person, self-definition requires a sense of coherency, i.e. knowing oneself sufficiently well to have a confident sense of uniqueness, who one is, who one has been and with whom one belongs. The objective historical truth may be less important than the conviction of coherency that is yearned for and needed, and that is essential for the mastery of most developmental tasks after infancy.

This need for coherency, requiring a delicate balance of historical truth and subjective processing, refers to the development of a sense of personal history that serves adaptation and progressive development. Either too little or too complete a foundation in objective historical fact may mislead the quest for inner coherency and impede developmental progress.

Thus, a person's reliance on a partial history—i.e. too incomplete and fragmented, or one comprised of significant, persistent distortions of reality—is likely to lead to unrealistic assessments of self-worth and is bound to fail, fostering a sense of inner chaos or a fragile 'pseudo-coherency'. This false coherency usually serves neurotic rather than healthy defenses and renders unavailable a more authentic sense of coherency, that inner confidence that expresses conviction about one's personal integrity. Without this reality-based inner conviction, the individual cannot attain a realistic sense of his self-esteem and confidence in his own present and future.

On the other hand, coherency does not evolve from a complete and accurate memory of historical fact. The unyielding imposition of such 'total' facts may, indeed, become an unhealthy burden to the individual when total recall dominates and restricts his life and replaces his capacity to discern the available choices and to use his free will to select the alternative he prefers.

DP—H*

We are not striving for the full recovery of historical truth, but rather for a knowledge of one's life and family that may serve sufficiently as the logical latticework for each person's 'narrative'. The personal, descriptive narrative, a mix of subjective and objective accounts of one's life experiences, is modified, condensed, and at times reduced in proceeding through the developmental landscape, enabling each person to approximate the story of his or her life with a sense of coherency.

Ernst Kris (1956b), distinguished psychoanalyst and art historian, took up the same issues when he said,

> The bent to link present to past experience reflects the very structure of man's mental apparatus. It is part and parcel of many types of introspection and in higher civilizations, part of the tradition of contemplative and speculative thinking. The study of the *interaction* between past and present stood at the beginning of psychoanalytic work and has remained *alive* throughout its development. An *interaction* it is. Not only does the present experience rest on the past, but the present supplies the incentive for the viewing of the past; the present selects, colours and modifies. Memory, at least autobiographical or personal memory, i.e. the least autonomous area of memory function, is dynamic and telescopic ... . the earliest memory functions arise in the refinding of the needed and later of the *beloved* object. 'Out of this matrix all memory functions emerge.

In conclusion

Remembering the process that leads to memory has two important functions: the first is coping for mastery, and the second is to prepare for future events and development. As Milos Kundera (1980) says in *The Book of Laughter and Forgetting*, 'The future is an apathetic void of no interest to anyone'. Whereas, 'The past is full of life eager to irritate us, provoke and insult us, tempt us to destroy or repaint it. The reason people want to be masters of the future is to change the past'. He then states that forgetting is '. . . the great private problem of man; a death as the loss of the self. But what is the self? It is the sum of everything we remember. What terrifies us about death is not the loss of the future, but the loss of the past'.

Thus each person, child and adult seeks to know himself as worthwhile and to feel that he is in charge of himself at various levels of development and within the context of social, historical and cultural reality. A crucial aspect of the individual's sense of free will is a knowledge of his own history that does not dominate, overburden, or destroy him. As the only creatures capable of knowing their past, the story of their lives, human beings use the constructions and reconstructions of the past in valuing themselves in coping with their present and in anticipating and influencing their future. Philosophically, we can say that each child and adult is entitled to a useful and self-respecting past, one that gives him a sound sense of his worth and of a future worth anticipating.

NOTES

1. Rosa's husband had become an asymptomatic malaria carrier. His history revealed he had suffered from typical malaria attacks in Sicily; these had subsided and he felt perfectly well once he moved to Brooklyn, New York. Despite this he continued to carry the malaria organism, and when his blood was injected into Rosa, clinical malarial attacks were activated in her.
2. The absent skull bone was not replaced until she was 14 years of age.
3. There was no evidence that Chrissy remembered the accident or what happened just before it.
4. A construction worker in the vernacular.

CHAPTER THIRTEEN

The id—
or the child within?

Joseph Sandler

It is proper, I believe, for an inaugural lecture of this sort to give an indication of where a new incumbent of a Chair places himself in relation to the body of ideas which constitutes his specialized field. I shall try to do this in fairly general terms, so I hope I will be forgiven if I do not go directly to the subject matter indicated by the title of this paper, but approach it by a somewhat roundabout route. I shall begin with some reflections on the way in which psychoanalytic concepts have developed, with particular attention to the role of the instinctual drives—mistakenly called instincts in the English translation of the German *Trieb*—in the psychoanalytic theory of conflict. I shall then put forward some thoughts of my own related to the future development of psycho-analytic theory.

A version of this paper was given at Clark University, Massachusetts, at the celebrations marking the 75th anniversary of Freud's visit there.

Since the time Freud put forward his first psychoanalytic for-mulations, the theory of psychoanalysis has been in a state of continuous but even development, for as one aspect of the theory was modified or refined, others were not always brought into correspondence with it. The consequence has been that every new development has inevitably imposed a conceptual strain on other elements of the theory. In Freud's lifetime this led to two radical reformulations of his psychoanalytic model of the mind—very early the topographical (Freud, 1900a) and later what came to be called the structural (Freud, 1923b, 1926d). These revisions have in turn engendered tensions in the theory which are, in one form or another, still with us, and which continue to provide a powerful but constructive stimulus to the further development of psycho-analytic thinking.

The path of development of psychoanalytic theory has been such that the theory has moved forward first in one direction and then in another, and this is perhaps the main reason for the curious fact that very few textbooks of psychoanalysis have been published, and most of those that have been produced are as well known for their limitations as for their merits. It would seem that we can only present a relatively integrated view of psychoanalytic theory if we mark each segment of it with the date when it was introduced, and if we build into it a temporal dimension, so that each aspect can be placed in its historical context. This runs counter to the natural inclination of the textbook writer who wants to produce a clear-cut and systematic exposition of the current psychoanalytic model. Of course, some of the difficulties can be avoided if the theoretical account is presented from one point of view only—if, for example, it is written entirely from the standpoint of so-called ego psychology, or of Kleinian theory. The brilliance and clarity of Freud's own various overviews of psychoanalytic theory were in part due to the fact that on each occasion he spoke or wrote of psychoanalysis as he saw it at the time. I have in mind here Freud's Clark lectures (1910a), and other overall presentations such as the *Introductory Lectures* (1916–17), the *New Introductory Lectures* (1933a) and the *Outline of Psychoanalysis* (1940a). Since Freud, perhaps the most successful account of the theory was Otto Fenichel's *The Psycho-analytic Theory of Neurosis*, published in 1945. But this was, however, essentially an encyclopaedia rather than a textbook, an encyclopaedia in which numerous and (I would argue) inevitable theoretical contradictions were entrenched. The sheer volume of subsequent psychoanalytic writings would make it impossible to produce a comparable work today.

In 1947 Ernst Kris commented as follows:

> Current psychoanalytic terminology is, by and large, that used by Freud. Freud's language bears the imprint of the physiology, neurology, psychiatry, and the classical education of his age. It is coloured by its use in the therapeutic procedure, hence the richness of metaphors. Freud was not concerned with semantics. The correct use of a term had little meaning to him; it was the context that mattered. One might say that such insouciance is the hallmark of a genius; it undoubtedly is its prerogative. When a generation or two of scientists arrogate such a prerogative the lack of concern for semantics may well lead to confusion . . .

He went on to say:

> Even more urgent is the [need for] systematic clarification. Throughout fifty years, psychoanalytic hypotheses have frequently been revised and reformulated. Rarely, however, have all previous findings been integrated with new [pieces of] insight. In 1926[d], in *Inhibitions, Symptoms and Anxiety*, Freud reformulated a considerable set of his previous hypotheses. I am convinced that this reformulation reaches further than was realized at the time of publication, possibly by Freud himself. At present, hypotheses in psychoanalysis are formulated in various terminologies according to the various stages of the development of psychoanalysis in which they were suggested. [Kris, 1947]

Throughout the history of psychoanalysis there has been a constant interaction between psychoanalytic theory and clinical practice. This has been a two-way process, with each side influencing the other, but the strongest force in this interaction has been the effect of clinical insights (and accompanying changes in psychoanalytic technique) on the theory of psychoanalysis, rather than the other way around. It is well known how Freud's clinical perception, in the late 1890s, of the important role played in the pathology of his hysterical patients by the wish-fulfilling daydream phantasies of childhood (Freud, 1897) led him to the topographical model of the mind in *The Interpretation of Dreams*, published in

1900(a). The topographical theory divided the mind into three parts, varying in psychological 'depth'. Closest to the surface was the *Perceptual-Conscious* system, then the *Preconscious* and, finally, in the depths, the system of the *Unconscious*, in which the persisting childhood sexual drives and wishes were located. The notion of drives is, of course, a very important one in psychoanalysis, and these contents of the *Unconscious*, and of what was later to be called the id, were seen as the driving forces which, when they were unsatisfied, created states of tension that were unpleasant. On the other hand, activity that satisfied the drives brought about pleasure. For Freud, each drive (oral, anal, phallic, etc.), and each component of a drive, had a source, a pressure, an aim and an object. And, as the child developed, the drives were seen as being increasingly connected with wishful content. Drives were, as Freud was at pains to point out, entirely hypothetical constructs, and for practical purposes we can regard the basic elements in the system Unconscious as wishes of one sort or another.

The lengthy phase in the development of psychoanalysis that followed the publication of *The Interpretation of Dreams* was dominated by the idea that unconscious childhood sexual wishes, which aroused conflict and were, as a result, defended against, found surface expression in a variety of disguises. If the sexual drives involved had been allowed to find direct (rather than disguised) surface expression, then the outcome would have been sexual activity that was regarded as perverse.

This phase of psychoanalysis was marked by intense interest in interpreting surface phenomena in terms of deep unconscious urges. Almost everything expressed on the surface (in the consulting room or outside it) was thought to have an unconscious symbolic meaning—ultimately a sexual meaning. Early in the century Freud was able to show, simply and convincingly, how unconscious libidinal wishes showed themselves overtly in a variety of forms—as dreams, jokes, symptoms, slips of one sort or another, and as transference in the analysis. What is quite remarkable is how accurately the theory of psychoanalysis reflected the special technical emphasis at that time on the close and detailed analysis of the material brought by the patient in his dreams and free associations. The work of interpretation was largely a work of translation, and in this translation both individual and social behaviour and attitudes tended to be seen as the expression of instinctual drive forces that had become involved in unconscious conflict.

The emphasis on the drives and on the Oedipus complex has continued to the present, but inevitably theoretical and clinical problems have arisen. We know that increasing clinical experience during the phase following the publication of *The Interpretation of Dreams* (1900a) brought many pressures to bear on psychoanalytic theory, with resulting changes in a number of its aspects. Thus, for example, Freud found it necessary to take the role of reality into account more than before, and to postulate a reality principle, while experience of transference phenomena (or their absence) stimulated formulations regarding narcissism and object-love, and the relation between the two. For a while the aggressive tendencies in mental life had been subsumed under the self-preservative drives, the so-called 'ego-instincts'. Very few years later, the understanding of melancholia and observation of the horrors of the First World War, among other things, led Freud to theories concerning aggression turned against the self and to his famous excursion into the theory of the death drive. By the beginning of the 1920s it was clear that although the basic principles of psychoanalytic theory retained their overall coherence, the topographical model, which to some extent was by now theoretically overloaded and coming to resemble a patchwork quilt, was quite inadequate as an integrated psychoanalytic theory of the mind. In 1923 Freud put forward, in *The Ego and the Id* (1923b), the structural theory with its notion of the three metal agencies of id, ego and superego interacting with one another and with external reality.

When Freud published the structural theory of the mind, he introduced it by reference to clinical observations. He noted how patients sometimes became worse following the elucidation of their unconscious incestuous and murderous wishes in analysis— the so-called negative therapeutic reaction—and from this inferred the existence of an unconscious sense of guilt, the source of which was, in Freud's new theory, the superego. This largely unconscious agency was seen as coming into being at about the age of five, as a consequence of the struggle to resolve the Oedipus complex. The superego was the internal, structured—but distorted—representative of the parents, a combination of the ideals derived from those parents and the conscience, which operated to enforce these ideals. The id, in contrast, represented the intrinsically unconscious life and death instinctual drives that press forward for gratification and for the discharge of their energies according to the pleasure principle and through appropriate action on their objects. The id was in many respects similar to the system Unconscious of the topographical model but now contained the aggressive and destructive, as well as the libidinal drive forces. It was, in a sense, the sexual and aggressive animal part of the personality. The ego, caught in the middle, was the servant that had to serve three masters—id, superego and external reality—and had to adapt to their conflicting demands. Like the superego, the ego was seen as having been derived from the primitive id. In this conception the ego has at its disposal various defences that are used to deal with conflict, and a very large part of it operates unconsciously.

I do not want to say any more about the ego as a structure at this point, except to add that before the introduction of the structural theory the term 'ego' had a spectrum of meanings, including consciousness and what we might now call the self (in the sense of oneself as an object). Much of the previous meanings of 'ego' remained attached to the term, and Freud saw no contradiction in 1923 (and after) in seeing the ego both as an apparatus—a large-scale structure, an agency—and as the object of narcissistic self-love. He would speak of loving the object—the unfortunate psychoanalytic term for the person—and loving the ego (nowadays we would say the 'self'). It was inevitable, of course, that this was later to be a source of major theoretical confusion and difficulty.

There can be little doubt that the introduction of the structural model was a radical step forward in psychoanalytic thinking, a quite remarkable reformulation by Freud of his psychoanalytic theory of the mind. It was to be followed in 1926, in *Inhibitions, Symptoms and Anxiety* (1926d), by a revision of his previous theory of anxiety, in which anxiety had been regarded as a transformation of libidinal energy that had been denied direct discharge. Prompted again by clinical observation, anxiety was now seen by Freud as a signal to the ego of a threatening situation of danger. This formulation has enormous implications, as yet relatively unexplored, for the psychoanalytic theory of motivation, but the topic has, of necessity, to be left for another occasion. By now, too, Freud had taken into account, far more than before, the ego's role in processes of internalization—identification and introjection—which had considerable relevance for the psychoanalytic understanding of the individual's social relationships.

Given that Freud's own formulations did not unfold in a straight line, it is not surprising that the work of other analysts has not proceeded entirely along a direct path from Freud. I want only to touch very briefly on some of these other developments in psychoanalysis, insofar as they bear on the theme of this paper.

In 1936 Anna Freud published *The Ego and the Mechanisms of Defence*, and in 1937 Heinz Hartmann *Ego Psychology and the Problem of Adaptation*. The work of Anna Freud and of Hartmann and his collaborators has led to substantial developments in psychoanalytic psychology, in particular to what came to be called ego psychology in the United States, where the ideas of the famous trio of Hartmann, Kris and Loewenstein tended to dominate the psychoanalytic scene for many years until their deaths. Although they shared a substantial common basis of theory, there were some significant differences between the ego psychologists and Anna Freud and her co-workers, for although both groups espoused the structural model and elaborated it, Anna Freud was less rigorous theoretically and did not abandon the topographical model. Her remarks in this context are interesting.

> Different from the people who found the structural theory existing when they entered psychoanalysis and saw the topographical scheme as a thing of the past, I grew up with the topographical scheme, and had a gradual transition to the structural in my own psychoanalytic development. I must say that in my writing I never made the sharp distinction between the two that later writers made, but according to my own convenience I used the one or the other frame of reference. I definitely belong to the people who feel free to fall back on the topographical aspects whenever convenient and to leave them aside and to speak purely structurally when that is convenient. I agree that what I describe here [in *The Ego and the Mechanisms of Defence*, 1936, p. 16] as id content is, if one takes it very sharply and seriously, preconscious, and one would say, therefore, that it is ego content. ... this bad habit of mine of living between the two frames of

reference—the topographical and the structural—is much to be recommended because it simplifies thinking enormously and simplifies description when necessary. ... I tried to keep what has been lost [with the structural theory] by reverting whenever I feel it necessary to the former, because we got along quite well with the former model for a long time. [Sandler, 1985]

In contrast, the ego psychological establishment in the United States—particularly in New York—maintained strict adherence to Freud's structural theory, and the use of the topographical model was frowned upon. The structural theory was developed into a rather formal (some would say even rigid) system which placed much emphasis on the vicissitudes of mental energies, on the development of different aspects of the structural ego, and little on life before the Oedipus complex. However, among their other major contributions—and there have been many—the ego psychologists have made an extremely valuable theoretical distinction between the ego as a structure and the ego as the mental representation of the self, which had also been (and sometimes still is) called ego. This has facilitated much theoretical clarification.

Following the deaths of Hartmann, Kris and Loewenstein, the stresses and strains that had built up within psychoanalysis in the United States became more noticeable, and ego psychology was not as securely established as in the past. Much more prominence has been given in recent years to the study of early (i.e. pre-oedipal) development. Many analysts have turned to the theories and techniques of self psychology put forward by Heinz Kohut, which have grown out of clinical work with patients with narcissistic personality disorders, and which have contributed to greater flexibility of psychoanalytic approach. To this we must add the influence of Margaret Mahler (Mahler et al., 1975), Otto Kernberg (1975), Roy Schafer (1976) and a number of others. In the United States there has also been, in recent years, an increased interest in the work of the British object-relations theorists—in particular Melanie Klein, Ronald Fairbairn and Donald Winnicott.

In contrast to the ways in which psychoanalysis has developed in the United States, the theories of Melanie Klein, which she began to develop in the 1920s, have placed much the greatest stress on the development of the infant's phantasy life during the first year. For Mrs Klein drives were of central and supreme importance, and particular significance was attached to the death drive. Both the life and death drives were seen as being linked from the beginning of life to the infant's objects, and to object-related phantasy. The notion of the superego, which was regarded by Freud as a structure formed from the internalized parent figures, was looked at by her from an object-relational perspective rather than from a structural one. In fact, the idea of mental structure, in the sense in which it has been used by Freud or the ego psychologists, tended to be de-emphasized or even ignored by Kleinian theorists, who were not interested in the ego as an apparatus but tended to conceive of mental organization in terms of 'positions' and unconscious infantile phantasies, which included interaction with the so-called internal objects—the internalized parents or parts of the parents. These internal figures are distorted because they are vehicles of the child's projections, especially projections of destructive parts of the self. Apart from the Kleinian analysts on the one hand, and the more 'classical' analysts associated with Anna Freud on the other, there has always been in Britain a substantial group of 'independent' analysts, whose theories vary from near-Kleinian to near-classical, and who have been much influenced by Jones, Strachey, Fairbairn, Winnicott, Bowlby, Balint and others.

Let me emphasize once more that the differences in theories are not purely semantic but reflect differences in clinical and technical orientation. For example, Mrs Klein and her followers systematically emphasized the interpretation of early unconscious phantasies in the transference, whereas Anna Freud and those who worked with her, because they took a very different approach to the technique of child analysis, attached greater significance to development over the whole of the first five or six years and stressed the role of external reality, both in the past and in the present. But it should be said that the situation in 1985 is different from that of 10 or 20 years ago, and there appears to be an increased interaction between the proponents of different points of view.

I hope that I have been able to convey a sense of some of the movement and change that occurred in psychoanalysis over the years and to have shown the need to look at these from a historical perspective. In a paper on the relation of psychoanalytic concepts to psychoanalytic practice I put forward the view that

> There are advantages to emphasizing the developmental–historical dimension in psychoanalysis when we think of theoretical matters. It allows us to escape—if we want to—quarrels about which theory is 'right' and which is 'wrong' . . . [and to ask rather which is the more useful in a particular context. It also] . . . puts us in the position of asking '*Why* was this, that or the other formulation put forward?' and '*What* did its authors mean?' It is of some interest that whenever an aspect of theory has emphasis transferred from it to some new formulation, so the hiatuses and weak areas in the theory which follow (if only because the new theory never encompasses exactly the same area as the old) attract counterforces aimed at filling the gaps or remedying the weaknesses. It is characteristic of these counterforces that they inevitably push forward a core of ideas which are useful and important; equally inevitably they represent an over-reaction, an over-filling of the empty spaces. Gaps and weaknesses in theory also follow changes in specific areas resulting from advances in clinical psychoanalysis and in technical procedures; again, sooner or later, over-reactions occur. And if the proponent of the new ideas is a charismatic leader, then a new 'movement' in psychoanalysis may result. It may split from the mainstream of psychoanalysis, or remain within it, contributing to the dialectic of theoretical development. [Sandler, 1983]

Because psychoanalytic theory constitutes a loosely linked but organically coherent body of ideas rather than a well-integrated whole, what appears to be most critical 'is not what psychoanalytic theory *should* be, but what should be emphasized within the whole compass of psychoanalytic thinking. And what should be emphasized is that which relates to the work we have to do.' In this connection, we can observe that

> the analyst, as he grows more competent, will [unconsciously] construct a whole variety of theoretical segments which relate directly to his clinical work. They are the products of unconscious thinking, are very much partial theories, models or sche-

mata, which have the quality of being available in reserve, so to speak, to be called upon whenever necessary. That they may contradict one another is no problem. They coexist happily as long as they are unconscious. They do not appear in consciousness unless they are consonant with official or public theory, and can be described in suitable words. Such partial structures may in fact represent better (i.e. more useful and appropriate) theories than the official ones, and it is likely that many valuable additions [to psychoanalytic theory] have come about because conditions have arisen that have allowed preconscious part-theories to fit together and emerge in a plausible and psychoanalytically socially acceptable way. ... The analyst can be regarded as ... a sort of probe into the psychoanalytic situation, that organizes the experience that [he] has in interaction with his patients. ... The probe can be withdrawn from the situation and the theories which have been formed can be examined ... the more access we gain to [these] theories of experienced analysts, the better we can help the advancement of psychoanalytic theory. [Sandler, 1983]

Having said all this, it is necessary to state that the basic core of agreement within psychoanalytic thinking is substantial. In a complex field like psychoanalysis, the real problems relate to where emphasis should be put. What may look like a profound theoretical disagreement may be quite irrelevant to the practical task of the analyst. I remember very well witnessing, as a very young analyst, a violent argument between two distinguished senior members of the British Psycho-Analytical Society, Willi Hoffer and Michael Balint, over the question of whether or not a state of primary narcissism could be said to exist in the earliest period of life. Nowadays, in Britain at least, few people would bother with such a controversy; different problems have come to the fore.

In the next part of this chapter I want to come rather closer to the question raised in its title, but the path I shall pursue is still, I am afraid, a rather indirect one. It has been said by Freud that the aim of the psychoanalytic process is to make the unconscious conscious, and few analysts would disagree with that. Freud later stated the aim of analysis as 'Where id was, there ego shall be' (1933a), and while some of us might have reservations about this latter formulation on theoretical grounds, it is clear that Freud meant that we should aim to bring the individual to a condition in which he is more in control of his unconscious drives than before and, as a result, need not resort to pathological solutions in order to deal with them.

My own preference for a formulation of the analytic aim has been put in the following way:

> One of the main aims of our analytic endeavours is to help the patient eventually to accept the infantile wishful aspects of himself which have aroused painful conflict and have become threatening during the course of his development. As a consequence they have been defended against, possibly with pathological results. We strive to get the patient to tolerate these parts of himself in his conscious thinking and phantasies, so that he is not compelled to act them out or to extend pathogenic efforts to keep them in check. To put it another way: a major analytic goal is to get the patient to become friends with the previously unacceptable parts of himself, to get on good terms with previously threatening wishes and phantasies. To do this means that we have to provide, through our interpretations and the way we give them, an atmosphere of tolerance of the infantile, the perverse and the ridiculous, an atmosphere which the patient can make part of his own attitude towards himself, which he can internalize along with the understanding he has reached in his joint work with the analyst. [Sandler & Sandler, 1983]

In order to achieve the analytic aim, to bring the patient to the point where he or she can tolerate the previously unacceptable aspects of himself in a safer and friendlier way, he will need to gain emotionally convincing insight in the course of the analytic work. Such insight is most effectively obtained through the patient's experience and understanding of what has been relived in his relation to the analyst in the transference. He will need to gain insight, not only into the content of his unconscious phantasies, but also into the nature of what can be referred to as his 'inner world', which includes his unconscious relation to his introjects (about which I shall say a little more later) with whom he can be said to have a continual unconscious inner dialogue. He will need as well to have insight into his unconscious anxieties and conflicts, and into the methods he uses to resolve such conflicts. His insight will, we hope, include an understanding of his own defensive mechanisms and manoeuvres, particularly the projections and externalizations that occur in his unconscious phantasy life. To the extent that the analytic aims can be achieved, it will be possible to bring about reduction of conflict and of associated painful emotions, and to permit a deflection of those mental contents that were previously not tolerated near consciousness, into conscious or preconscious thought and phantasy.

The material available to the analyst for the analytic work is that which the patient can allow to come to the surface in one form or another. This can be regarded as consisting of disguised derivatives of and allusions to what is uppermost in the unconscious part of the patient's mind. It is the analyst's task to work with the patient in such a way that as much as possible of this current unconscious content can be made readily available to consciousness.

The analyst aims to anchor the progressive analytic mapping of the patient's inner world, particularly as it has emerged through its externalization in the transference. In order to do this anchoring, in order to consolidate an emotionally meaningful perspective on the central and recurring patterns and themes in the patient's inner world, we have to provide a reconstruction of his or her past in a meaningful and relevant way, just as we have to make constructions about the patient's current inner world. And we link the two, the constructions and the reconstructions, together. But the elucidation and interpretation of the past can be regarded as being of value in the analytic process primarily because of the light it throws on the present, and there must be few analysts who still subscribe to the archaeological aim of the psychoanalytic method—i.e. who aim in their analytic work to analyse the present ultimately to uncover and reconstruct the past (Sandler & Sandler, 1984).

As I have indicated, the introduction of the structural model was undoubtedly a major step forward, particularly because it gave prominence to the role of the unconscious sense of guilt, which is certainly a factor of the greatest importance in the development of psychological disturbance. However, Freud's view that '. . . neurosis is the result of conflict between the ego and its id' (1924b) has proved to be in need of substantial revision, even though we can agree that sexual and destructive wishes and wishful phantasies play a major role in normal and pathological mental life. The application of the structural model to clinical material has been increasingly criticized on clinical and theoretical grounds in recent years, especially as psychoanalysts have become more aware of the fact that early pre-oedipal influences play a significant role in pathological development and that by the time the child enters the oedipal phase his or her conflicts cannot be reduced to simple clashes between id and external or internalized authority. These developments in psychoanalysis have undoubtedly been influenced, directly or indirectly, by the Kleinians and by child analysts such as Anna Freud and Margaret Mahler, who have been particularly interested in direct child observation and in pre-oedipal developmental disturbances, disturbances that have assumed greatest significance in the work that has been done in recent years on narcissistic and borderline character disorders.

At this point I should like to interpose the story of David Rapaport's definition of id and ego. Rapaport was a gifted psychologist who has justifiably been regarded as an outstanding psychoanalytic theoretician, although he never actually engaged in psychoanalytic practice. In 1959 he suggested that 'In contrast to the id, which refers to peremptory aspects of behaviour, the ego refers to aspects which are delayable, bring about delay, or are themselves products of delay'. This formulation was widely accepted in psychoanalytic circles, especially in the United States, but it only makes sense if we equate all peremptory aspects of behaviour with the instinctual drives or their close derivatives. This is manifestly not the case, but it is curious that Rapaport's much-quoted definition was not questioned for many years. Incidentally, this demonstrates how easy it is for a gap to develop between the 'official' psychoanalytic theory and the private theories more closely linked to clinical experience.

We can agree with Rapaport in the idea that unconscious conflict occurs between peremptory tendencies and urges on the one hand, and tendencies that work in the direction of delay, which aim at preventing these peremptory impulses from finding overt expression, on the other. However, as I hope to show, these peremptory impulses or tendencies need not be instinctual in nature. In other words, *not every unconscious impulse is an instinctual impulse*, and we can say this without minimizing the importance of the roles of sexuality and aggression in mental life. And, as you may have divined by now, I want to suggest that we shall find it necessary to make increasing use in our psychoanalytic psychology of some concept of 'the child within'.

Consider the following case: Mrs M, a successful professional woman in her mid-thirties, who had been in analysis for about a year, arrived a few minutes late at her analytic session. It was a Monday, and the summer vacation was due to start at the end of the week. She lay on the couch without talking, but after about 10 minutes she told me that she had not felt like coming because her children had been very demanding over the week-end. She had tried to gratify them but now felt exhausted. There was too much for her to do at home and at work, and she hesitated to get involved in any new project in case she did not have time to carry it through. I commented that perhaps the same feelings applied to the analysis because of the forthcoming holiday. Possibly this had contributed to her being late. She was silent for a few moments and then told me that she had, in fact, been early for her session and had decided to go for a walk around the block. Unfortunately she had misjudged the distance, and that had made her late. After a further short silence she told me of a colleague of hers who had irritated her that morning by repeatedly asking for help and who did not allow her the time to do her own work. Normally she could cope with this, but it had been particularly difficult that day. Things would certainly be worse for her during the holiday, when the children would be at home and she would have to get extra help. As I saw it, the conflict she was experiencing at the time was between a wish to cling to me, to ask for my help, support and protection on the one hand, and a feeling that this was improper, unfair and childish, on the other. There was a demanding part of her that she did not like at all. She had dealt with the conflict over her demandingness, when faced with the prospect of the holiday, by criticizing the demandingness of others. Following my interpretation she told me that she now recalled that she had had the phantasy, when she had left home that morning, that I would be staying at home for the summer, that she would be taken ill, and that I would offer to see her during the holiday because of this.

Later in the analysis we were able to see, once Mrs M had, so to say, made friends with her clinging wishes—with the demanding aspects of herself—how these had arisen in childhood as a defensive clinging whenever she was to be left alone. She could recall how she had been a very clinging child, and how her parents had reproached her for this. What emerged in the analysis now was that as a child she had had multiple fears of being attacked by an intruder when left alone and had experienced nightmares throughout her childhood from which she would awake just when she was about to be injured or killed. This material was elicited when she became frightened of coming to the sessions, being convinced that my interpretations might hurt or damage her in some way. The analytic work at that time disclosed that she was experiencing considerable unconscious conflict over hostile feelings towards me and towards my other patients, and that she dealt with the conflict over these feelings by projection in the transference, so that she saw me as a threatening, aggressive figure, just as she had experienced the intruders who threatened her in her nightmares. The analytic task was now for her to become friendly (if I may use the phrase again) towards her hostile wishes or, one could say, with the aggressive part of herself. Whether this hostility should be called id or not is an open question, for not all aggression need be considered to be instinctual aggression, but we should not exclude the possibility that the question itself is irrelevant to the practical analytic task. What *is* relevant is that the patient progressed from being an angry child to being a frightened and clinging one and, in turn, moved on to being a defensively independent adult. Some time later her mother told Mrs M that at the age of 2½ Mrs M had been extremely upset and angry when a baby brother had been born and her mother had had to stay in hospital because of complications. Mrs M had some memories of temper tantrums, and recalled episodes of angrily competing with her brother. This, together with her rivalry with my other patients, enabled us to provide her with a historical perspective for her understanding of herself.

I remarked a few moments ago that the question of whether Mrs M's hostile feelings were id or not was perhaps irrelevant. From a clinical point of view what we *actually* see in our patients as unconscious conflict is *a conflict between some tendency or urge that was once acceptable (or at least accessible) to the patient's consciousness, and a counterforce that came into existence during the course of development.* I believe this formulation to be of the greatest importance, because the impulse that enters into the conflicts we see in our patients need not be an instinctual one, the direct expression of a sexual or aggressive drive, but it may readily have a forceful, peremptory quality quite equal in intensity to any instinctual urge (Sandler, 1974). When, as analysts, we bring to consciousness the impulses or urges that our patients have defended against, we do not find that we are dealing with id alone, or even with id at all. Perhaps what follows may make this a little clearer.

In the case of Mrs M, the developmental thread that was followed in the analysis may indeed have had substantial instinctual drive roots—in, for example, childhood feelings of envy and wishful phantasies of sadistic attacks upon the brother, and perhaps earlier hostility towards the parents. But this patient has been able, during the course of her development, to find solutions to the conflicts she experienced over her more primitive impulses. One such solution was to become phobic, to project her aggressive wishes, which included both her hostility towards her baby brother and her anger with the mother who left her. She could then feel the hostility as belonging not to herself but to someone else and could use phobic avoidance and clinging to protect herself. The defensive impulse to cling when anxious soon acquired the quality of peremptoriness, as indeed do all successful ways of coping with anxiety or with any other painful feeling. We can say that the more violent the threat, the more peremptorily are the defences against the threat applied. The urgent need to impose a specific defence can by no means be regarded as the expression of a drive. From the point of view of the structural model, defensive behaviour is ego rather than id!

A male patient habitually and insistently accused others of being guilty of misdemeanours. During analysis it became clear that this was a defence against sharp and sudden feelings of guilt and consequent self-reproaches, which occurred whenever he thought affectionately of his father, who had deserted the family in the patient's childhood. The initially unconscious self-reproaches were seen quite clearly to have a peremptory quality, but as they, in turn, came into conflict with his ideals for himself, they were defended against by accusing others of crimes that were very similar to those he felt he had committed. Of course, the self-reproaches had a history of their own, but the conflicts that resulted in their production in childhood could not be analysed until the patient had been able to accept his tendency to self-reproach as part of himself.

There are many examples one can give of unconscious urges that are not directly instinctual in nature. Perhaps the most striking of these are the unconscious and very forceful strivings to recreate some earlier relationships with a love object or with an ambivalently loved person. Here, again, it would be a gross over-simplification to say that the urges to recreate the presence of the object are always fashioned out of sexual and aggressive drives. The need to set up external representatives of one's so-called 'internal objects' is very strong in all of us, particularly in situations where one's feelings of safety are threatened; and this is nowhere better evident than in the analytic transference.

I hope that by now it has been possible to discern some connection between what I have been saying and the title of this chapter. I hope, too, that I have made a convincing case for considering unconscious mental conflict as involving peremptory urges that cannot simply be equated with an instinctual 'id' (see Hayman, 1969, for a discussion of some of the difficulties associated with the notion of an 'id'). Such urges can be looked on as unconscious impulses of the adult patient to behave as if he were at an earlier stage of development—*as if* he were a child. So an unconscious urge reflected in an impulse to cling, of the sort we saw in Mrs M, can be regarded as *the adult version of the urgent clinging impulse of 'the child within'*. We should be mindful of the fact, of course, that 'the child within' is a concept, and we should be careful not to reify it—except temporarily for purposes of convenient communication. 'The child within' that is active at any particular time *can* be an instinctual drive-dominated child. He *can* be sexual or destructive in a whole variety of ways (which can be quite perverse), but he can also be, and very often is, a frightened and defended child. Above all, he (or she) is an object-related child. He carries with him an internal world of childhood and attempts to externalize, to actualize this world (and all the various phantasies he has about it), in the present. And, like any other child, he has a history of past conflicts and adaptations. The pressure to re-establish our relations with internal or internalized objects by setting them up outside is all the greater the more anxious we are, the more we are threatened, and the less in control of ourselves or our environment we feel. Indeed, we could not exist with any degree of sanity at all if we did not succeed in bringing our inner and outer object worlds into some sort of harmony, and the pressure to do this has as peremptory a quality as any instinctual drive.

I want to suggest that we have reached a stage in the development of psychoanalytic thought that is comparable to that which existed in the few years before the introduction of the structural theory by Freud in 1923. I am reminded here of Thomas Kuhn's (1962) notion of a pre-revolutionary stage in scientific development, and it seems possible that we are in such a phase in psychoanalysis—if we are, it is very likely that it is a phase that may last a long time.

What I want to do in the final part of this chapter is to formulate a few ideas that relate to what I have been talking about, in the hope that they may stoke the fires of the theoretical revolution. In the first place, no matter how much we may swing away from the mechanistic formulations of the structural model, we shall always need some model of mental organization that is relevant to the work we do and to the things we are interested in as psychoanalysts. In regard to such an organization, it is useful to think in terms of mental structure—not the large-scale structures of id, ego and superego, but structure in the more general sense of an enduring psychological organization. We can assume that behaviour and subjective experience can be related to structures of this sort and be involved with them. We can assume, too, that with the infant's interaction with the external world, his psychological structures increase in complexity. Thus the organization of the mind—of what Freud called the mental apparatus—is capable of modification, and its development is a function both of maturation and of the forces entering into psychological adaptation. This point may seem trivial, but it is important. It is perhaps one of the weaknesses of Kleinian theory that the notion of a mental organization is understressed, that mechanisms have not been differentiated from phantasies, so that, for example, the mechanism of projection is equated with the phantasy of expelling unwanted mental content. Although we can be deeply grateful to the Kleinian theorists for the emphasis they have placed on the existence of an object-related inner world in the child and in the adult and on the analysis of this inner world as it shows itself in the transference, to describe this world in terms of phantasies and internal objects leaves us without a clear picture of its organization, for man's mind is not made of phantasies alone. In this context it may be found useful to conceive of internal objects or introjects as hypothetical structures representing internal figures to whom we relate, just as we relate to objects in the external world. In a sense we live simultaneously in two worlds—and we spend much of our lives trying to reconcile the one with the other. Whatever form any new overall psychoanalytic theory will take, it will need to have at its centre the idea of an organized, unconscious, internal world and unconscious, internal, object relationships.

Psychological structures are continually being modified during development, but at the same time no structure is, by definition, ever lost. The apparent contradiction can be resolved by assuming that modification comes about by the superimposition of further structures. However, if a point is reached when a later or higher-order solution does not function as well, from the point of view of psychological adaptation, as a more primitive one, it will be abandoned in favour of the earlier mode of functioning. Thus, if a child finds that a particular solution to a conflict works well internally and satisfies the criteria for internal adaptation, he or she will continue to apply it, until perhaps for some reason it does not work so well. He will then find some new solution to his conflict, but the tendency to function in the old way will always be there, and he will allow himself to make use of the older mode of functioning if the newer and higher-order solutions do not work. This means that we are constantly inhibiting childhood impulses, thoughts, phantasies and conclusions based on primitive theories of the world. So the past is very actively alive in the present. The earlier tendencies may break through when we are tired, when we do not monitor ourselves sufficiently attentively or when we are faced with painful new conflicts (Sandler & Joffe, 1967).

The idea of persistence of the past in the way I have just described leads us, for example, to the conclusion that regression is not a revival of something that has been buried, but a *disinhibition* of something that continues to be active in the present. It also allows us to look at the mechanism of cure or change through psychoanalysis as involving inhibition of the use of structured pathological solutions, which nevertheless always retain the potential for being used again.

Let me conclude by giving an example of the tendency to persistence from my own experience. When I was a boy, I had a very thick head of hair, which always required thinning by the barber. With the passage of time I became very noticeably less well-endowed with hair, although I still find it necessary to pay an occasional visit to the hairdresser. On a recent occasion I fell asleep in his chair and was awakened by his saying 'anything else, sir?' In my drowsy state I immediately answered 'yes, thin it out a bit on top'—a remark I had not made for some decades. What had happened was that I had failed to inhibit the emergence of a structured response that had once been appropriate but now was not, to inhibit 'the child within'.

REFERENCES

Ainsworth, M. D. S. (1977). Social development in the first year of life: maternal influences on infant–mother attachment. In J. M. Tanner (ed.), *Developments in Psychiatric Research*. London: Hodder and Stoughton.

Anderson, J. R., & Bower, G. H. (1973). *Human Associative Memory*. New York: Wiley.

Anderson, J. W. (1972). Attachment behaviour out of doors. In N. Burton Jones (ed.), *Ethological Studies of Child Behaviour*. Cambridge: Cambridge University Press.

Ashby, W. R. (1960). *Design for a Brain: The Origin of Adaptive Behavior*. New York: Wiley.

———. (1963). *An Introduction to Cybernetics*. New York: Wiley.

Auden, W. H. (1940). In *Collected Short Poems, 1927–1957*. New York: Random House.

Bagshaw, M. H., & Pribram, J. H. (1965). Effect of amygdalectomy on transfer of training in monkeys. *Journal of Comparative Physiological Psychology, 59*: 118–121.

Barrett, T. W. (1969). Studies of the function of the amygdaloid complex in Macaca Mulatta. *Neuropsychologia, 7*: 1–12.

Bender, L., & Yarnell, H. (1941). An observation nursery. *American Journal of Psychiatry, 97*: 1158–1174.

Benjamin, J. (1978). Authority and the family revisited; or, in a world without father. *New German Critique*, no. 13: 57.

Bernfeld, S. (1932). Der Begriff der 'Deutung' in der Psychoanalyse. *Zeitschrift der angewandten Psychologie, 42*: 448–487.

Bible (1944). *King James Bible*. Cambridge: Cambridge University Press.

Bohm, D., Hiley, B. J., & Stuart, A. E. G. (1970). On a new mode of description in physics. *International Journal of Theoretical Physics, 3* (3): 171–183.

Bowlby, J. (1940). The influence of early environment in the development of neurosis and neurotic character. *International Journal of Psychoanalysis, 21*: 154–178.

———— (1944). Forty-four juvenile thieves: their characters and home life. *International Journal of Psychoanalysis, 25*: 19–52 and 107–127.

———— (1958). The nature of the child's tie to his mother. *International Journal of Psychoanalysis, 39*: 350–373.

———— (1969). *Attachment and Loss. Volume 1. Attachment*. London: Hogarth Press.

———— (1973). *Attachment and Loss. Volume 2. Separation: Anxiety and Anger*. London: Hogarth Press.

———— (1979). Psychoanalysis as art and science. *International Revue of Psychoanalysis, 6*: 3–14.

———— (1980). *Attachment and Loss. Volume 3. Loss: Sadness and Depression*. London: Hogarth Press.

Breuer, J., & Freud, S. (1893–95). *Studies on Hysteria. Standard Edition, 2*.

Brillouin, L. (1961). *Science and Information Theory*. New York: Academic Press.

Brindley, G. S., & Merton, P. A. (1960). The absence of position sense in the human eye. *Journal of Physiology, 153*: 127–130.

Broadbent, D. E. (1977). The hidden preattentive process. *American Psychologist, 32*: 109–118.

Brobeck, J. R. (1948). Food intake as a measure of temperature regulation. *Yale Journal of Biology & Medicine, 20*: 545–552.

Brown, N. O. (1959). *Life against Death: The Psychoanalytic Meaning of History*. Middletown, CT: Wesleyan University Press.

Cannon, W. B. (1929). *Bodily Changes in Pain, Hunger, Fear and Rage*. New York: D. Appleton and Company.

Chasseguet-Smirgel, J. (1974). Perversion, idealization and sublimation. *International Journal of Psychoanalysis, 55*: 349–357.

———— (1976a). Freud and female sexuality. *International Journal of Psychoanalysis, 57*: 275–286.

——— (1976b). Some thoughts on the ego-ideal. *Psychoanalytic Quarterly, 45*: 346–373.

——— (1978). Reflexions on the connexions between perversion and sadism. *International Journal of Psychoanalysis, 59*: 27–35.

Chin, J. H., Pribram, K. H., Drake, K., & Green, L. O., Jr. (1976). Disruption of temperature discrimination during limbic forebrain stimulation in monkeys. *Neuropsychologia, 14*: 293–310.

Chodorow, N. (1978). *The Reproduction of Mothering: Psychoanalysis and the Sociology of Gender.* Berkeley, CA: University of California Press.

Deleuze, G., & Guattari, F. (1977). *Anti-Oedipus: Capitalism and Schizophrenia* (R. Hurley et al., trans.). New York: Viking Press.

Deutsch, A. (1976). *Manuel d'Instruction Religieuse Israelite.* Paris: Fondation Sefer.

Dinnerstein, D. (1976). *The Mermaid and the Minotaur: Sexual Arrangements and Human Malaise.* New York: Harper & Row.

Dixon, N. F. (1971). *Subliminal Perception: The Nature of a Controversy.* London: McGraw-Hill.

Dostoevsky, F. (1873). *Les Demons.* Paris: Fernand Hazan, 1963.

Eigen, M. (1977). The origin of life. In *The Search for Absolute Values: Harmony Among the Sciences, Vol. II,* Proceedings of the Fifth International Conference on the Unity of the Sciences, November 1976. New York: ICF Press.

Eliade, M. (1956). *Forgerons et Alchimistes.* Paris: Flammarion, 1977.

——— (1956). *Mephistopheles et l'Androgyne.* Paris: Gallimard.

Ellenberger, H. F. (1970). *The Discovery of the Unconscious.* London: Allen and Unwin.

Engel, S. (1980). Femininity as tragedy: re-examining the 'new narcissism'. *Socialist Review,* no. 53 (September–October).

Erdelyi, M. H. (1974). A new look at the New Look: perceptual defense and vigilance. *Psychological Review, 81,* 1–25.

Fairbairn, W. R. D. (1940). Schizoid factors in the personality. In *Psychoanalytic Studies of the Personality.* London: Tavistock Publications, 1952.

Fancher, R. (1971). The neurologic origin of Freud's theory. *Journal of the History of the Behavioral Sciences, 7,* 59–74.

Fenichel, O. (1941). *Problems of Psychoanalytic Technique.* New York: The Psychoanalytic Quarterly Press.

——— (1945). *The Psychoanalytic Theory of Neurosis.* New York: Norton.

Frank, A. (1979). Two theories or one? or none? *Journal American Psychoanalytic Association, 27*: 169–207.

Freud, A. (1936). *The Ego and the Mechanisms of Defence.* New York: International Universities Press.

———— (1965). *Normality and Pathology in Childhood.* New York: International Universities Press.

Freud, S. (1887–1902). *The Origins of Psychoanalysis: Letters to Wilhelm Fliess, Drafts and Notes.* London: Imago, 1954.

———— (1897). Letter to Fliess, 24 January, 1897. *Standard Edition, 1.*

———— (1900a). *The Interpretation of Dreams. Standard Edition, 4–5.*

———— (1901b). *The Psychopathology of Everyday Life. Standard Edition, 6.*

———— (1905c). *Jokes and Their Relation to the Unconscious. Standard Edition, 8.*

———— (1905d). *Three Essays on the Theory of Sexuality. Standard Edition, 7.*

———— (1907b). Obsessive actions and religious practices. *Standard Edition, 9.*

———— (1909d). Notes upon a case of obsessional neurosis. *Standard Edition, 10.*

———— (1910a). Five lectures on psycho-analysis. *Standard Edition, 11.*

———— (1911b). Formulations on the two principles of mental functioning. *Standard Edition, 12.*

———— (1912b). The dynamics of transference. *Standard Edition, 12.*

———— (1915a). Observations on transference-love (further recommendations on the technique of psycho-analysis, III). *Standard Edition, 12.*

———— (1916–1917). *Introductory Lectures on Psycho-Analysis. Standard Edition, 15–16.*

———— (1917c). On transformations of instinct as exemplified in anal eroticism. *Standard Edition, 17.*

———— (1918b). From the history of an infantile neurosis. *Standard Edition, 17.*

———— (1920g). *Beyond the Pleasure Principle. Standard Edition, 18.*

———— (1923a). Two encyclopaedia articles. *Standard Edition, 18.*

———— (1923b). *The Ego and the Id. Standard Edition, 19.*

———— (1924b). Neurosis and psychosis. *Standard Edition, 19.*

———— (1924e). The loss of reality in neurosis and psychosis. *Standard Edition, 19.*

———— (1925d). *An Autobiographical Study. Standard Edition, 20.*

———— (1925j). Some psychical consequences of the anatomical distinction between the sexes. *Standard Edition, 19.*

———— (1926d). *Inhibitions, Symptoms and Anxiety. Standard Edition, 20.*

———— (1926e). *The Question of Lay Analysis. Standard Edition, 20*.

———— (1933a). *New Introductory Lectures on Psycho-Analysis. Standard Edition, 22*.

———— (1937c). Analysis terminable and interminable. *Standard Edition, 23*.

———— (1937d). Constructions in analysis. *Standard Edition, 23*.

———— (1939a). *Moses and Monotheism. Standard Edition, 23*.

———— (1940a). *An Outline of Psycho-Analysis. Standard Edition, 23*.

———— (1940b). Some elementary lessons in psycho-analysis. *Standard Edition, 23*.

———— (1940e). Splitting of the ego in the process of defence. *Standard Edition, 23*.

Galambos, R., Norton, T. T., & Frommer, C. P. (1967). Optic tract lesions sparing pattern vision in cats. *Experimental Neurology, 18*: 8–25.

Gedo, J. E. (1979). *Beyond Interpretation: Toward a Revised Theory for Psychoanalysis*. New York: International Universities Press.

Gill, M. (1975). What is metapsychology? In M. Gill and P. Holzman (eds.), *Meaning and Mechanism in Psychoanalytic Theory*. New York: International Universities Press.

Goldfarb, W. (1943). The effects of early institutional care on adolescent personality. *Journal of Experimental Education, 12*: 106.

Grossman, S. P. (1967). *A Textbook of Physiological Psychology*. New York: Wiley.

Grunberger, B. (1966). Oedipe et narcissisme. In *Le Narcissisme*. Paris: Payot, 1971. [Translated in *Narcissism*. New York: International Universities Press, 1979].

Guntrip, H. (1975). My experience of analysis with Fairbairn and Winnicott. *International Revue of Psychoanalysis, 2*: 145–156.

Harré, R. (1970). *Principles of Scientific Thinking*. London: Macmillan Press.

Hartmann, H. (1937). *Ego Psychology and the Problem of Adaptation*. New York: International Universities Press.

———— (1939). *Ego Psychology and the Problems of Adaptation*. New York: International Universities Press, 1958.

Hayman, A. (1969). What do we mean by 'id'? *Journal of the American Psychoanalytic Association, 17*: 353–380.

Head, H. (1920). *Studies in Neurology*. London: Oxford University Press.

Heinicke, C. (1956). Some effects of separating two-year-old children from their parents: a comparative study. *Human Relations, 9*: 105–176.

Heinicke, C., & Westheimer, I. (1966). *Brief Separations*. New York: International Universities Press.

Hilgard, E. R. (1977). *Divided Consciousness: Multiple Controls in Human Thought and Action*. New York: Wiley.

Holst, E. von, & Mittelstaedt, H. (1950). Das Reafferenzprinzip. *Naturwissenschaften, 37*: 464–476.

Holt, R. R. (1962). A critical examination of Freud's concept of bound vs. mobile cathexis. *Journal of the American Psychoanalytic Association, 10*: 475–525.

Home, H. J. (1966). The concept of mind. *International Journal of Psychoanalysis, 47*: 43–49.

Jahoda, M. (1972). Social psychology and psychoanalysis: a mutual challenge. *Bulletin of the British Psychological Society 25*: 269–274.

James, W. (1901). *The Principles of Psychology*. London: MacMillan and Company.

Janik, A., & Toulmin, S. (1973). *Wittgenstein's Vienna*. New York: Simon and Schuster.

Jones, E. (1953). *Sigmund Freud: Life and Work, Vol. 1*. London: Hogarth Press.

———— (1957). *Sigmund Freud: Life and Work, Vol. 3*. London: Hogarth Press.

Jung, C. G. (1907). *The Psychology of Dementia Praecox*. New York and Washington: Nervous and Mental Disease Publishing Co., 1909.

Kahneman, D. (1973). *Attention and Effort*. Englewood Cliffs, NJ: Prentice-Hall.

Karplus, J. P., & Kreidl, A. (1909). Gehirn und Sympathicus. *Arch. ges. Physiol. Pflugers, 129*: 138–44.

Kernberg, O. (1975). *Borderline Conditions and Pathological Narcissism*. New York: Jason Aronson.

Klein, G. S. (1976). *Psychoanalytic Theory: An Exploration of Essentials*. New York: International Universities Press.

Klein, M. (1948). *Contributions to Psycho-Analysis, 1921–1945*. London: Hogarth Press.

———— (1957). Envy and gratitude. In *Envy and Gratitude and Other Works, 1946–1963*. London: Hogarth Press, 1975.

Kohut, H. (1971). *The Analysis of the Self*. New York: International Universities Press.

Kris, E. (1947). Problems in clinical research: discussion remarks. *American Journal of Orthopsychiatry, 17*: 210.

———— (1956a). On some vicissitudes of insight in psycho-analysis. *International Journal of Psychoanalysis, 37*: 445–455.

———— (1956b). The recovery of childhood memories in psycho-analysis. *Psychoanalytic Study of the Child, 11*: 54–88.

Kuhn, T. S. (1962). *The Structure of Scientific Revolutions*. Chicago, IL: University of Chicago Press.

———— (1970). *The Structure of Scientific Revolutions,* second edition. Chicago, IL: University of Chicago Press.

———— (1974). Second thoughts on paradigms. In F. Suppe (ed.), *The Structure of Scientific Theory*. Urbana, IL: University of Illinois Press.

Kundera, M. (1980). *The Book of Laughter and Forgetting*. New York: Knopf.

Lassonde, M. C., Ptito, M., & Pribram, K. H. (1981). Intracerebral influences on the microstructure of visual cortex. *Experimental Brain Research, 43*: 131–144.

Loewald, H. (1978). *Psychoanalysis and the History of the Individual*. New Haven, CT: Yale University Press.

Lorenz, K. Z. (1935). Der Kumpan in der Umwelt des Vogels. *J. Orn. Berl., 83* [English translation in C. H. Schiller (ed.), *Instinctive Behaviour*. New York: International Universities Press, 1957].

Mackay, D. M. (1966). Cerebral organization and the conscious control of action. In J. C. Eccles (ed.), *Brain and Conscious Experience*. New York: Springer-Verlag.

McCulloch, W. S., & Pitts, W. (1943). Logical calculus of the ideas immanent in nervous activity. *Bulletin of Mathematical Biophysics, 5*: 115–133.

McFarland, D. J. (1971). *Feedback Mechanisms in Animal Behaviour*. New York: Academic Press.

Magendie, F. (1822). Experiences sur les fonctions des racines des nerfs rachidiens. *J. Physiol. Exp., 2*: 276–279.

Mahler, M. S., Pine, F., & Bergman, A. (1975). *The Psychological Birth of the Human Infant*. New York: Basic Books; London: Maresfield Library, Karnac Books.

Malcolm, H. (1971). *Generation of Narcissus*. Boston: Little, Brown.

Marcuse, H. (1962). *Eros and Civilization*. New York: Vintage Books.

———— (1964). *One-Dimensional Man*. London: Routledge and Kegan Paul.

Matte-Blanco, I. (1975). *The Unconscious as Infinite Sets: An Essay in Bi-Logic*. London: Duckworth and Co.

Meissner, W. W. (1979). Critique of concepts and therapy in the action language approach to psychoanalysis. *International Journal of Psychoanalysis, 60*: 291–310.

Melzack, R., & Wall, P. D. (1965). Pain mechanisms: a new theory. *Science, 150*: 971–979.

Meyer, J. (1963). Regulatory and metabolic experimental obesities. In M. A. B. Brazier (ed.), *Brain and Behaviour*. Washington, DC: American Institute of Biological Sciences.

Miller, G. A. (1956). The magical number seven, plus or minus two, or, some limits on our capacity for processing information. *Psychological Revue, 63*: 81–97.

Muller, G. A., Galanter, E. H., & Pribram, K. H. (1960). *Plans and the Structure of Behaviour*. New York: Holt and Company.

Mintz, T. (1976). Contribution to panel report on effects on adults of object loss in the first five years. *Journal of the American Psychoanalytic Association, 24*: 662–665.

Mitchell, J. (1974). *Psychoanalysis and Feminism*. New York: Pantheon Books.

Mittelstaedt, H. (1968). Discussion. In D. P. Kimble (ed.), *Experience and Capacity*. New York: New York Academy of Science.

Money-Kyrle, R. E. (1952). Psycho-analysis and ethics. *International Journal of Psycho-Analysis, 33*: 225–234.

———— (1961). *Man's Picture of His World*. London: Duckworth.

Moss, H. (1963). *The Magic Lantern of Marcel Proust*. London: Faber.

Newson, J. (1977). An intersubjective approach to the systematic description of mother–infant interaction. In H. R. Schaffer (ed.), *Studies in Mother–Infant Interaction*. New York: Academic Press.

Offer, D. (1969). *The Psychological World of the Teenager: A Study of Normal Adolescent Boys*. New York: Basic Books.

Pantin, C. F. A. (1968). *The Relations Between the Sciences*. Cambridge: Cambridge University Press.

Peterfreund, E. (1971). *Information, Systems, and Psychoanalysis*. New York: International Universities Press.

———— (1980). On information and systems models for psychoanalysis. *International Revue of Psychoanalysis, 7*: 327–345.

Philippides, C., Dewdney, C., & Hiley, B. J. (1979). Quantum interference and the quantum potential. *Nuovo Cimento, 52B*: 15–28.

Popper, K. (1963). *Conjectures and Refutations*. London: Routledge and Kegan Paul.

Pribram, K. H. (1954). Concerning three rhinencephalic systems. *EEG and Clinican Neurophysiology, 6*: 708–709.

———— (1958). Neocortical function in behaviour. In H. F. Harlow and C. N. Woolsey (eds.), *Biological and Biochemical Bases of Behavior*. Madison, WI: University of Wisconsin Press.

———— (1959). On the neurology of thinking. *Behavioral Science, 4*: 265–284.

———— (1969). The amnestic syndromes: disturbance in coding? In G. A. Talland and M. Waugh (eds.), *The Psychopathology of Memory*. New York: Academic Press.

———— (1971). *Languages of the Brain*. Englewood Cliffs, NJ: Prentice-Hall [2nd ed., Monterey, CA: Brooks/Cole, 1977].

———— (1976). Self-consciousness and intentionality. In G. E. Schwartz and D. Shapiro (eds.), *Consciousness and Self-Regulation, Vol. 1*. New York: Plenum.

———— (1977). Peptides and protocritic processes. In L. H. Miller, C. A. Sandham and A. J. Kastin (eds.), *Neuropeptide Influences on the Brain and Behavior*. New York: Raven Press.

———— (1980a). The place of pragmatics in the syntactic and semantic organization of language. In *Temporal Variables in Speech: Studies in Honour of Frieda Goldman-Eisler*. The Hague: Mouton.

———— (1980b). Cognition and performance: the relation of neural mechanisms of consequence, confidence and competence. In A. Routtenberg (ed.), *Biology of Reinforcement: Facets of Brain Stimulation Reward*. New York: Academic Press.

———— (1980c). The brain as the locus of cognitive controls on action. In G. d'Ydewalle & W. Lens (eds.), *Cognition in Human Motivation and Learning*. Leuven, Belgium: University of Leuven Press.

Pribram, K. H., & Gill, M. M. (1976). *Freud's 'Project' Reassessed: Preface to Contemporary Cognitive Theory and Neuropsychology*. London: Hutchinson Publishing Group.

Pribram, K. H., & Kruger, L. (1954). Functions of the 'olfactory' brain. *Annals of the New York Academy of Science, 58*: 109–138.

Pribram, K. H., & McGuinness, D. (1975). Arousal, activation and effort in the control of attention. *Psychological Revue, 82* (2): 116–149.

Pribram, J. H., & Weiskrantz, L. (1957). A comparison of the effects of medial and lateral cerebral resections on conditioned avoidance behaviour of monkeys. *Journal of Comparative Physiological Psychology, 50*: 74–80.

Prigogine, I. (1980). *From Being to Becoming*. New York: Freeman.

Proust, M. (1981). *Time Regained*, Vol. 3 of *Remembrance of Things Past*. London: Chatto and Windus.

Rapaport, D. (1959). A historical survey of psychoanalytic ego psychology. *Psychological Issues, 1*: 5–17.

Rickman, J. (1941). A case of hysteria: theory and practice in the two wars. *Lancet, 240*: 785–786.

Ricoeur, P. (1970). *Freud and Philosophy: An Essay in Interpretation* (D. Savage, trans.). New Haven, CT: Yale University Press.

Robertson, J. (1952). Film: *A two-year-old goes to hospital* (16mm : 45 min.; sound; guidebook supplied; also abridged version, 30 min.). London: Tavistock Child Development Research Unit.

———— (1953). Some responses of young children to loss of maternal care. *Nursing Times, 49*: 382–386.

Robertson, J., & Bowlby, J. (1952). Responses of young children to separation from their mothers. *Courr. Cent. int. Enf., 2*: 131–142.

Rosenblatt, A. D., & Thickstun, J. T. (1977). *Modern Psychoanalytic Concepts in a General Psychology, Parts 1 & 2*. New York: International Universities Press.

Rubinstein, B. B. (1967). Explanation and mere description: a metascientific examination of certain aspects of the psychoanalytic theory of motivation. In R. R. Hold (ed.), *Motives and Thought: Psychoanalytic Essays in Honor of David Rapaport*. New York: International Universities Press.

———— (1976). On the possibility of a clinical psychoanalytic theory: an essay in the philosophy of psychoanalysis. In M. M. Gill and P. S. Holzman (eds.), *Psychology Versus Metapsychology*. New York: International Universities Press.

Ruch, T. C. (1951). Motor systems. In S. S. Stevens (ed.), *Handbook of Experimental Psychology*. New York: Wiley.

Sade, D. A. F., Marquis de (1966). *The 120 Days of Sodom and Other Writings*. New York: Random House.

———— (1967). *Marquis de Sade—Oeuvres Complètes*. Paris: Cercle de Livre Précieux.

Sander, L. W. (1964). Adaptive relationships in early mother–child interaction. *Journal of the American Academy of Child Psychiatry, 3*: 231–264.

———— (1980). New knowledge about the infant from current research: implications for psychoanalysis. Report of panel held at the Annual Meeting of the American Psychoanalytic Association, Atlanta, Georgia, May 1978. *Journal of the American Psychoanal. Association, 28*: 181–198.

Sandler, J. (1959). On the repetition of early childhood relationships in later psychosomatic disorder. In *The Nature of Stress Disorder*. London: Hutchinson.

———— (1974). Psychological conflict and the structural model: some clinical and theoretical implications. *International Journal of Psychoanalysis, 55*: 53–62.

———— (1976). Countertransference and role-responsiveness. *International Revue of Psychoanalysis, 3*: 43–47.

———— (1983). Reflections on some relations between psychoanalytic concepts and psychoanalytic practice. *International Journal of Psychoanalysis, 64*: 35–45.

Sandler, J., with A. Freud (1985). *The Analysis of Defense.* New York: International Universities Press.

Sandler, J., & Joffe, W. G. (1967). The tendency to persistence in psychological function and development. *Bulletin of the Menninger Clinic, 31*: 257–271.

Sandler, J., & Sandler, A.-M. (1978). On the development of object relationships and affects. *International Journal of Psychoanalysis, 59*: 283–296.

———— (1983). The 'second censorship', the 'three-box model' and some technical implications. *International Journal of Psychoanalysis, 64*: 413–425.

———— (1984). The past unconscious, the present unconscious and interpretation of the transference. *Psychoanalytical Inquiry, 4*: 367–399.

Schachter, S., & Singer, T. E. (1962). Cognitive, social and physiological determinants of emotional state. *Psychological Revue, 69*: 379–397.

Schafer, R. (1976). *A New Language for Psychoanalysis.* New Haven, CT: Yale University Press.

Schrodinger, E. (1944). *What is Life? Mind and Matter.* Cambridge: Cambridge University Press.

Shannon, C. E., & Weaver, W. (1949). *The Mathematical Theory of Communications.* Urbana, IL: University of Illinois Press.

Simon, H. A. (1974). How big is a chunk? *Science, 183*: 482–488.

Skinner, B. F. (1969). *Contingencies of Reinforcement: A Theoretical Analysis.* New York: Appleton-Century-Crofts.

———— (1971). *Beyond Freedom and Dignity.* New York: Alfred A. Knopf.

Smets, G. (1973). *Aesthetic Judgment and Arousal.* Leuven, Belgium: Leuven University Press.

Solnit, A. J. (1960). Hospitalization: an aid to physical and psychological health in childhood. *American Medical Association Journal of Diseases of Children, 99*: 155–163.

Spence, D. P. (1982). *Narrative Truth and Historical Truth.* New York/London: W. W. Norton & Co.

Spinelli, D. N. (1970). Occam, a content addressable memory model for the brain. In K. H. Pribram and D. Broadbent (eds.), *The Biology of Memory.* New York: Academic Press.

Spinelli, D. N., & Pribram, K. H. (1966). Changes in visual recovery functions produced by temporal lobe stimulation in monkeys. *Electroenceph. clin. Neurophysiol., 20*: 44–49.

——— (1967). Changes in visual recovery function and unit activity produced by frontal and temporal cortex stimulation. *Electroenceph. clin. Neurophysiol., 22*: 143–149.

Spitz, R. A. (1946). Anaclitic depression. *Psychoanalytic Study of the Child, 21*: 313–342.

——— (1957). *No and Yes.* New York: International Universities Press.

Strachey, J. (1959). Editor's Introduction to the Standard Edition of Freud's *Inhibitions, Symptoms and Anxiety. Standard Edition, 20.*

——— (1964). Editor's Note to the Standard Edition of Freud's *Moses and Monotheism. Standard Edition, 23.*

Strouse, J. (ed.) (1974). *Women and Analysis.* New York: Grossman.

Sulloway, F. (1979). *Freud, Biologist of the Mind.* New York: Basic Books.

Teitelbaum, P. (1955). Sensory control of hypothalamic hyperphagia. *Journal of Comparative Physiological Psychology, 48*: 156–163.

Teuber, H. L. (1960). Perception. In J. Field, H. W. Magoun and V. E. Hall (eds.), *Handbook of Physiology, Neurophysiology III.* Washington, DC: American Physiological Society.

——— (1964). The riddle of frontal lobe function in man. In J. M. Warren and K. Akert (eds.), *The Frontal Granular Cortex and Behavior.* New York: McGraw-Hill.

Tolstoy, L. (1903). *Resurrection.* London: Grant Richards.

Trevarthen, C. (1979). Instincts for human understanding and for cultural co-operation: their development in infancy. In M. von Cranach, K. Foppa, W. Lepenies, and D. Ploog (eds.), *Human Ethology.* Cambridge: Cambridge University Press.

Waddington, C. H. (1957). *The Strategy of the Genes.* London: Allen and Unwin.

Weber, M. (1961). *General Economic History* (Frank H. Knight, trans.). New York: Collier Books.

Weisstein, N. (1970). Kinder, Küche, Kirche as scientific law: psychology constructs the female. In R. Morgan (ed.), *Sisterhood is Powerful.* New York: Random House.

Weizsacker, E. von (1974). *Offene Systeme I.* Stuttgart.

Wiener, N. (1948). *Cybernetics.* New York: Wiley.

Wigner, E. P. (1969). Epistemology of quantum mechanics: its appraisals and demands. In M. Grene (ed.), *The Anatomy of Knowledge.* London: Routledge and Kegan Paul.

Will, D. (1980). Psychoanalysis as a human science. *British Journal of Medical Psychology, 53*: 201–211.

Winnicott, D. (1960). Ego distortion in terms of true and false self. In *The Maturational Processes and the Facilitating Environment*. London: Hogarth Press.

———— (1974). Fear of breakdown. *International Revue of Psychoanalysis 1*: 103–107.

Woolf, M. (1945). Prohibitions against simultaneous consumption of milk and flesh in orthodox Jewish Law. *International Journal of Psychoanalysis, 26*: 160–176.

INDEX